The Imagined Sky

The Imagined Sky

Cultural Perspectives

Edited by

Darrelyn Gunzburg

Equinox Publishing Ltd

eϙuınox

SHEFFIELD UK   BRISTOL CT

Published by

Equinox Publishing Ltd
Office 415, The Workstation, 15 Paternoster Row, Sheffield, South Yorkshire S1 2BX, UK
SD, 70 Enterprise Drive, Bristol, CT 06010, USA

www.equinoxpub.com

First published 2016

© Darrelyn Gunzburg and contributors 2016

British Library Cataloguing-in-Publication Data
A catalogue record for this book is available from the British Library.

   ISBN   978-1-78179-167-7 (hardback)
          978-1-78179-168-4 (paperback)

Library of Congress Cataloging-in-Publication Data
A catalog record for this book is available from the Library of Congress.

Typeset by Forthcoming Publications Ltd (www.forthpub.com)
Printed and bound by Lightning Source

CONTENTS

ACKNOWLEDGMENTS

It is my pleasure to acknowledge those who helped the idea for this book become a reality. Five chapters in this volume were first presented as papers *at Imagining Astrology: Painted Schemes and Threads of the Soul*, a conference that I co-convened with Liz Greene at The University of Bristol, 10–11 July 2010. That conference benefitted from the financial support of the Centre for Medieval Studies, the University of Bristol Alumni Foundation, the Graduate Dean's Fund, and the financial and administrative assistance of the Bristol Institute for Research in the Humanities and Arts (BIRTHA), in particular, the substantial help of Samantha Barlow. Thank you James Clark, Ronald Hutton, Ad Putter, and Beth Williamson for your astute advice and wise counsel in helping to bring that conference into fruition. Thank you Janet Joyce at Equinox Publications for your enthusiastic response to the idea of this book and for encouraging its growth by publishing those five papers as a Special Issue of the *Journal for the Study of Religion, Nature and Culture* 7.4 (December 2013). Thank you Bron Taylor, Editor in Chief of *JSRNC*, for your generosity and support of my guest editorship of that volume. From that seed I then sought a further six chapters to complete this book, for which thanks and gratitude are due to Peter Dent, Duane W. Hamacher, Gillian Hutchinson, Ed Krupp, Genevieve Liveley, Frank Prendergast, and Anthony Thorley for your work as peer reviewers. Thank you, Valerie Hall at Equinox Publications for your steady hand on the publishing side of this volume. Finally, Bernadette Brady, thank you for all your patience and enthusiasm during the organising of the conference and the publication of this book without which neither would have come into being.

INTRODUCTION

Whether by day or by night, the sky has a visual impact on us, forming fifty percent of our visual world. Paired with the earth, it creates an impression of two separate yet inseparable expanses. Little attention nevertheless has been paid to the sky as a presence in its own right. We locate ourselves externally and internally, physically and symbolically, by the sky, and humanity uses it to judge its time and set its courses geographically and culturally. By its imagery, transmitted through text, image, oral tradition, physical mapping, and painted description, the sky has reflected our place in the cosmos. Its internalised impressions provide the foundation of much of our philosophical and theological insights. The sky explored within all its connotations offers us both outer world examination and inner world philosophy. As Immanuel Kant (1724–1804) wrote in 1788:

> Two things fill the mind with ever new and increasing admiration and reverence, the more often and more steadily one reflects on them: *the starry heaven above me and the moral law within me.* I do not need to search for them and merely conjecture them as though they were veiled in obscurity or in the transcendent region beyond my horizon; I see them before me and connect them immediately with the consciousness of my existence (Kant 1788, *Critique of Practical Reason* 5:162:133, italics original).

This volume, written by some of the most eminent scholars in their fields, explores the visual complexity of the sky and its importance, how the sky has been imagined, and the cultural implications and consequences that have arisen as a result, from the sky's movement mirrored in the archoeastronomy of British prehistory, the apocalyptic myths of comets and meteors, sky cartography reflected in European globes and medieval frescoes, Australian aboriginal sky myths, the issue of disappearing dark skies, contemporary reflections on the sky, to the recognition that sky imagery has persisted in similar forms since its potential roots in the Palaeolithic period. These eleven chapters thus offer a wide-ranging understanding of, and critical engagement with, the sky in human imagination and culture and contribute to this new field emerging within the academy.

Ronald Hutton's chapter 'The Strange History of British Archaeo-astronomy' examines the rise of the relatively new study of archaeo-astronomy, or astro-archaeology, the discipline that scrutinises how people of the past have understood the sky and the role it played in their cultures. Archaeoastronomers posit that prehistoric monuments aligned on a star could situate them in a landscape, and Hutton's chapter considers in particular the prehistoric monuments of Britain and the debates around their precise alignments upon heavenly bodies. This new area of academic study rose to prominence in Britain in the 1970s and 1980s on the heels of archaeology, itself a relatively new discipline formed and shaped between the 1920s and 1950s. Yet archaeoastronomy was to disappear from the academic discourse by the 1990s. Astronomy, mathematics, and statistics became estranged from archaeology, and prehistory remained in the hands of the excavators. Whilst acknowledging the rise of archaeoastronomy in the New World, which emerged from scholars investigating the astronomies and the role of cosmology in native North, Meso-, and South American cultures, Hutton has deliberately focused on the development of British archaeoastronomy, tracing its history and the people who played key roles in attempting to advance it as a recognised academic discipline, as well as those who stymied its forward movement. His chapter contributes a strong analysis and review of the history of the discipline, and he raises key questions that have not yet been asked in the debate, such as: Why has the sky become invisible to archaeologists when it forms part of the landscape they investigate, and why has the cultural impact, the way ancient people perceived and experienced their world, been marginalised from their thinking? Hutton's incisive questioning offers ways of considering what he notes is 'the process of history' and the study of the remote past, and highlights how viewing past cultures with contemporary attitudes can block a debate. (Archaeo-astronomy is now placed within the academy at the University of Wales Trinity Saint David as a module taught through the MA in Cultural Astronomy and Astrology.)

Patrick McCafferty's chapter 'Comets And Meteors: The Ignored Explanations for Myths and Apocalypse' argues that although myths about comets and meteors have the capacity to inform us about our world, they have been ignored in many areas of scholarship. Comets have been feared due to their unpredictability. McCafferty observes how collisions with earth have produced catastrophic effects in the past and ancient prophecies presage future impacts with devastating consequences. He notes how the transposition of astronomic events into mythic narratives suggests that such events have been alive in history, yet their content and function has been overlooked due to the form in which they have been presented. McCafferty suggests that the implications of this symbolic nature of cometary myth should be a central part of any critical inquiry. In this regard the controlled touchdown of Philae, a robotic lander accompanying the European Space Agency (ESA)'s Rosetta spacecraft, onto the surface of Comet 67P/Churyumov-Gerasimenko on 12 November 2014, has been timely. Taking our cue from McCafferty, if this narrative was written as a myth, it might take the form of a heroic figure who sets out on a quest to find a grey stone monster who holds valuable knowledge. After ten non-productive years, the hero sights the monster far in the distance, hurtling headlong through the sky. The hero adjusts his path and with split-second timing, leaps onto the back of the monster. Locked together at high speed, the hero manages to wrest some of the knowledge from the monster and to communicate this knowledge to his people before he is rendered mute. The hero knows that he must wait until the stone monster draws closer to the sun god before he can plead for the gift of sunlight and once more gain the power to speak.

If prehistoric cultures believed that structures aligned on a star created a necessary focus that connected them in a substantial and meaningful way with the heavens, then Roger Beck's chapter 'Imagery and Narrative in an Ancient Horoscope: P.Lond. 130 (*Greek Horoscopes* No. 81)', an exploration of the 'star-talk' written into a Greek papyrus horoscope from the first century CE, illuminates how that sky was meaningful for a culture thousands of years on in time. Beck describes star-talk as 'a celestial language spoken by the stars themselves in their motions'. The horoscope may have been a flat two-dimensional map of the heavens, but in replacing the usual matter-of-fact listing of longitudes with a written narrative, Titus Pitenius, the author-narrator of the horoscope, told us he saw the heavens as alive and ensouled. Beck skilfully demonstrates how Titus Pitenius weaves two narratives for his client: the sky as he saw it made up of the five planets and two lights, and the other the vivid literary telling of the account that he saw in that configuration. The Greek author-narrator, through the vibrant richness of his language, tells us that he was exploring far more than just the movements of the stars. For him, this was a sky that was alive to planetary movement in ways that our contemporary eyes have lost. Beck calls our attention to the fact that the five planets and the two lights are 'actors in the celestial field' in the true sense of the word—those who act and those who take action—and that this was expressed in the verbs that Titus Pitenius used. Symbols and images derive meaning from context, and we are reminded by Beck that the Greek astrologer saw the field of the sky as rich and inhabitable as the earthly world in which his client lived and worked. That the story should be conveyed with opulent language offers us an insight into the Greeks' connection with the sky, for as Beck attests, 'the astrologer invites his client not merely to *hear* his story but to *visualize* it'.

The next four chapters take an art historical approach to this visualisation of the heavens and the figures connected with the constellations. Kristen Lippincott, in her chapter 'Reflections on the Farnese *Atlas*: Exploring the Scientific, Literary and Pictorial Antecedents of the Constellations on a Graeco-Roman Globe', raises concerns regarding the frameworks that are used to derive our understanding of the depiction of the heavens on the globe itself. No longer requiring the language used by the Greek author-narrator described by Beck to evoke the celestial narrative in the imagination of the listener, now the constellations relative to the celestial circles are carved onto a marble globe 65 cm in diameter held by the towering figure of Atlas, the whole figure standing 2.1 metres tall. The question Lippincott poses is, whose understanding of the heavens shaped the sky constellations depicted on the globe? If one attempts to date the work by anchoring it to an Hipparchan astronomical model, as some scholars have done, one may be led astray, Lippincott cautions, since the makers may have utilised obsolete astronomical information. Instead she suggests that greater attention should be paid to the largely independent pictorial tradition that was prevalent in image representation from the fourth century BCE onwards. This shift of focus from astronomically led imagery to an artist-driven figurative language in representing these early forms of sky constellations moves the discussion from a reliance on star-catalogues and/or iconography to one that acknowledges a recognised, commonly understood pictorial tradition whose vocabulary was conveyed from artist to artist and which helped shape the representation of constellations.

In my chapter 'Giotto's Sky: The Fresco Paintings of the First Floor Salone of the Palazzo della Ragione, Padua, Italy', considering the art historical culture of medieval Italy, I faced no lack of texts to inform the images of the first floor Salone of the Palazzo della Ragione, the law courts, in Padua, Italy, and their depiction of the night sky. Indeed, my contention is that too many texts can lead the contemporary scholar astray and place an emphasis on meaning when none may be meant. In the past, scholars focused on a convenient image-filled book to explain the images. Yet approaching the scheme with a practical, contemporary understanding of the techniques of medieval astrology and naked eye astronomy—the observer's view of the sky—provides fresh insights into the messages of this medieval fresco scheme of 319 images and what it was saying about the role of the sky in medieval cosmology. I suggest that there is a deeper astrological and cosmological meaning to the building that accounted for the way the Paduan Commune wanted the fresco scheme to explain their experiences. I further argue that in the top register of this fresco scheme it is possible to see the sky over Padua in the fourteenth century in its seasonal and calendrical cycle, suggesting that the Paduan community's relationship with the sky was as alive and vital as Beck suggests Titus Pitenius saw it with his Greek papyrus horoscope from the first century CE.

Geoffrey Shamos's chapter 'Astrology as Sociology: The "Children of Planets", 1400–1600' examines another art historical approach to astrological images in their popular bearing via the pictorial convention known as the 'Children of the Planets' and how they acted as a social framework in the Early Modern period. Shamos clearly points out how astrology at this time was being utilised to reflect, represent, and possibly comment on society. This reflection of the sky flourished across Europe during the fifteenth and sixteenth centuries, appearing in a variety of media, appealing to a broad audience, and disseminating a common conception of this period's social world. By examining the changing imagery of the planets and the two lights across a two-hundred-year period, Shamos is able to identify how the sky via the 'Children of the Planets' reflected the cultural milieu and social relations and in many ways confirmed their prejudices. Shamos argues that, unlike cast horoscopes that required specialised knowledge and investigated astrological questions in depth, the 'Children of the Planets' acted as astrology for the layman, enabling it to be read and understood pictorially and offering information regarding a person's health, physique, behavioural tendencies, craft and profession, and class and rank. Shamos explores how planetary deities in the sky were placed into popular culture through representation. In this regard one could argue that the 'Children of the Planets' play an important role in the discourse of the imagined sky as the precursors of modern sun-sign astrology and in keeping the sky alive via the planetary deities in the Early Modern period. Expressed in woodcuts and engravings, Shamos notes how the images of the planetary deities often riding in chariots above the social world below reflected society and its social distinctions and reinforced for its clients and users the social hierarchies they already recognised. In the process, he shows how the social implications of the sky, in particular the role of Mercury in the city of Antwerp, maintained the belief that the sky was alive and threaded into the social fabric, no matter how simplified.

Shamos's historical analysis is followed by Emily Urban's research into the decoration of the Sala Bologna, originally a small dining room located on the Terza Loggia of the Cortile di San Damaso in the Vatican Palace in 'Mapping the Heavens: The Ceiling of the Sala Bologna in the Vatican Palace'. In exploring this decoration, commissioned for the Jubilee of 1575 by Pope Gregory XIII, mastermind of the reformed calendar, Urban identifies that it articulates a sophisticated treatment of the sky in a ceiling fresco, along with an extraordinarily high level of accuracy in its celestial cartography. She argues that, since the *sala* was used to entertain illustrious guests, it not only represented the Church's official attitudes towards sixteenth-century astronomy, it became a state-of-the-art showpiece of current astronomical thinking. Urban suggests that, whilst Gregory XIII may have been quoting an ancient Roman artistic heritage both in depicting celestial iconography on the *sala*'s dining room ceiling and taking an outer-celestial positioning, a perspective that originated in antique celestial globes and was common in Renaissance globe making, another important function was at stake. Urban argues that Gregory XIII was making use of leading edge celestial knowledge to reinforce the erudition of the Counter Reformation. Furthermore, Urban notes, rather than demonstrating ownership of and dominion over the powers of the skies, as much scholarship regarding medieval and Renaissance astronomical wall and ceiling frescoes has suggested, such a ceiling reflected instead Gregory XIII's desire to be in accordance with the heavens, just as medieval astrological authors, such as Avraham Ibn Ezra (born 1089–1092, died after 1160) and Guido Bonatti (c. 1207–died between 1281 and 1296), dedicated their works to God in order to be in harmony with the divine. Urban goes on to argue that this night sky fresco in the Sala Bologna offers the viewer an understanding of Counter Reformation connectivity between religion and astrology/astronomy, between earth and sky.

Moving across the boundaries of visual depiction on a ceiling to the sky physically experienced, John Goldsmith's chapter 'Cosmos, Culture and Landscape: Documenting, Learning and Sharing Australian Aboriginal Astronomical Knowledge in Contemporary Society' considers two groups of people in our contemporary environment for whom the sky has not yet dimmed: indigenous Australians whose oral tradition of sky knowledge gives rise to the community's sense of belonging and relationships, rather than ownership and individuality; and radio astronomy scientists who view the sky through telescopes and communicate that knowledge through written text. Through the Cosmos, Culture and Landscape project, Goldsmith's research reveals how, whilst counterpointing each other culturally, bringing two such groups together to share their diverse experiences has a positive effect for both cultures. In the dark countryside, using naked eye astronomy and sitting around a campfire, Aboriginal people shared their stories of the sky with radio astronomy scientists. They then looked at the sky through a telescope. Radio astronomy scientists, on the other hand, saw the skies for the first time through the eyes and stories of Aboriginal people. Goldsmith's analysis shows how both groups were enriched by the experience. As Aboriginal participant Charmaine Green observed: 'People like talking about the sky and just like looking at the stars. So the connection there was when the sun came down, people had lots to talk about.' Goldsmith argues that the implications of this cross-cultural experience of sharing and learning about sky knowledge between Aboriginal and non-Aboriginal people in the Murchison region of Western Australia, which then translated into the creation of Western Australia's largest Aboriginal art exhibition primarily based on astronomical themes, are fundamental in encouraging the appreciation and respect of Aboriginal astronomical knowledge.

In 'At Night's End', Tyler Nordgren is primarily concerned with how we can reclaim that sky bright with stars in our contemporary world where fifty percent of the world's population lives in cities and are thus subject to light pollution. Indeed Nordgen points out how the idea of a sky full of stars has become transformed into a tourist attraction, placed high on the priority list of park visitors to two western U.S. parks, and thought to be as instrumental to their park experience as seeing wildflowers and waterfalls. In defence of dark skies, Nordgren develops a careful historical analysis of the role played by the visibility of the Milky Way. He notes how the sky has defined our cardinal directions perhaps for as long as humans have existed and may explain why stones, rooms, buildings, or other structures are often aligned with the sky. For Nordgren, this also raises the questions of glare and sky glow, both of which deprive the viewer of truly natural night. Yet, Nordgren argues, although the places where one can experience truly natural, night skies are diminishing, the natural nocturnal sky is fully recoverable. The rise of the International Dark-Sky Association (IDA) in 1988 has taken on the challenge of reducing the amount of unwanted light flooding the world's skies and creating International Dark-Sky Parks and Nordgren teases out some of the implications of this move for returning the planet to one that includes the nightly presence of stars.

Tim Ingold's chapter 'Reach for the Stars!—Light, Vision and the Atmosphere' reveals a different set of associations connected with the sky simply by shifting the attention to the perspective of phenomenology, the conscious experience of being outside, whether by day under the azure firmament or at night under the celestial vault. In a discussion closely informed by James Gibson's ecological approach to visual perception and Maurice Merleau-Ponty's philosophical considerations, Ingold asks the question: What is the sky? In so doing he considers the nature of light and what it is that we see in the night sky, parsing the line and colour of Vincent van Gogh's *The Starry Night* (*De sterrennacht*) in order to understand what it feels like to be under the stars. Light in the night sky, Ingold concludes, is atmospheric and when this light becomes the light of the sun then he disputes whether Gibson is correct to state that 'You cannot draw the sky, but you can paint it.' Ingold builds on Merleau-Ponty's point that 'to see the sky—just as to see the sun—is to experience its luminosity from within' and he argues for blue sky being considered atmosphere, suggesting that there is no such thing as an empty sky, rather the sky is full of the material stuff of air. By focusing on the interrelationship of inhalation and exhalation, Ingold shifts our perspective so that we find ourselves experiencing the sky rather than observing it.

The final chapter by Bernadette Brady, 'Images in the Heavens: A Cultural Landscape', completes a circle. In the same way that Hutton recognises that there is a created dialogue between monument and sky that is culture-specific, Brady distinguishes how the sky itself holds cultural specificity. Her chapter outlines how the relatively unchanging nature of the sky—its deterministic rules of movement—combines with human imagination, to produce a stability of sky imagery across time. In tracing the history of the sky via constellation images from the earliest Elamite seals of the fourth millennium BCE to the invention of printing and the age of the great star atlases of the sixteenth to nineteenth centuries, Brady posits a sky that is alive with narrative, just as Beck found with his Greek papyrus horoscope from the first century CE. Brady argues for the robustness of these constellation images, that the relatively unchanging sky over time means that constellation images formed millennia ago are still with us today. As Brady notes, the sky has 'scattered its symbols across time into diverse objects, ranging from precious manuscripts and ceilings to mouse mats and coffee cups'. Thus the sky imagery represents a culture of humanity without the borders of tribes, clans, nations, languages, or religions. Where Hutton offered circumspection in viewing past cultures with contemporary attitudes in the area of archaeoastronomy, recognising that it stifled debate, Brady suggests that constellation images can offer a bridge in allowing us to recognise a continuum of our humanity.

The visual complexity of the sky and its importance in culture has generally been on the fringes of other subjects. Yet cultural studies of the sky is an emerging academic discipline of relevance to the fields of archaeoastronomy, history, art history, cartography, cultural astronomy, cultural astrology, and religious studies in anthropology. *The Journal of Skyscape Archaeology*, edited by Fabio Silva and Liz Henty, and focusing on the role and importance of the sky in the interpretation of the material record, was launched in 2014. The eleven chapters in this volume suggest that, whilst the cultures that created the images or monuments may have had different reasons for and different ways of expressing their ideas about the heavens, they were all engaged with the sky. This commonality can therefore be understood as a doorway, a Rosetta Stone, a universal thread that we can use to enter diverse cultures, providing us with a tool to help recognise similarities and differences between civilisations. The intention of this volume is to give centrality to the sky in order to understand its relevance in culture. This volume offers critical engagement with ways of understanding the sky and the images perceived in it, which will continue to inform, underpin, and encourage research of the subject within the academy.

References

Kant, Immanuel. 1997 [1788]. *Critique of Practical Reason*, ed. Mary Gregor, Cambridge Texts in the History of Philosophy, Cambridge: Cambridge University Press.

THE STRANGE HISTORY
OF BRITISH ARCHAEOASTRONOMY

Ronald Hutton

University of Bristol, School of Humanities, Department of History,
11 Woodland Road, Bristol BS8 1TB, England, UK
R.Hutton@bristol.ac.uk

Abstract

Between 1965 and 1985, British archaeologists found themselves obliged to study the skies as well as the evidence beneath the earth. The sciences of astronomy, mathematics, and statistics bore down on the study of prehistoric monuments as never before, and a series of impressive books and conferences explored the alignments and proportions of ancient ceremonial sites. A quarter of a century later, all this excitement has arguably evaporated. The four different disciplines have largely separated again, and prehistory has been handed back to the excavators. These developments can be characterised as the result of a series of complex relationships between established experts in British prehistory, academic scholars from other disciplines, and members of a radical counter-culture. Archaeoastronomy became presented as a challenge to the credentials of the established experts, and the apparent lack of absolute proof to its conclusions enabled them to reject it wholesale. In Britain it has effectively been handed over to the counter-culture in which it is retained as a tradition.

Keywords

Archaeoastronomy, anthropology, megalithic, alignments, pagan Britain, orientation, ethnoastronomy, Oxford conferences, methodology, astronomical heritage, British history.

The subject matter of this article is designed to represent a parallel study to the history of astrology. It does so in that it similarly considers ways of looking at the cosmos, focused on the patterns of heavenly bodies, which raise questions about the relationship between orthodoxy and unorthodoxy in modern professional scholarship. Its intention is to examine two specific problems. The first is what has happened in Britain to the discipline of archaeoastronomy, or astro-archaeology, the study of ancient responses to the heavens. The subject was established in the 1970s and 1980s on a wave of excitement created by pioneering works of the 1960s. It was confidently expected then to become an integral and important component of the investigation of prehistory. Instead it has shrunk into a small sub-discipline, isolated both from most archaeo-logists and from an enthusiastic movement existing largely outside the academy, which focuses on alignments between prehistoric monuments and the sky. The second question is why current archaeologists should be so uninterested in the sky, even though the two movements that have dominated the development of their discipline since the 1990s should have enhanced their consciousness of it.[1] One of those movements has been landscape archaeology, and the sky is not only a major component of any landscape but the only one that remains much as it was during prehistory. The other has been cognitive archaeology, the study of the way in which ancient people perceived and experienced their world, and the sky, again, must have formed a major aspect of both processes. Instead it usually plays at most a minor part in the interpretation of archaeological sites.

To set about providing some answers, it is necessary to explain the fortunes of archaeoastronomy itself. In order to do that, attention should be paid to the context in which it appeared and had to operate, and there were four significant features to that.[2] The first was the admiration for big science that has pervaded modern Western society and peaked at certain moments, such as the late nineteenth and the mid-twentieth century. A widespread belief, which had commenced under Queen Victoria, was that scientists would eventually find remedies for virtually all human ills and limitations and reveal all of the workings of the universe. As people almost invariably search for kindred spirits in the past, this created a disposition to detect and praise anybody in history or prehistory who

---

1.   However, in the case of O'Connell (2013), the role of archaeoastronomy in formulating a likely interpretation for the monument at Lismullin, County Meath, Ireland, has been significant.

2.   All four have been investigated in more detail, with regard to parallel issues, in Hutton 2009a: 210-417; 2009b.

seemed capable of anticipating or matching modern scientific achievements. The second relevant development was the professionalisation of the discipline of archaeology between the 1920s and the 1950s. Until then it had been carried on mostly by amateurs. Now it became rooted in university courses and the qualifications that they gave, and its prime tool, excavation, was reserved for those equipped with such qualifications. The higher the academic status of archaeologists, the more dominant they were in the discipline (Stout 2008). For those with a passionate interest in prehistory who were unable or unwilling to join this exclusive club, only two aspects of the subject remained which were not under the latter's control. One was the relation of prehistoric monuments to other landscape features; the other was their relation to heavenly bodies.

Built into the development of professional archaeology was a third contextual feature: the belief in evolution as the motor force of natural development, which had appeared under Victoria. It was coupled with another major feature of Victorian thought: a cult of moral and techno-logical progress as an admirable, and perhaps divinely inspired, phenomenon. This created a tendency to regard ages that were techno- logically primitive as debased in their social and moral characteristics as well. The twin words habitually employed for more traditional societies—savages and barbarians—summed up this attitude. It was embodied in the works of some of the most prominent archaeologists of the early twentieth century. It was also, and perhaps more influentially for the general public, personified in the illustrations provided for works on prehistory. The ubiquitous drawings of Alan Sorrell (1980), for example, provided for the readers of the 1950s and 1960s a succession of prehistoric Britons with unkempt hair and beards, dressed in animal skins.[3] This last, intellectually dominant view of the remote past ran counter to an older one, which remained significant in twentieth-century Britain, especially outside the academy. It was ultimately derived from the Bible, which had remained the basis for a general understanding of history and prehistory until the 1860s. Even among people who had themselves ceased to be Christian, it was a potent instinctual position a hundred years later: a belief that in the remote past humanity had shared a single, primal, good religion, perhaps based on divine revelation or a deep instinctual knowledge of the truths of the cosmos. In this view, the religion and the knowledge concerned had been fractured and mostly forgotten in the course of the millennia. Many people who held it brought with them a desire, to a greater or lesser degree, to recover this lost wisdom and

3. See also Sorrell's illustrations to Atkinson 1959.

revive this good primal religion in the modern age. Some felt, echoing the Christian apocalyptic tradition, that the survival of humanity depended on this achievement.

The professional archaeologists of the early twentieth century were certainly aware that some of Britain's prehistoric monuments—and some elsewhere—had important alignments with the sky. The most famous of all was Stonehenge's orientation on the midsummer sunrise, but there were others. Scotland's greatest single Neolithic monument, the passage grave of Maes Howe, was aligned with the midwinter sunset. None of these leaders of the new profession, however, were much interested in astronomy, mathematics, or engineering. This was partly because those are simply different disciplines but also because the elements of all those in prehistoric structures seemed simple enough to require no special study. Occasionally an outsider had taken an interest in them, and this sometimes had spectacular effects. The most distinguished was the great research scientist Sir Norman Lockyer, who was, among other achievements, the discoverer of helium, and who published a series of works on the astronomical significance of ancient monuments between 1894 and 1907. In the process he fixed the date of Stonehenge at around 1680 BCE and informed the leaders of the Welsh national cultural institution, the Eisteddfod, that the ceremony that opened it was proven by its orientations to be about 4000 years old. By studying the layout of ancient buildings, he declared his discovery of a universal ancient religion of sun-worship, carried across Europe by the Phoenicians. These had brought it to Britain and founded the religious tradition that entered history as the Druids (Lockyer 1906).[4]

All of this was eventually proved completely wrong. The earliest phase of Stonehenge is about a thousand years older, and the ceremony that opens the Eisteddfod was invented by an eighteenth-century forger. The Phoenicians never got near Britain, and the buildings which Lockyer linked together in his universal sun-worship are completely unrelated. It took, however, until the late twentieth century for each suggestion to be decisively disproved, and, in addition, Lockyer found a number of apparent alignments between specific monuments and different annual movements of the sun that are more difficult firmly to refute. The archaeologists of the first three decades did not know what to make of any of his suggestions. Most decided to ignore them, while a few dismissed them and indeed went a great deal further to reject all attempts to

4. Lockyer's work is considered with full references in Hutton 2009a: 314-15, 333, 366, 404. Much of the latter two-thirds of that book are concerned with the context in which these ideas of Lockyer's came to be refuted.

characterize ancient monuments regarding astronomical orientation in general and contemptuous terms (Michell 1977: 45-47). This approach seemed effective: as the century wore on, such ideas slipped from public view. Initially Lockyer had inspired a number of other individuals with an interest in astronomy and surveying to turn their attention to ancient sites. The most significant of these was Rear-Admiral Boyle Somerville (1924, 1927), who claimed solar, lunar, and stellar alignments from several Irish and Scottish sites.

Somerville identified a problem for archaeoastronomy which had appeared as soon as it took shape, and which was to shadow it ever since (Somerville 1924, 1927). He noted that 'discredit and derision' had already been brought on it

> ...through the visionary ideas of some enthusiasts, who have tried to import into the subject far more than the cold facts of science can sustain; so that with them, we become confronted by numbers of [Neolithic] 'astronomer priests' sacrificing to the Sun, singing psalms to the Moon, and saluting the Stars. Even the number of stones compassing a Circle, and the 'cubits' that are comprised in its dimensions, have been called upon to provide mystical figures and proportions—an entire prehistoric arithmetic and astrology. It is no wonder, then, that the unmathematical, but otherwise scientific, archaeologist has repelled any suggestion of orientation in these ancient structures (Somerville 1924: 193).

Somerville published in the main journals of archaeology, but after his death this momentum was not continued; by the mid-twentieth century a few people, notably Alexander Thom and C.A. ('Peter') Newham were still publishing articles on the subject in learned journals and local newspapers but creating no controversy and receiving little attention.

This situation ended dramatically in the years between 1963 and 1965, when a professor of astronomy at an American university, Gerald Hawkins, published a series of works leading up to a book, written with some assistance from his friend John White, called *Stonehenge Decoded*.[5] It became a rapid best-seller on both sides of the Atlantic and continued to be one, in paperback, into the 1970s. Deliberately pitched to a popular market, its selling point was that it was the first attempt to apply computer technology systematically to an archaeological problem. In this case the problem was the purpose of Stonehenge, which Hawkins

---

5. The most celebrated of his early publications was also called 'Stonehenge Decoded', and appeared in *Nature*, the science magazine founded by Lockyer, issue 200 (Hawkins 1963). The book was first published in New York by Doubleday. An English edition followed in 1966, and a Fontana paperback in 1970.

declared to have been built with extraordinary skill and precision and aligned with the movements of sun and moon. He thought that it had certainly been a calendar, and perhaps a kind of computer, designed among other things to predict eclipses. Hawkins was respectful to archaeologists and used their work, but clearly believed that he had surpassed them in determining at last why the monument was built. He also implicitly challenged their depiction of prehistoric people as savages when the latter had apparently possessed scientific knowledge and ability only equalled again in modern times. The result was a division of expert opinion. One of the most respected of British astronomers, Sir Fred Hoyle of Cambridge University, disagreed with Hawkins's calculations. Hoyle made some of his own calculations, however, and concluded that Stonehenge had indeed been a major scientific instrument, arranged to test new theoretical ideas in a way not known again until modern times (Hoyle 1966a, 1966b). Some prominent writers on archaeology, including the established authority on Stonehenge, Richard Atkinson, condemned Hawkins for making constant mistakes in his use of archaeology and basing his data on inaccurate plans of the monument. Hawkins's critics could not, however, refute the mathematical and astronomical reasoning itself, arguing only that it was possible but not certain, and that different scientists seemed to be reaching different conclusions based on individual selections of data and reconstructions of Stonehenge (Atkinson 1966; Hawkes 1967; Hoyle 1967).

Moreover, the archaeologists concerned failed to express their ideas in populist works to rival *Stonehenge Decoded*, leaving a large general public to assume that it had been proven. In addition, and almost immediately, they had a yet more formidable challenger with whom to reckon in the same field: a retired academic Alexander Thom (Thom 1988, 1995).[6] Thom was a very distinguished scholar, having been the Professor of Engineering Science at Oxford University, where a building is named after him. Ever since the 1930s he had been interested in the astronomical and mathematical properties of prehistoric monuments and had devoted many holidays to surveying them, especially in his native Scotland. In 1954 he began to publish his ideas regarding prehistory, but in journals only read by astronomers and statisticians. It was probably the example of Hawkins that made Thom turn to books, releasing in

---

6.   Biographical sketches of Thom with a bibliography of his works are provided by his son Archie Thom, 'A Personal Note about my Late Father' (1988) and Hans Metz, 'A Personal Appreciation of Professor Alexander Thom' (1988). Archie Thom later published a biography, *Walking in All of the Squares* (1995), and there are further valuable details in Heath 2007: 1-24.

1967 the first of a series which brought his theories before a large public: indeed, Hawkins had actually cited Thom's earlier work and called for more of it (Hawkins 1963).[7] These books were the first to support the hypothesis that prehistoric monuments were aligned with the heavens using statistical evidence from many sites, produced by extensive field-work of high quality. What Thom argued from this was that the stone circles and rows of Neolithic and Bronze Age Britain had primarily been observatories for studying the night sky in particular with considerable sophistication and precision. He also believed that these observations were used to construct and maintain a general prehistoric calendar of eight annual festivals. Furthermore, he contended that the monuments had been laid out with marvellous mathematical ability, using a standard unit of measurement that he termed the 'megalithic yard'.

Thom did not mock archaeologists for failing to perceive all this, nor did he make any attempt to integrate it with their own findings and their reconstructions of prehistoric culture and society. Instead, he left it to his readers to decide whether the two could be reconciled, and many concluded that he had rendered those reconstructions redundant. As a result, his work was immediately and enthusiastically taken up, together with that of Hawkins, by the Earth Mysteries movement that appeared in Britain at the end of the 1960s. This movement was explicitly opposed to scholarly orthodoxies, being closely allied with the hippy counter-culture of the period and largely inspired by the writings of John Michell, especially his book *The View Over Atlantis*, which was published in 1969. This introduced a wide public to the concept of leys—straight lines of mysterious natural energy covering the surface of the earth along which ancient monuments had been aligned. Three points should be emphasised about this concept and the movement with which it was associated in the present context. The first is that it was initially bound up with a post-Christian religiosity and in particular with the biblical concept of a single, primordial true religion from which humanity had deviated at great cost. Michell set the tone for subsequent writers by avoiding any definition of the nature of this religion while employing terms to describe it taken from Christianity. He used apocalyptic lan-guage, declaring that acceptance of his ideas represented 'the rediscovery of access to the divine will' and 'the restoration of the Holy Spirit' (Michell 1973 [1969]: 185). The second pertinent point was that it was

7. The best known were *Megalithic Sites in Britain* (Thom 1967), *Megalithic Lunar Observatories* (Thom 1971), and (with Archibald S. Thom) *Megalithic Remains in Britain and Brittany* (Thom and Thom 1978).

explicitly hostile to orthodox prehistory as part of a general condemna-
tion of established ideas and institutions. Michell sneered at professional
archaeologists as treasure-hunters and grave-robbers who had to be
thrown from power (Michell 1973 [1969]: vi, 64).

The third point is that it is most unlikely that Michell and those like
him would have written with such enthusiasm had it not been for the
apparent discoveries of Alexander Thom. To them, Thom provided a
classic example of an outsider who had shown the whole of orthodox
prehistory to be flawed. As such, he was hailed as a hero by Michell and
other authors such as Screeton (1974: 22-26), Graves (1976), Hitching
(1976: 1-24), and Pennick (1979: 31-34), who followed him in the
Earth Mysteries tradition (or as many practitioners called it, 'alternative
archaeology') through the 1970s and produced classic works of the
genre. Thom's own relationship with this movement was complex. His
idea did not reflect its mysticism and its contempt for most academics.
On the other hand, his ideas, consciously or not, sometimes drew on
those of the counter-culture or reinforced them. For example, he pro-
claimed that Neolithic Britain had observed a ritual calendar of eight
festivals, composed by blending the solstices and equinoxes with the
quarter days, which started the seasons. He found apparent indications of
this in the alignments of megalithic monuments. Lockyer (1906) had
drawn attention to such alignments but suggested that the quarter days,
solstices, and equinoxes formed not one sacred calendar but two, used by
successive prehistoric ages. The only religions known definitely to have
observed such an eight-point system are those that constitute modern
Paganism. Although claimed by Pagans to be prehistoric, this cycle of
feasts had actually been adopted by the first of those traditions to appear,
Wicca, in 1958 (Hutton 2008). Thom (1971: 9) also gave support to the
idea of ley lines by declaring in 1971 that Neolithic engineers could
survey straight paths between mutually invisible points.

Thom's claims were, of course, a great deal less convenient to professional archaeologists, especially as the latter had no skills with which
to test them. To do that would require an expertise in astronomy,
mathematics, and statistics, and these were all separate sciences. In 1975
Richard Atkinson became the first leading member of his discipline to
declare an acceptance of Thom's basic principle that megalithic
monuments were bound up intrinsically with astronomical observations.
In a book in which he exulted over what he called Atkinson's 'public
confession of his former errors' and termed him the first to abandon the
'sinking ship' of conventional archaeology, Michell (1977: 85) swiftly
took full advantage of this opportunity. Michell made archaeoastronomy
his key example of an apparent heresy that had turned out to prove

established scholarship completely wrong and that had become an orthodoxy itself. The lesson was that other unorthodox theorists, like Michell himself, would become the acclaimed experts of the future. By the late 1970s, therefore, two things had become very clear. One was that Thom's claims needed to be examined properly by experts in all of the necessary branches of knowledge. Thom himself was now leaving the field, for by the mid-1970s he had become too old to engage in further research. The other lesson was that established experts in prehistory now had the strongest possible reason to hope for a disproof of Thom's ideas. As the latter had been set up, especially by Earth Mysteries authors, as the test case of the value of professional archaeology, archaeologists needed to face up to that test and vindicate themselves and their discipline. Nonetheless, two further elements in the situation weighed against any simple need, desire, or ability on the part of practitioners of archaeology to defend their traditional attitudes against Thom's ideas. One was that, contrary to the assertions of some of their non-academic critics, they could actually adapt to fundamental challenges to their received views both speedily and effectively. In exactly the same period during which Thom published his findings, the method of dating upon which they relied, based on radiocarbon analysis, was revealed to be faulty, and the resulting revision altered the whole conventional interpretation of European prehistory. This was also a change brought about by external, scientific research, and it was rapidly and effectively assimilated by archaeologists. The second point to be emphasised is that the decision regarding the worth of Thom's theories could not be made by archaeologists themselves. The span of scientific expertise required for the task required a coalition of practitioners, most of them trained in disciplines other than archaeology.

It was this requirement that engendered the new academic discipline or 'interdiscipline' of archaeoastronomy. This secured something like official recognition in 1979, when the *Journal for the History of Astronomy* created a supplement for it. The first full-scale conference officially devoted to the subject was held at Oxford in 1981, and in the course of the 1980s a coalition of experts emerged within it. Some, like Douglas Heggie, were respected scientists, and some, such as Aubrey Burl, had an existing fame in archaeology. Others, such as John Barnatt, Gordon Moir, and Clive Ruggles, were scholars who were in the process of establishing careers. None of them could have been considered to belong to any existing 'establishment' of experts in prehistory: the nearest to such a figure in the list was Burl, who held a post at what was then a polytechnic and not a university. By contrast, Lockyer, Hawkins, Hoyle, and Thom were all, or had been, prominent members of the 'establishment' of academic pure or applied science.[8] A few of the new group of archaeoastronomers had personal connections with Thom: indeed, Burl had collated his plans for publication and added approving comments (Thom, Thom, and Burl 1980, 1990). Their investigations had been anticipated during the 1970s by a series of scholars who had accepted Thom's ideas and built upon them, and a few of these continued to do so in later decades (Critchlow 1973; MacKie 1977, 2000, 2002; Wood 1978; Thom, Ker, and Burrows 1988).

Nonetheless, the cluster of experts described above came to out-number these earlier workers in the field and to outrank them, and in the first half of the 1980s, these experts seemed to reach a consensual and negative verdict on Thom's theories, including his mathematical theorising (Burl 1980; Heggie 1981, 1982; Ruggles and Whittle 1981; Barnatt and Moir 1984; Ruggles 1984). Stone circles that he claimed to have been laid out with marvellous precision could, it seemed, have been built without it; nor was good evidence found for a common system of geometry or for a common system of measurement. Their verdict on his astronomical arguments was more mixed. Many stone circles and rows appeared to have no proven alignments with any heavenly bodies, which in itself seemed to overturn Thom's central thesis. The associations between megaliths and stars could not be tested adequately because the latter move so frequently and swiftly that any correlation could not be established without knowing a more precise date for the construction of the monument than present techniques permitted. On the other hand, a significant number of structures did seem to be built to correspond to the movements of the sun or moon, and some to both. This, however, fitted perfectly well the traditional model for prehistoric society that had been assembled by archaeologists. That model had always accepted that certain monuments, including some of the greatest, such as Stonehenge, had clear alignments with bodies in the sky. It had accepted these as significant components of the religion or religions, in most respects mysterious, which had partially inspired the construction of those monu-ments. Thom's argument had been that the same structures had primarily been astronomical observatories, erected by people with a shared scientific knowledge that had been marvellous even by the standards of the modern age. It was this that had appealed so much to the Earth Mysteries movement, seeming as it did to prove the existence of an impressive and universal ancient wisdom.

---

8. Archaeology is sometimes called a science, but in practice the discipline is almost always classed among the arts and humanities subjects of universities.

A close examination of these critiques suggests that Thom's conclusions were not, in fact, clearly refuted. What they revealed instead was that, at each point, Thom's suggestions were susceptible to challenge and alternative readings: they were not 'hard' science of the kind represented by the correction of the radiocarbon dating process. For virtually all professional archaeologists, this was sufficient to make it permissible to discard them as a contribution to the study of prehistory, justifying their desire to get back to business as usual. By the end of the 1980s, the coalition of experts who had investigated Thom's ideas more or less dispersed, and only one of them continued to make a reputation in the field. This was Ruggles, who emerged during the 1990s as the most respected archaeoastronomer in Britain. As well as being, in the long term, the most dedicated academic scholar of the subject, he had also been the most inclined to emphasise the difficulties and subtleties in it. He had emphasised, for example, that there are actually two different kinds of basic theoretical approaches to statistics, which get significantly different results. He had recognised that apparent scientific results may not always match up to cultural realities. When he investigated the stone rows and aligned pairs of North Mull and the Kilmartin Valley in Scotland, he found that all had a similar orientation. The only celestial event that matched it was the major southerly lunar standstill. What worried him about this was that there are no traditional peoples on earth in recorded history that have shown an interest in movements of the moon along the horizon. A conclusion from this that the Neolithic British were somehow cleverer and more scientifically minded than any other such people seems counter-intuitive. Ruggles got around it by suggesting that in Scotland's latitude alone the moon might seem to move along the horizon at major standstills. He was still plainly unhappy, however, and admitted what he called 'the fundamental problem…that evidence acceptable to a numerate scientist is of a very different nature from that acceptable to his counterpart trained in the humanities' (Ruggles 1988a).

By the end of the 1990s, Ruggles had effectively summed up archaeoastronomy in Britain for his academic peers (see in particular Ruggles 1999). He ruled decisively against any high-precision alignments with heavenly bodies in British or Irish prehistoric monuments. Instead, he found evidence for rough and symbolic alignments with either the sun or the moon among regional traditions that inclined to one or the other. These were fairly clear expressions of a belief system focused upon ritual and cosmic truths rather than observation for its own sake. He also pointed out a logical maw at the heart of Thom's labelling of megalithic monuments as observatories: that prehistoric farmers could determine the time of year quite easily by watching the horizon. They had no need for any markers to do so, let alone massive stone structures requiring huge efforts to build. In addition, Ruggles had acquired the knowledge of anthropology needed to raise one further concern: that many modern indigenous peoples have taboos against pointing directly at sacred things, so all of the alignments may be deceptive. Equipped with these arguments, he opened the new century by becoming Britain's only professor of archaeoastronomy, a fitting symbol of his pre-eminence in the field.

It seems that for many archaeologists Ruggles's conclusions represented not just the end of the debate but the end of the subject, an effect neatly illustrated by the most high-profile British prehistoric site of all: Stonehenge. In 1996 a respected academic historian of astronomy, John North, published a book in which he suggested that most Neolithic monuments were aligned with precision on heavenly bodies. Those from the earlier part of the period were targeted on stars, while the large enclosures of the later part, including Stonehenge, to which he devoted most attention, were more oriented with the movements of sun and moon. North (1996) emphasised that the essential purpose of the structures was religious but still insisted that they represented a scientific knowledge extraordinary for the time. The next year, a compilation of essays on the subject of *Science and Stonehenge* appeared under the auspices of the Royal Academy, and Ruggles was invited to write for it on astronomy. Without concentrating on North's book, he managed nonetheless to answer all its arguments, holding that they were hard to prove and suggesting that Stonehenge had only a single undoubted axis based on the solstices and a possible lunar component, neither requiring much grasp of science (Ruggles 1997). In 2007 Julian Richards, at that time probably the leading archaeological authority on the site, produced a book aimed at a large readership and entitled *Stonehenge: The Story So Far*. This did not mention North at all: he was clearly not part of 'the story'. Instead, it summed up Lockyer, Hawkins, and Thom as misguided, and introduced Ruggles as 'the voice of reason' before quoting his views at length (Richards 2007: 217-19). Two years before, Richards had rewritten the official guidebook to the monument, and briefly summarised Ruggles's ideas as all that was needed to be said about the astronomical aspects (Richards 2005: 17). In 2009 the Royal Astronomical Society issued a booklet to the general public which summed up those aspects in a few pages, compiled by a group of members led by Ruggles and once more repeating his views (Ruggles et al. 2009).

To his credit, Clive Ruggles himself was clearly uneasy about the situation that had developed, especially concerning the lack of interest in astronomy that British archaeologists had displayed since 1990. Many had ceased, in fact, to give any special consideration to possible heavenly alignments at the sites that they investigated (Ruggles 2001; Ruggles et al. 2009: 6-11). Ruggles suggested three reasons for this. One was that archaeologists had a new enthusiasm for setting prehistoric sites in their landscapes, which had distracted their focus. Another was that archaeo-astronomers drew their language from modern Western science, and so much of the earlier discourse grated on the ears of archaeologists as both ethnocentric and anachronistic. The third reason, in the eyes of profes-sional archaeologists, was that academic archaeoastronomy had been contaminated by confusion with what Ruggles termed a booming 'popular archaeoastronomy' that had blended indissolubly with paganism and New Age ideas (Ruggles 2001; Ruggles et al. 2009: 6-11).

It may be suggested here that there is truth in all three reasons, but, nevertheless, each can bear further consideration. Ruggles himself noted the logical maw in the first: that the sky is part of the landscape which archaeologists claimed to be studying. The language of archaeoastron-omy may well grate on the ears of professional archaeology. What is possibly more significant, however, is that so many aspects of archaeo-astronomy now seem so conjectural and inconclusive that British archaeologists in general now shy away from it.

The major exception to this rule in the years around 1990 was prob-ably the interpretation of a Bronze Age enclosure with wooden posts at Godmanchester near Huntingdon. The excavators proposed alignments from several of the posts upon movements of the sky, only to have their suggestions slammed by Ruggles himself as 'ill-advised', 'dangerous', and 'unconvincing', thus providing an example potent enough to deter others (Ruggles 1999: 128). In this situation, it is all too easy for archaeologists to leave the whole problem to archaeoastronomers, even forgetting in the process to supply the latter with any data. If they take any notice of archaeoastronomy, then the default position is more obviously to repeat the views of Ruggles, not because he is seen as occupying an extreme, sceptical end of a spectrum, but because he is regarded as the opposite: as the main representative of a cautious and consensual position with which virtually all archaeoastronomers should agree, even if some would like to go much further.

The terms which Ruggles has used for the more unorthodox and unofficial forms of archaeoastronomy may also need some refinement. To call them 'popular' is perhaps questionable, in both senses of the word: there is no sign that they attract more public interest or enthusiasm than mainstream archaeology, that they are representative of the populace as a whole, or that they arose from mainstream popular culture. Rather, they are generated by a relatively well-defined minority interest and sub-culture within the UK, which overlaps with the Pagan and New

Age movements, shares their opposition to traditional social and cultural norms, but is distinct from the mainstreams of both. The obvious source of it is in neither of the two movements named by Ruggles, but in the former Earth Mysteries, of which in many ways it is a continuation: now that ley lines drawn straight between ancient monuments on the earth have largely fallen out of fashion, the interest has shifted to straight lines in the air, drawn between monuments and heavenly bodies. This interest is propelled by the same impulse that gave rise to a new interest in archaeoastronomy itself in the 1960s: surveying the sky is one apparent way of coming up with new ideas about the prehistoric past which requires no excavation and no acquaintance with current thinking about prehistory. The force that has recently given it fresh vigour is the microchip revolution, which has provided exciting new tools, including software, that represent the configuration of the night sky during different eras of prehistory, as well as satellite pictures of sites. The simplest name for it, which accurately reflects its most obvious characteristic while being value-free, is 'Thomite'.[9] To give some sense of the range of approaches at present existing within it, three different bodies of work will now be considered as examples.

The first is that of Robin Heath, who has emerged as the most prominent and prolific recent figure in the field, with a series of books issued since the late 1990s and his own web site (1998, 1999, 2002, 2009, and www.skyscript.co.uk). He is an engineer who has taught at various colleges and recently held an honorary research fellowship at the University of Wales, Lampeter—a reminder that the boundary between mainstream archaeoastronomers and Thomites is not straightforwardly one between academics and non-academics. Heath's heroes are Hawkins, Michell, and Thom, and in his earlier work he restated their claim to have proved the existence of a worldwide, ancient, awe-inspiring scientific wisdom. From the geometrical and mathematical properties of stone circles, especially Stonehenge, he concluded that the builders used them to predict eclipses, calendar dates, tides, and phases of the moon. Heath has also asserted, in partnership with Michell, that Neolithic people accurately calculated the dimensions of the planet. In that earlier work he made no attempt to integrate any of this information with the findings of archaeologists, and indeed he had no time for the latter, dis- missing them collectively as characterised by 'ignorance and prejudice' (Heath 1998: xiii). Instead, the supporting evidence that he employed for his interpretations of measurements and calculations was taken from a

9. 'Thomist' is more elegant, but is already current among intellectual historians for the followers and thought of the medieval theologian Thomas Aquinas.

personal reinterpretation of medieval Christian legends and of selected parts of the Bible and Apocrypha. In many ways his work has been firmly in the older Earth Mysteries tradition, arguing both for an equal validity of the insights of 'dowsers, ley hunters, sacred geometers, psychics, and shamans' with those of archaeology, and for the valuable lessons to be drawn today about 'living on the earth' from a true understanding of ancient wisdom (Heath 1998: 138, 183). His most substantial recent book has been an extended defence of the work of Alexander Thom (Heath 2007).[10] Although this book is much more respectful to archaeologists than before, it is still only interested in them and their publications inasmuch as they relate directly to Thom's ideas. Yet Heath still clearly regards a rejection of those ideas as moral failings rather than simply a difference of scholarly opinion. The principal villain of his story, predictably, is Ruggles.[11]

Heath is, in my opinion, the most typical as well as the most prominent of my three case-studies. The other two, in different ways, buck the normal trend. One is a recent arrival on the scene, a computer programmer named Thomas William Flowers Junior, who has published two booklets and more information on a web site since 2008 (Flowers 2008, 2009).[12] His starting point is also the work of Thom, but he has attacked the latter as inadequate and set out to demonstrate his own surveys of Stonehenge and other major Neolithic sites to be superior. In particular, he has sought to establish a theory that the monuments concerned were designed to bring the sun and moon together to produce

10. My efforts to obtain this text illustrate well the difficulties experienced by mainstream scholars in trying to engage with such alternative viewpoints. The text did not exist in the copyright library nearest to me, at Oxford, and when I put in an order through the inter-library loan system, I was informed that none was held by any lending institution in the UK. A confined copy existed in the British Library in London, and there was one in a local branch library in Somerset, neither place easily reached from my home. The only other way to read the book was to locate, order, and purchase it on the Internet. I myself thought the effort and expense worth the trouble, in this case, but it would probably deter many mainstream scholars with doubts about the value of the exercise.

11. I am Heath's principal example of a collaborator with the forces of darkness, rather flatteringly in view of my position as an outsider to the field. My experience in this respect is part of a pattern: scholars who ignore the work of Thomites and other counter-cultural writers are only denounced by them in general and anonymous terms. Those who try to engage with their work, while disagreeing, are attacked by them in a direct and personal fashion. This acts as a further, powerful disincentive to any recognition of their existence.

12. In this case there was no difficulty in obtaining the booklets because the author sent copies himself to a string of prominent prehistorians.

a baby sun. He in turn has shown no real interest in the recent findings of archaeology. Instead, Flowers has announced that, on sending his conclusions to English Heritage, the administrative body that cares for Stonehenge, he received a polite acknowledgment but it did not adopt his views. He has therefore condemned archaeologists in general as 'stuck in the past'. He has advanced various reasons for a neglect of Thomite work by archaeologists since the 1980s. A further one is that Thomites seem to disagree with each other, while being in general equally hostile towards orthodox scholarship.

The third example is a different sort of exception to the current Thomite rule. It is a lengthy study of the Neolithic monuments of the Boyne Valley, the most famous in Ireland, which appeared in 2006 (Murphy and Moore 2006).[13] Anthony Murphy and Richard Moore are, respectively, a journalist and an artist from that district. In many ways the book is absolutely typical of the Thomite canon. Its inspiring figure is (again) Thom himself, and it proposes, after his manner, a large number of alignments between the different monuments and the sun, moon, and stars. It is also rooted firmly in the Earth Mysteries tradition, drawing straight lines on the ground between the various sites and finding a giant figure picked out in the landscape. Both are classic phenomena that Earth Mysteries researchers claim to have detected elsewhere, and the book likewise treats the ancient world as having wisdom to teach the present. It also, like Heath, places an emphasis on medieval legends as supporting evidence for these claims. What is so distinctive about it is that the authors have made every effort to understand archaeologists, to incorporate their findings, and to show respect for them. They never, in fact, abuse any opponents and their work is proportionately free of evangelical rhetoric. They admit that their arguments are speculative and offer them as a contribution to a general debate. Nothing quite like their work seems to have appeared in Britain. The difference is not a national one, because relations between archaeologists and Thomites in Ireland seem to have been as strained as those in Britain.[14] It seems to be simply one of personality.

13. This would have passed me by completely had I not met Anthony Murphy at a conference of Earth Mysteries enthusiasts at which we were both invited to speak, found him as charming in person as in print, and promptly bought his book.

14. For example, the archaeologist Muiris O'Sullivan spoke bitterly of the 'pseudo-scientific literature' of Earth Mysteries and Thomite writers about Irish Neolithic monuments, and accused them of being 'almost paranoid about archaeologists' (O'Sullivan 1993: 36).

To broaden and balance the argument, on the other side of the Atlantic a different story about archaeoastronomy was emerging, one that shall be touched on only briefly here. Archaeoastronomy in the New World was spawned in an environment investigating the astronomies and the role of cosmology of native North, Meso-, and South American cultures. The two most prominent researchers working with this Mesoamerican material were Anthony Aveni and Edwin Krupp, both highly regarded scholars throughout the Americas and significant in founding the discipline of archaeoastronomy during the 1970s (Aveni 1975; Krupp 1977). Aveni, an astronomer researching the astronomical history of the Maya Indians of ancient Mexico, recognised a complex and fundamental difference between astronomical systems developed by indigenous civilisations of the tropical latitudes versus those based in temperate latitudes. This difference was based on distinctly different visible skies as caused by significant latitudinal difference, which his research indicated gave rise to different cosmologies (Aveni 1981). Furthermore, having access to resources such as ethnographies and the historical records of the early colonisers, unavailable to their European counterparts, meant New World archaeoastronomers were able to make claims for the motives behind the construction of monuments and building orientations that were underpinned by anthropological enquiry (Aveni 2008: 8). Such assertions in the Old World would have been considered mere speculation. In 1982 Aveni was made Russell Colgate Distinguished University Professor of Astronomy and Anthropology and Native American Studies at Colgate University in Hamilton, New York, and still holds that position. Krupp is an astronomer whose early research sought both a commonality in the use of sky myths in a diverse set of cultures, including the indigenous peoples of the American plains, northwest, and southwest, and a synthesis of the study of the heavens with archaeology (Krupp 1977, 1984). Since 1974 Krupp has been Director of the Griffith Observatory in Los Angeles, which is owned and operated by the City of Los Angeles Department of Recreation and Parks.

The first large-scale meeting of scholars interested in Pre-Columbian Archaeoastronomy, defined as 'the study of the extent of the astronomical knowledge and practice of the ancient people of Mesoamerica' (Aveni 1975: xii), was convened in Mexico City in June 1973, organised jointly by Mexico's Consejo Nacional de Ciencia y Tecnologia (CONACYT) and the American Association for the Advancement of Science (AAAS). The meeting was designed to investigate whether Mesoamerican archaeoastronomy as a bona fide interdisciplinary field that had relevance to the understanding of development of civilisation and culture existed, and the overwhelming response was that it did.

In 1981 Michael Hoskin, then President of the history section of the International Astronomical Union (IAU), organised a conference in Oxford to bring together scholars conducting research in archaeo-astronomy in both the Old and New Worlds. The result was electric. Those studying Mesoamerican cultures were 'scandalized at the gulf between Thom and his sympathizers on the one hand and European archaeologists on the other' (Hoskin 2001: 2). The only evidence Old World Thomites could bring to bear on ancient sites was the precise measurement of stones. This contrasted with those in the New World using a range of ethnographical evidence. To quote Ignacio Bernal: 'Astronomy and the calendar are aspects of mathematics and function on the basis of numbers. Whence the dangerous fascination of playing with figures. By moving them from here to there or giving them different meanings, they apparently can be used to prove any hypothesis' (in Aveni 1975: x-xi). The methodologies and research questions of the participants were considered so different that the conference proceedings were published as two volumes (Aveni 1982; Heggie 1982), giving rise to Old World (a green-coloured volume) or green archaeoastronomy, based primarily on alignment-orientated statistics, versus New World (a brown-coloured volume) or brown archaeoastronomy, which drew on historical and ethnographic records to enrich its understanding of early astronomies and their relationships to calendars and ritual (Aveni 1980). Yet from this grating mix arose a continuing series of Oxford Inter-national Conferences on Archaeoastronomy, held every four to five years, designed to share methodologies and processes. As a result, more interdisciplinary approaches that include archaeologists, ethnographers, anthropologists, and historians have underpinned and informed the current discipline of archaeoastronomy (Aveni 1989: xi-xiii). Rather than merely establishing the existence of ancient astronomies, contemporary archaeoastronomers are more open to seeking explanations within a broader cultural context of why ancient peoples would have harboured an interest in the sky. Published proceedings from the 2011 Oxford IX conference held in Lima, Peru (Ruggles 2011) offered a far more global collection of scholarly papers on the development of archaeoastronomy.

In conclusion, this contribution to the subject does not itself attempt to make any intervention in the debates over archaeoastronomy; the author lacks any of the scientific qualifications needed to become a participant in them. They are viewed here instead as an exercise in cultural history, focusing on what they tell us about modern British people and perhaps even about the processes of history themselves. One suggestion is that the various arguments provide powerful support for the concept of great personalities as motive forces in human development. Without the towering figure of Alexander Thom, neither academic nor popular interest in the field would have taken off as it did, and it may be that the Earth Mysteries would not have developed into a coherent movement at all. The same story also reveals some interesting differences between approaches to data on the part of scientists and of scholars in the humanities. It throws into high relief the basic problem of how truth can be established in scholarship and especially in the study of the remote past. Perhaps, however, it is most revealing as a lesson in the power politics of knowledge, expressed here in the relationships between different kinds of professional scholar, between popular and academic culture, between secularism and Christianity in the modern age, and between mainstream society and a counter-culture. One of the lessons of postmodernity is that academics should look more at the way in which their own perceptions are affected by the times and places in which they live. In this particular case, the interaction between academic and counter-cultural attitudes to the past, and between those engendered by different academic disciplines, seems to have been more important than has generally been acknowledged.

Acknowledgments

I am very grateful to Professor Clive Ruggles for reading through this piece of work in draft form and for making several invaluable suggestions for improvement.

References

Atkinson, R.J.C. 1959. *Stonehenge and Avebury and Neighbouring Monuments* (London: Her Majesty's Stationery Office).
Atkinson, J.C. 1966. 'Moonshine on Stonehenge', *Antiquity* 40: 212-16.
———. 1975. 'Megalithic Astronomy: A Prehistorian's Comments', *Journal of the History of Astronomy* 6: 51.
Aveni, A.F. 1980. *Skywatchers of Ancient Mexico* (Austin, TX: University of Texas Press).
———. 1981. 'Tropical Archeoastronomy', *Science* 213.4504: 161-71.
———. 1982. *Archaeoastronomy in the New World: American Primitive Astronomy: Proceedings of an International Conference Held at Oxford University, September 1981* (Cambridge: Cambridge University Press).
———. 1988. *New Directions in American Archaeoastronomy: Proceedings [of the] 46th International Congress of Americanists: Amsterdam, Netherlands 1988* (Oxford: B.A.R.)

———. 1989. *World Archaeoastronomy: Selected Papers from the 2nd Oxford International Conference on Archaeoastronomy Held at Merida, Yucatan, Mexico, 13–17 January 1986* (Cambridge: Cambridge University Press).

Aveni, A.F., ed. 1975. *Archeoastronomy in Pre-Columbian America* (Austin, TX: University of Texas Press).

———. ed. 2008. *Foundations of New World Cultural Astronomy: A Reader with Commentary*, Science. Boulder: University Press of Colorado, 2008.

Barnatt, John, and Gordon Moir. 1984. 'Stone Circles and Megalithic Mathematics', *Proceedings of the Prehistoric Society* 50: 197-216.

Burl, Aubrey. 1980. 'Science or Symbolism', *Antiquity* 54: 191-200.

Critchlow, Keith. 1973. *Time Stands Still: New Light on Megalithic Science* (London: Gordon Fraser Gallery).

Flowers, Thomas William. 2008. *Woodhenge Embryology* (private publication).

———. 2009. *Alexander Thom's Megalithic Yard* (private publication). Online: http://www.delnitivestonehenge.com.

Graves, Tom. 1976. *Dowsing* (Penzance, UK: Turnstone).

Hawkes, Jacquetta. 1967. 'God in the Machine', *Antiquity* 41: 174-80.

Hawkins, Gerald S. 1963. 'Stonehenge Decoded', *Nature* 200: 306-308.

Heath, Robin. 1998. *Sun, Moon and Stonehenge* (Cardigan, Wales: Bluestone Press).

———. 1999. *Sun, Moon and Earth* (Glastonbury, UK: Wooden Books).

———. 2002. *Stonehenge* (Glastonbury, UK: Wooden Books).

———. 2007. *Alexander Thom* (Cardigan, Wales: Bluestone Press).

———. 2009. *The Moon and Ancient Calendars* (Cardigan, Wales: Bluestone Press). Online: http://www.skyscript.co.uk.

Heggie, Douglas C. 1981. *Megalithic Science* (London: Thames & Hudson).

Heggie, Douglas C., ed. 1982. *Archaeoastronomy in the Old World* (Cambridge: Cambridge University Press).

Hitching, Francis. 1976. *Earth Magic* (London: Cassell).

Hoskin, Michael. 2001. *Tombs, Temples and Their Orientations: A New Perspective on Mediterranean Prehistory* (Bognor Regis, UK: Ocarina Books).

Hoyle, F. 1966a. 'Speculations on Stonehenge', *Antiquity* 40: 262-76.

———. 1966b. 'Stonehenge: An Eclipse Predictor', *Nature* 211: 454-56.

———. 1967. 'Hoyle on Stonehenge: Some Comments', *Antiquity* 41: 92-95.

Hutton, Ronald. 2008. 'Modern Pagan Festivals: A Study in the Nature of Tradition', *Folklore* 119: 251-73.

———. 2009a. *Blood and Mistletoe: The History of the Druids in Britain* (New Haven, CT: Yale University Press).

———. 2009b. 'Modern Druidry and Earth Mysteries', *Time and Mind* 2.3: 313-32.

Krupp, E.C. 1977. *Skywatchers, Shamans, and Kings: Astronomy and the Archaeology of Power* (New York: Wiley).

———. 1984. *Archaeoastronomy and the Roots of Science* (Epping, UK: Bowker).

Lockyer, Sir J.N. 1906. *Stonehenge and Other British Stone Monuments Astronomically Considered* (London: Macmillan).

MacKie, Euan. 1977. *Science and Society in Prehistoric Britain* (London: Paul Elek).

———. 2000. 'Maeshowe and the Winter Solstice', *Antiquity* 74: 62-74.

———. 2002. 'The Structure and Skills of British Neolithic Society', *Antiquity* 76: 666-68.

Metz, Hans. 1988. 'A Personal Appreciation of Professor Alexander Thom', in Ruggles 1988b: 14-30.

Michell, John. 1973 [1969]. *The View Over Atlantis* (London: Sphere Books).

———. 1977. *A Little History of Astro-Archaeology* (London: Thames & Hudson).

Murphy, Anthony, and Richard Moore. 2006. *Island of the Setting Sun* (Dublin: Liffey Press).

North, John. 1996. *Stonehenge: Neolithic Man and the Cosmos* (London: HarperCollins).

O'Connell, Aidan. 2013. *Harvesting the Stars: A Pagan Temple at Lismullin, Co. Meath*, NRA Scheme Monographs, 11 (Dublin: National Roads Authority).

O'Sullivan, Muiris. 1993. *Megalithic Art in Ireland* (Dublin, UK: Town House & Country House).

Pennick, Nigel. 1979. *The Ancient Science of Geomancy* (London: Thames & Hudson).

Richards, Julian. 2005. *Stonehenge* (London: English Heritage).

———. 2007. *Stonehenge: The Story So Far* (London: English Heritage).

Ruggles, Clive. 1984. *Megalithic Astronomy: A New Archaeological and Statistical Study of 300 Western Scottish Sites*, British Archaeological Reports, 123 (Oxford: B.A.R.).

———. 1988a. 'The Stone Alignments of Argyll and Mull', in Ruggles 1988b: 232-50.

———. 1997. 'Astronomy and Stonehenge', in *Science and Stonehenge*, ed. B. Cunliffe and C. Renfrew (Oxford: Oxford University Press): 203-29.

———. 1999. *Astronomy in Prehistoric Britain and Ireland* (New Haven, CT: Yale University Press).

———. 2001. 'Astronomy, Cosmology, Monuments and the Landscape in Prehistoric Ireland', in *Astronomy, Cosmology and Landscape*, ed. C. Ruggles, F. Prendergast, and T. Ray (Bognor Regis, UK: Ocarina): 51-52.

———. 2011. 'Pushing Back the Frontiers or Still Running around the Same Circles? "Interpretative Archaeoastronomy" Thirty Years on', *Proceedings of the International Astronomical Union* 7 (Symposium S278): 1-18.

Ruggles, Clive, ed. 1988b. *Records in Stone: Papers in Memory of Alexander Thom* (Cambridge: Cambridge University Press).

———. 2011. *Archaeoastronomy and Ethnoastronomy: Building Bridges between Cultures: Proceedings of the 278th Symposium of the International Astronomical Union and 'Oxford IX' International Symposium on Archaeoastronomy Held in Lima, Peru, January 5–14, 2011* (Cambridge: Cambridge University Press).

Ruggles, Clive, and Alisdair Whittle, eds. 1981. *Astronomy and Society in Britain during the Period 4000–1500 BC*, British Archaeological Reports, 88 (Oxford: B.A.R.).

Ruggles, Clive, Bill Burton, David Hughes, Andrew Lawson, and Derek McNally. 2009. *Stonehenge and Ancient Astronomy* (London: Royal Astronomical Society).

Screeton, Paul. 1974. *Quicksilver Heritage* (Wellingborough, UK: Thorsons).

Somerville, H. Boyle. 1924. 'Orientation in Prehistoric Monuments in the British Isles', *Archaeologia* 73: 193-224.

———. 1927. 'Orientation', *Antiquity* 1: 31-41.

Sorrell, Alan. 1980. *Early Wales Recreated* (Cardiff: National Museum of Wales).

Stout, Adam. 2008. *Creating Prehistory* (London: Blackwell).

Thom, Alexander. 1967. *Megalithic Sites in Britain* (Oxford: Oxford University Press).

———. 1971. *Megalithic Lunar Observatories* (Oxford: Oxford University Press).

Thom, Alexander, and Archibald S. Thom. 1978. *Megalithic Remains in Britain and Brittany* (Oxford: Oxford University Press).

Thom, Alexander, Archibald S. Thom, and Aubrey Burl. 1980. *Megalithic Rings* (Oxford: British Archaeological Reports).

———. 1990. *Stone Rows and Standing Stones* (Oxford: British Archaeological Reports).

Thom, Archibald S. 1988. 'A Personal Note about My Late Father', in Ruggles 1988b: 3-13.

———. 1995. *Walking in All of the Squares: Alexander Thom, Engineer and Archaeo-astronomer* (Glendaruel, Scotland: Argyll Publishing).

Thom, Archibald S., J.M.D. Ker, and T.R. Burrows. 1988. 'The Bush Barrow Gold Lozenge', *Antiquity* 62: 108-19.

Wood, John Edwin. 1978. *Sun, Moon and Standing Stones* (Oxford: Oxford University Press).

COMETS AND METEORS: THE IGNORED EXPLANATIONS FOR MYTHS AND APOCALYPSE

Patrick McCafferty

Universität Leipzig / Philologische Fakultät, Institut für Sorabistik,
Beethovenstr. 15, 04107 Leipzig, Germany
megalithed@yahoo.co.uk

Abstract

In their attempts to understand the origins of humanity's corpus of otherworldly tales, scholars of mythology have recognised deities of the sun, moon, planets and stars. Comets and meteors have been largely ignored, however, despite their importance in human culture, their obvious parallels with many aspects of myths, and their known physical effects. Of all the celestial bodies, comets and meteors have the greatest ability to inspire the imagination, leaving us with myths of monsters and dragons, of thunderbolt-throwing deities, of fallen angels wielding swords of light, and of battles between forces of good and evil in the heavens. Comets and meteors are clearly important contributors to the development of mythology (the Cometary Paradigm). When we consider myths in the light of the Cometary Paradigm, important conclusions are reached about the role of comets and meteors in human culture, the value of mythology to modern society, the origins of apocalyptic fears, and humanity's role on this planet.

Keywords

Celestial bodies, comets, meteors, mythology, Cometary Paradigm, apocalypse imagery, comparative mythology.

There appeared a star of wonderful magnitude and brightness, darting forth a ray, at the end of which was a globe of fire in the form of a dragon, out of whose mouth issued forth two rays, one of which seemed to stretch towards the Irish, so ending in seven lesser rays. Said Merlin to Uther: 'the star, and fiery dragon under it, signifies yourself'. Uther commanded two dragons to be made of gold, in likeness of the dragon which he had seen at the ray of the star. From this time he was called Uther Pendragon. (Geoffrey of Monmouth, in Giles 1900: 220-21).

Comets in Human Culture

If the sky is a tapestry embroidered by the human imagination, then the stars might be viewed as bright dots that can be joined to create a sky-scape of characters and imaginary objects. Across this map of the otherworld, familiar characters such as planets and the moon make regular appearances on predictable paths. Our stellar tapestry is unfurled each evening by the sun, and obscured each morning by light. Continuing our analogy, comets are scary, unpredictable characters who appear suddenly, behave unpredictably, warn of disaster, and change the plot. Scariest of all are meteors and fireballs, who spring to life, jump off the stellar cloth, and come down to Earth and into human lives.

In cultures around the world, sky gods play a prominent role: 'The worship of the Sky-god in its long and chequered history and its many ramifications and manifestations has been a basic element in the history of religion' (James 1963: 169). The sun and moon, as the brightest objects in the heavens, were worshipped in antiquity. Planetary deities, such as the Roman gods Mercury, Venus, Mars, Jupiter, and Saturn, are also recognisable in myths and in culture. Mythical characters can be linked to stars, with stories that seem to match the annual, apparent movement of the constellations (Monroe and Williamson 1987: 16). In almost every treatment of mythology, however, comets and meteors have been largely ignored. A search for the word 'comet' in the index of any major book on world mythology, for example by Mircea Eliade (1958) or C. Scott Littleton (2002), will invariably find that the word is missing.

This absence is both surprising and unjustifiable for a number of reasons. First, we know from history that comets, more than any other heavenly body, could inspire terror in human society: 'right up to medieval times, comets were a source not just of confusion but of terror. They seem to have engendered a feeling of virtual helplessness as if in the presence of superhuman forces' (Clube and Napier 1982: 158). Comets could sometimes appear to be the largest objects in the night sky.

Unlike all other bodies in the heavens (the sun, moon, planets, and stars), which are reasonably predictable, comets seemed to appear at will and could change their size and shape from one night to the next. As objects signifying disorder in the heavens, comets symbolised negative changes on Earth (Calder 1980: 12). Comets warned of the deaths of kings, as William Shakespeare wrote in *Julius Caesar* (Act 2, Scene 2): 'When beggars die, there are no comets seen; the heavens themselves blaze forth the death of princes'. They have also been blamed for bringing plagues, and for causing wars and famines:

> These Blazeing Starrs! | Threaten the World with Famine, Plague, & Warrs | To Princes, Death: to Kingdoms, many Crosses: | To all Estates, inevitable Losses ! | To Herds-men, Rot; to Plowmen, hapless Seasons | To Saylors Storms; to Cityes, Civill Treasons (Gadbury 1665: frontispiece).

Most ancient comets travelled on remote paths that could cause no physical effects on Earth (Kronk 1999–2009), so their ominous appearance at times of disaster was often coincidence and the human fear of comets was, apparently, mere superstition. As Nigel Calder (1980: 10) wryly commented:

> Comets drive people dotty. Like the emperors and priests who used to tremble when they appeared, some members of the public are still eager to be duped by charlatans selling protection against the evil influence of comets, or pamphlets proclaiming the end of the world.

Widespread, superstitious fear nevertheless has a power of its own. Comets posed a particular hazard for Roman Emperors, being seen as warnings of death and encouraging plots against their lives. The emperor Augustus (63 BCE–14 CE) was murdered in 14 CE after the appearance of a blood-red comet (Schechner-Genuth 1997: 25). Pliny (23–79 CE) (*Historia Naturalis* Book 2 §22) noted a comet in 54 CE, about the time that Claudius (10 BCE–54 CE) was poisoned (Rackham 1949: 235). Vespasian (9 CE–79 CE), too, died after the appearance of a comet: 'And at the fatal sight of a comet he cried: "Look at that long hair! The King of Parthia must be going to die"' (Graves and Grant 2003 [1957]: 294). Tacitus (56 CE–117 CE) described how a comet inspired an assassination plot against Nero (37 CE–68 CE): 'A brilliant comet now appeared. Since the general belief was that a comet meant a change of emperor, people speculated on Nero's successor as though Nero were already dethroned' (Grant 1996 [1956]: 324).

All too often, however, classical historians focus primarily on humans and ignore the role played by comets in ancient Rome. Historians William Smith (1913: 350), Christopher Mackay (2004: 203-207), and David Potter (2007: 68) described the humans who plotted Nero's assassination, yet disregarded the comet. This is a pattern all too familiar in history. Although the writings of Cassius Dio (c. 150–c. 235 CE) refer to multiple comets—Book 56 §24 noted how, in 9 CE, 'showers of comets appeared at one and the same time' (Scott-Kilvert 1987: 240)—the index to translations of Dio by both Earnest Cary (1968 [1918]: 487-89) and Ian Scott-Kilvert (1987: 338) fail to list the words 'comet', 'meteor', or even 'omen', focusing primarily on people and places. As a result, the historical and cultural importance of comets in ancient Rome has been overlooked. To paraphrase Oscar Wilde (1917 [1893]: 69), those who look only in the historical gutter will never see the stars.

The Origins of Mythology

Similarly, in the field of mythology, scholars have repeatedly ignored the contribution of comets and meteors to the development of myths. Global mythology identifies heroes who embark on otherworldly journeys, dragons and thunderbirds, giants and wizards, warriors who wield death-dealing weapons, angels and gods who interfere in human affairs. Over the centuries, scholars have suggested that comets and meteors could explain these myths, but their arguments have been dismissed or ignored by the mainstream. Max Müller (1899: 409-10) and George Cox (1870: 168), for example, attributed the numerous mythical motifs describing bright, fiery entities in the sky to the sun, though it is difficult to imagine how a single sun could give rise to such a multitude of sun-gods. Where Müller had seen sun-gods, Robert Graves (1961 [1948]: 9-10) saw a moon-goddess, worshipped across Europe, and James Frazer (1922: 144) saw a god of nature, or vegetative deity. Similarities between motifs and structures in many European tales (Mallory and Adams 1997: 331-32) were attributed to European society (Dumézil 1958). When Europeans encountered remarkably similar motifs in stories on other continents, however, another explanation was needed. Heyerdahl (1950; 1978: 50, 184) offered a model of cultural diffusion and contact. Sigmund Freud (1960: 3), Carl Jung (1964: 67), Joseph Campbell (1975 [1949]: 18), and Claude Lévi-Strauss (1970) explained the similarities between far-flung myths as the products of comparable human minds. Noting that many myths around the world referred to gods travelling in chariots in the sky and, tapping into the 1950s fascination with UFOs, Erich Von Däniken (1968) cynically attributed these to aliens in spaceships.

As a result, Western societies have become increasingly dismissive of myths. Indeed, in addition to its conventional definition of myth as 'a traditional story...typically involving supernatural beings or events', the Oxford dictionary online (2014) also defines 'myth' as 'a widely held but false belief or idea'. The Oxford thesaurus offers words such as 'delusion' and 'falsehood' as alternatives to 'myth'. For a society that no longer believes in giants or dragons, gods and goddesses, these semantic associations encourage a view of myths as mistaken views of the world, the products of imaginative or primitive or drug-altered minds, disconnected from reality.

It was not always so. There was a time when myths were believed to contain truth. The word 'myth' comes from the Greek word *muthos*, which Plato distinguished from *logos*: *muthos* was 'story' or unverifiable discourse whereas *logos* (the origin of our word 'logic') was rational argument, or verifiable discourse (Buxton 1994: 12). Karen Armstrong (2005: 135) argues that we need to have greater appreciation for the value of myth: 'We must disabuse ourselves of the nineteenth century fallacy that myth is false or that it represents an inferior mode of thought'.

The Cometary Paradigm

The above attempts to explain the origin of myths have, in my opinion, failed to address one key aspect: most tales are not cyclical but recount a chronology of events: a hero such as Achilles, Cú Chulainn, or Rama is born in auspicious circumstances, embarks on a journey at a young age, then returns for a pivotal event on a particular day a specified number of years later. These tales are presented as 'history', not as abstract depictions of the seasonal movements of the sun or moon, or the interplay between archetypes. Another explanation is required.

There is a simple explanation for the similarities between myths from around the world that I call the Cometary Paradigm. This explanation does not require a panoply of suns or moons, remote contact by raft, disturbed psyches, or gods in alien spacecraft. Rather, it suggests that if people witnessed, and were inspired by, similar events in the sky involving comets and meteors, and their associated phenomena of meteor showers or fireballs, then their stories describing those incidents would contain common features. Thus stories involving a dragon, a mythical beast that reputedly flew through the air, breathing its destructive fire on the landscape beneath, may have been describing large meteors or fireballs. As Carl Sagan and Ann Druyan (1985: 197) noted,

> [in the year 1000] a kind of flaming torch fell upon the Earth, leaving behind a long track of light like a path of a flash of lightning. Its brightness was so great that it frightened not only those who were in the fields, but even those who were in their houses. As this opening in the sky slowly closed, men saw with horror the figure of a dragon, whose feet were blue and whose head seemed to grow larger and larger.

One finds a similar account for the year 735 from Ireland: *'Draco ingens in fine autumni cum tonitruo magno post se uisus est'* / 'A huge dragon was seen, with great thunder after it, at the end of autumn' (Mac Airt and Mac Niocaill 1983: 188-89). Umberto Dall'Olmo (1980: 23) commented, 'Terms like *serpens* (snake) and *draco* (dragon) may refer both to an aurora and to a sporadic meteor; the smoky remnants of a big sporadic meteor may take the twisted shape of a snake or of a dragon, due to the currents in the upper atmosphere'.

Comets also provide explanations for other mythical and cultural motifs (McCafferty and Baillie 2005). The global spread of the swastika as a religious symbol can be explained as a rotating comet with four jets (Sagan and Druyan 1985: 156-60; McCafferty 2007: 230). In the second century BCE, the Chinese produced a silk manuscript depicting twenty-nine different types of comets (Kiang 1984), one of which has the shape of a swastika. Comets may likewise have inspired the idea of heavenly horses such as Pegasus. Indeed, the Chinese compare the tail of a heavenly horse to a comet: 'From the Scythian cave came the heavenly horse…eyes bright as the Evening Star…his tail was like a comet' (Minford and Lau 2000: 731). In 2007, Comet McNaught appeared with a spectacularly maned dust-tail and was linked by Richard Jakiel (2008: 23-24) to the comet described as Hippias by Pliny (*Historiae Naturalis* Book 2 §22): *'hippeus equinas iubas celerrimi motus atque in orbem circa se euntes'* / 'like a horse's mane; it has a very rapid motion, like a circle revolving on itself' (Rackham 1949: 232). Comets offer a better explanation than the sun or moon for the concept of a destructive, one-eyed giant such as the Cyclops or Medusa: in 2007, Comet 17P/Holmes bore a striking resemblance to a giant eye in the sky (Fig. 1).

Figure 1: Comet 17P/Holmes, 2007. The ground-based image of Comet 17P/Holmes was taken 1 November 2007, by astrophotographer Alan Dyer. The observations were made in southern Alberta, Canada with a 105mm apochromatic refractor at f/5 with a Canon 20Da camera at ISO400. Field is about 2.5 × 1.5 degrees. Photo: Alan Dyer/NASA/ESA.

The word 'comet' means 'long-haired'. This characteristic may have led to comets being anthropomorphised or inspired accounts of bright-faced celestial deities (McCafferty and Baillie 2005: 28-29, 51-53). Pliny described 'a white comet with silver hair so brilliant that it could not be looked at, and having the face of a deity in human form' (Hellman 1944: 36). A more contemporary drawing of Comet Donati in 1858 resembles a wig (Fig. 2).

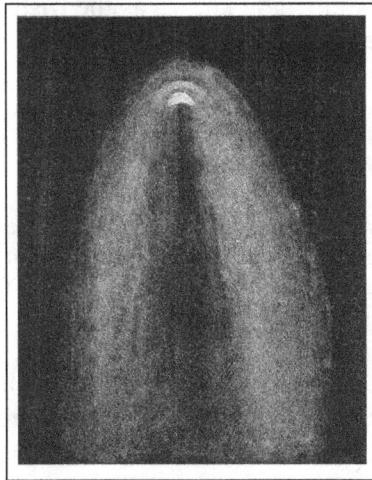

Figure 2: Comet Donati, 29 September 1858. Image: Guillemin 1875: pl. X (between pp. 222 and 223).

As entities known to have inspired terror in human populations, one might expect comets to have been not only feared but also propitiated and worshipped as deities. Cicero (106–43 BCE) included comets and meteors in his list of natural phenomena that inspire religion:

> The awe inspired by lightning, storms, rain, snow, hail, floods, pesti-
> lences, earthquakes and occasionally subterranean rumblings, showers of
> stones and raindrops the colour of blood, also landslips and chasms
> suddenly opening in the ground, also unnatural monstrosities human and
> animal, and also the appearance of meteoritic lights and what are called
> by the Greeks 'comets' and in our language 'long-haired stars' such as
> recently during the Octavian War appeared as harbingers of disasters…all
> of which alarming portents have suggested to mankind the idea of the
> existence of some celestial and divine power (trans. Rackham 1956
> [1933]: 137).

In Alexander Reed's anthology of myths from New Zealand (2004: 506, 514), deities such as Rongomai are openly recognised and described as cometary. Such recognition is exceptional, however. In most other traditions, mythologists never consider comets and this increases the chance of incorrect identification of the origins and attributes of gods. I have previously argued that the Egyptian goddess Hathor appeared as a red comet, not as the star Sirius (McCafferty 2007: 231-32). I have also, more tentatively, noted that the Aten, commonly interpreted as the sun, bears a striking resemblance to a comet (McCafferty 2007: 231). While it is difficult to be certain about the cometary aspect of the Aten, one can be sure of Lugh, the Celtic god known as the Irish sun god (Nutt 1895: 292) because he rose in the west, looking like the sun:

> Is iongnadh leam, ar se, an ghrian ag eirghe aniar aniu, agus anoir gacha
> laoi aile. Do budh fearr go mad í, ar na draoithe. Créad oile, ar sé.
> Dealradh aighthe Lóga Lamhfhada, ar siad.

> 'It is a wonder to me', said he, 'that the sun should rise in the west today,
> and in the east every other day'. 'It were better that it were so' said the
> Druids. 'What else is it?' said he. 'The radiance of the face of Lugh of the
> Long Arms', said they (O'Curry 1863: 176-77).

The fact that the sun never rises in the west, whereas a comet or meteor can, indicates that Lugh is not a sun god, but a comet deity (McCafferty and Baillie 2005: 48-50). Moreover, Lugh's epithet, Lugh of the Long Arm, is more consistent with a comet than the sun. Similarly, the Greek god Apollo, who, like a comet, shot death-dealing arrows and brought plague, is misinterpreted as a sun god because of his brightness, even though the Greeks already worshipped Helios. Many other celestial gods are known as planetary deities, but have characteristics that can best be explained by considering comets and meteors.

Like the ancient gods, and the planets, comets are celestial, bright and mobile. Unlike the planets, but like the gods, comets appear anthropomorphic, can feasibly cause destruction on Earth, and can split into pieces (Schaaf 1997: 261-66), apparently generating offspring. Thus it is possible for deities to have both planetary and cometary characteristics. Victor Clube and Bill Napier (1990: 85) drew attention to a drawing of planets with cometary tails and suggested that many of the divine names associated with planets may once have been the names of comets. In this way, a deity such as Quetzalcoatl may have ended up with both a planetary association (Venus) *and* clearly cometary attributes (the feathered serpent).

Similarly, the planet Jupiter may have become associated with a cometary god who threw thunderbolts. For ancient writers such as Seneca (*Naturales Quaestiones* Book 1 §5) thunderbolts had two potential causes: lightning and meteors (Clarke 1910: 40), perhaps due to the fact that in a world without light pollution, meteors were more common than lightning. Comets (and asteroids), however, are also capable of throwing meteoritic thunderbolts in Earth's path. The connection between comets and meteor showers was recognised in 1866 by Schiaparelli (1867), who showed that the August Perseids followed the orbit of comet Swift-Tuttle (1862 III).

Since comets look similar to meteors, with their bright head and tail, ancient people may have thought that both were celestial bodies capable of travelling to Earth. The Aztec Emperor Monteczuma II interpreted a comet as the return of the white-bearded god Quetzalcoatl, whom he mistook for the Spanish conquistador Cortes (Sagan and Druyan 1985: 27). Amédée Guillemin (1875: 6) noted that in Homer's *Iliad* (Book 4, §73), Athena shot to Earth, shooting sparks like a meteor:

> She came swooping down from the heights of Olympus like a meteor that Zeus, son of sickle-wielding Cronus, discharges as a warning to sailors or to some great army on the land: blazing, it shoots out a mass of sparks. That was how Pallas Athene looked as she sped to earth and leaped in among the troops (trans. Jones and Rieu 2003: 50).

The Siberian tale of Bukha-Noyon-babai descending from the sky as a bull was depicted as a fireball surrounded by meteors (Tashak 2004: 43). Similar imagery appears in Gilgamesh: when the goddess Ishtar sent the Heavenly Bull to fall on Uruk, the snorts from its nostrils killed hundreds of men (Sandars 1960: 86). Gilgamesh, who killed the bull, had meteoritic characteristics in a dream in which he:

> walked through the night under the stars of the firmament, and one, a meteor of the stuff of Anu, fell down from heaven. I tried to lift it but it proved too heavy... I brought it to you, and you yourself pronounced it my brother (trans. Sandars 1960: 64).

Eliade (1958: 54) reasoned, 'Everything that fell from above partook of the holiness of the sky; that is why meteorites, absolutely saturated with it, were venerated'. Religions often have strong associations with meteorites. The black stone in the Kabaa in Mecca is said to have been brought by an angel to Abraham, and is thought by Eliade to be a meteorite (1958: 277-79). A number of deities, such as Pallas Athena and Cybele, were represented by a stone that fell from heaven, a clear association with meteorites that should have informed mythologists of the strong links between these deities and comets and meteors.

Fireballs and Apocalyptic Battles

Although New Zealand is one of only a few places in the world whose gods have been clearly identified as comets and fireballs (Reed 2004: 506), we know from accounts of the Bamberg fireball of 28 December 1560 that humans have interpreted fireballs as an apocalyptic, destructive battle in the heavens (Bailey et al. 1990: 89). The day that Lugh rose in the west, Ireland experienced its mythical battle of *Magh Tuired*, between the divine Tuatha Dé Danann and the grotesque Fomhor, in which Lugh killed his grandfather Balor of the Evil Eye. Had Lugh not done so, Balor's eye would have burned all of Ireland (Gregory 1905: 51). In the book of Genesis (19.24), 'Then the LORD rained on Sodom and Gomor'rah brimstone and fire from the LORD out of heaven'. Extraordinarily violent battles occur in almost every mythological corpus. These generally take place a certain number of years after the birth of the divine hero and involve potent, meteoritic weapons. The Indian epic, the *Ramayana*, contains the following description of Ravana: 'Coursing through the sky in his celestial chariot, Ravana appeared like a blazing comet. His dark body shone with a brilliant aura. From his ten heads his reddish eyes darted about, scouring the mountains below' (Dharma 2000: 1). The *Ramayana* describes a fireball storm:

> Great meteors fell from the sky and the Earth shook. The sky became darkened even while the sun shone. Terrible thunderbolts and flashes of lightning fell upon the Rakshasa army. Ravana's steeds shed hot tears and emitted sparks from their mouths (trans. Dharma 2000: 400).

Hesiod's description of the mythical battle between the Gods and Titans is also replete with violent, meteoritic imagery:

> Then Zeus...showed forth all his strength. From Heaven and from Olympus he came forthwith, hurling his lightning: the bolts flew thick and fast from his strong hand together with thunder and lightning, whirling an awesome flame. The life-giving Earth crashed around in burning, and the vast wood crackled loud with fire all about (trans. Evelyn-White 1977: 128-31).

A similar apocalyptic battle appears in almost every strand of Indo-European mythology, from the Norse *Ragnarök* to the Persian *Shahnameh*. Some Indo-European scholars interpret these parallel accounts as a Proto-Indo-European 'War of the Functions' as if they are merely describing social struggles between kings, farmers, and warriors (Mallory 1989: 139). Such interpretation ignores the meteoritic and cometary imagery in the tales. Moreover, apocalyptic battles with meteoritic imagery also appear in tales outside the Indo-European realm: in Finland, the Americas, in Africa, in Egypt, the Middle East, in China, and New Zealand (McCafferty 2011). When these accounts are examined from an astronomical perspective, one can conclude that human cultures around the world witnessed spectacular comets and meteor showers, and fireballs as violent as the Tunguska blast in 1908.

Such events did not merely inform humanity's view of the sky: they also influenced our view of the future. In many cultures, there are predictions of the end of the world. The Greek Stoics and Epicureans predicted the end of the world in a cosmic fireball (Adams 2007: 126-27). The Celts who met Alexander the Great in 335 BCE informed him 'they feared nothing except that the sky might fall down on them' (Strabo 7.3.8 in Koch and Carey 2000: 7). In Rome, the Sibylline prophecies predicted that 'fiery swords shall fall from heaven on earth; and great bright lights shall come flaming down in the midst of men' (Book 3, 1. 841-43 in Terry 1899: 34). According to the Old Testament, civilisation had already been destroyed by the Deluge and prophets such as Enoch warned of a cosmic catastrophe. David Levy (2003: 10) interpreted an angel as a comet: 'And David lifted up his eyes, and saw the angel of the Lord stand between the Earth and the heaven, having a drawn sword in his hand stretched out over Jerusalem' (1 Chronicles 21.16). The angels of the Old Testament are not the friendly, benevolent beings of modern angelology but capable of coming from heaven to commit mass murder: 'Then the Angel of the Lord went out, and killed in the camp of the Assyrians one hundred and eighty-five thousand; and when people arose early in the morning, there were the corpses—all dead' (Isaiah 37.36). The book of Revelation contains numerous predictions of destructive angels blowing their trumpets to bring stars crashing onto Earth: 'And the stars of heaven fell to the earth' (Revelation 6.13); 'a great star fell from heaven, burning like a torch' (Revelation 8.10-11). Across a wide span of literature, apocalyptic imagery is intertwined with meteors.

The Threat from Above

This author is not the first person to draw attention to the similarities between comets and meteors and ancient accounts of heavenly battles. Throughout the centuries, numerous scholars and artists have concluded that myths were describing catastrophes caused by meteors or comets. In ancient Greece, the tale of Phaethon described his inability to control the horses pulling the sun's chariot. When Phaethon drove the sun so close to Earth that it was in danger of burning, Zeus knocked him to the ground with a thunderbolt. Plato (c. 428–c. 348 BCE) in his *Timaeus* §22C, recalled an Egyptian priest's opinion that the tale was a record of a catastrophe caused by the heavenly bodies:

> That story, as it is told, has the fashion of a legend, but the truth of it lies in the occurrence of a shifting of the bodies in the heavens which move round the earth, and a destruction of the things on the earth by fierce fire, which recurs at long intervals (trans. Bury 1929: 33-35).

Scientists such as Isaac Newton (1642–1727) and Edmond Halley (1656–1742) thought that comets and fireballs could provide an explanation for destructive events in myths and in the landscape. The comet of 1680 travelling on a sun-grazing orbit, convinced Newton that it had become superheated, and could extinguish life on Earth if it came too close (Martin 1757: 7). Halley (1724: 123) speculated that a comet could have caused the biblical deluge. Halley had identified a 575-year pattern for the comets of 1680, 1106, 531 (all CE) and 44 BCE (Cohen and Whitman 1999: 918), leading William Whiston (1708: 142) to connect a comet to the destruction of Troy and to Noah's deluge. Others feared that it would cause the Apocalypse on its next return in the year 2255 (Anonymous 1757: 6):

> When the blazing stars appear, like so many furies, with their lighted torches, threatening to set all on fire. For I do not doubt but the Comets will bear a part in this tragedy, and have something extraordinary in them, at that time; either as to number, or bigness, or nearness to the earth.

In 1777, observations of Comet Lexell showed that its nucleus held very little mass: comets were much smaller than planets and they seemed to be harmless (Schaaf 1997: 21). New discoveries, however, showed that the sky might, after all, provide an explanation for myths. One was the realisation that peasants who reported stones falling from the sky were not lying (Biot 1810: 9): meteorites could indeed strike Earth after a journey through space. Another was the discovery of asteroids, starting in 1800, bringing about the realisation that we live in 'the cosmic shooting gallery' (Asher et al. 2005). Today, we know that there are numerous asteroids, of which more than eleven thousand are on potentially catastrophic orbits in Earth's neighbourhood (NASA 2014). Increasing numbers of people connected myths to comets, asteroids, and meteors. In 1950, Immanuel Velikovsky notoriously concluded that the planet Jupiter somehow gave birth to the planet Venus which passed Earth as an enormous comet, causing the mayhem described in ancient texts (Velikovsky 1950: 173). Albert Einstein (1946) rejected Velikovsky's proposed planetary mechanism as impossible but largely agreed with his catastrophist interpretation of myths. Velikovsky did not need a planet-sized comet to explain events in myths: in 1828, David Milne (1828: 121) had won an astronomy prize at Edinburgh University for his Essay on Comets, in which he suggested that even though a comet nucleus is small, it could inflict tremendous damage on Earth due to its large velocity (of 10–70 km per second). In recent decades, the discovery of Iridium at the K-T boundary brought awareness that dinosaurs became extinct because of a cosmic impact (Alvarez et al. 1980: 1106). The collision of Comet Shoemaker-Levy 9 with Jupiter in 1994, causing explosions in the scale of millions of megatons (Crawford et al. 1995: 256), raised humanity's awareness of Earth's vulnerability to impact from space (Levy 1998: 213).

It is important not to exaggerate the effects of comets, asteroids, and meteors. Asteroids are most likely to miss us. Comets are usually remote from Earth and pose no danger. Even when changes in a comet's orbit bring it on a path that intersects Earth's orbit, there is very little danger of a direct collision. There is, however, an extremely high chance of encountering cometary debris. This is most likely to be just dust, causing a spectacular meteor shower. Unfortunately, numerous comets have been observed to split into large pieces, not just dust, and this makes them highly dangerous (Steel 1995: 257-58). It is now known that some comets travel in a trail of large particles (Sykes et al. 1986: 1115). In 2006, comet 73P/Schwassmann-Wachmann 3 (Fig. 3) was observed to have undergone a cascade of fragmentation, forming at least 60 large fragments (Fernández 2009: 1221). If a comet with a diameter of 10km were to split into 1km objects, it would form not just ten of these, but one thousand (10^3), each of which could, in turn, split into one thousand 100m objects and so on. If Earth were to encounter such a trail, the planet would experience a swarm of large chunks of cometary fragments, each causing enormous explosions.

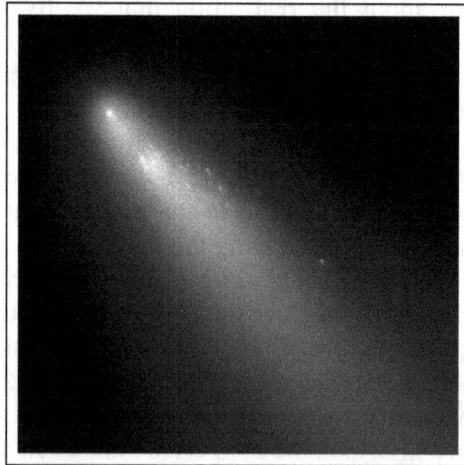

Figure 3: Comet 73P/Schwassmann-Wachmann 3, - Fragment B: 18 April, 2006. Photo: NASA, ESA, H. Weaver (APL/JHU), M. Mutchler and Z. Levay (STScI).

At Tunguska in 1908, an object just 35m in diameter (Boslough and Crawford 2008: 1442) felled roughly eighty million trees over an area of 2000 square kilometres, or roughly fifty kilometres in diameter (Kulik 1927). So there is no need to imagine comets striking Earth to explain myths: due to their velocity, small house-sized chunks of debris can cause widespread devastation. It is estimated that a Tunguska-scale event might occur just once per millennium (Brown 2002: 296), which would imply two events on land and three over the sea in the past five thousand years. Such a low frequency would not explain the development of myths. However, this estimate is almost certainly too low, as suggested by the 500-kiloton explosion of a 17m object over Chelyabinsk on 15 February 2013, injuring over 1000 people just a century after Tunguska (Malik 2013), and by a suspected explosion over Brazil in 1930 (Bailey et al. 1995: 250). During the Holocene (the geological epoch which began at the end of the last ice age, c. 11,700 years ago), at least eleven impact craters were formed by large iron-nickel objects at, for example, Morasko, Poland and Kaalijärv, Estonia (Hamacher and Norris 2010: 28-30). From meteorite discoveries, it is thought that stony chondrites (which generally do not cause impact craters) make up 80% of meteorite falls (Burbine et al. 2002: 656) and outnumber iron-nickel meteorites (which can cause craters) by at least five to one. On this basis alone, one would expect over fifty large airbursts during the Holocene. Moreover, the existence of comet trails shows that these events do not occur randomly. Like meteors, one might watch for ages and see none but then experience a major shower with thousands of shooting stars in a single hour. Mythical accounts of apocalyptic battles suggest that humans witnessed swarms of destructive fireballs and numerous Tunguska-scale blasts in one day. Although this has not yet been confirmed by archaeology, this interpretation of myths is consistent with astronomical discoveries.

Conclusion

We live in a world where the corpus of myths is often dismissed as fantasy fiction. Attempts to explain myths in terms of the sky have focused primarily on the regular, predictable motions of the heavens. As a result, myths seem to be the products of primitive minds or disturbed psyches and the celestial tapestry has been presented as a richly decorated but comparatively uneventful canvas. Myths are, in consequence, deemed irrelevant for many scholars in disciplines such as archaeology and history who are attempting to understand the past.

Surprisingly, comets and meteors have been ignored in many areas of scholarship, even though comets are known to have caused fear in societies across the world (Sagan and Druyan 1985). The word 'comet' is missing from the indexes of almost every book dealing with the human past, from anthropology to mythology, folklore, and archaeology. Yet, by examining myths for motifs that can be related to fireballs and comets, many tales that one would dismiss as impossible can, in fact, be understood. The tales suggest that cometary entities in the heavens (sky gods, armies, heroic warriors, dragons, and angels) occasionally rained destructive fire and brimstone on the Earth in great celestial battles, possibly on the same day across the world.

Whilst no comet has collided with Earth in recent millennia, a much less dramatic mechanism exists to explain the events in myths. In recent decades, through scientific observation of the skies, astronomers have discovered numerous potential hazards in space. We are now at a critical juncture, perhaps for the first time in centuries, where we can marry the ancient accounts of our ancestors with a new, scientific understanding of Earth's crowded neighbourhood in our busy solar system. These ancient tales seem to warn that spectacular, Tunguska-scale events occurred with a greater frequency and intensity than is currently appreciated even by many astronomers. Scientific observation of the skies offers a new way of understanding the human past. The picture of cometary catastrophe that emerges is a completely new paradigm that requires a major reassessment of previous theoretical approaches. It offers an explanation of myths and the origins of religion that fits the historically attested fear of comets. It matches the archaeological record with its gaps and evidence of the widespread simultaneous collapse of civilisations. It also offers a society that has grown dismissive of myths and religions a new alternative between the polar opposites of belief and disbelief: understanding and respect for traditions.

To conclude, only by uncovering the richly decorated tapestries of celestial events, only by connecting meteors to myths, and comets' tails to comet tales can we hope to appreciate the real significance of humanity's cultural compendium of legends and narratives. What is needed is a new engagement with myths and religions, and an exploration of their cometary significance to the human past. We may need to do this to determine our future. Ancient prophecies warn of the potentially apocalyptic effects of future impacts. For the first time in its long history, our solar system has nurtured a species with both the intelligence and nascent technological capability to observe the sky and to protect a planet from cometary and asteroidal impacts. Whereas all our ancestors could do was beseech the heavenly gods, we could take responsibility for our planet's future. Perhaps that is the significance of the biblical passage Genesis 1.26-28 granting humanity dominion over the Earth.

References

Adams, Edward. 2007. *The Stars Will Fall From Heaven: Cosmic Catastrophe in the New Testament and its World*, Library of New Testament Studies, 347 (London: T&T Clark).

Armstrong, Karen. 2005. *A Short History of Myth* (Edinburgh: Canongate).

Alvarez, Luis W., Walter Alvarez, Frank Asaro, and Helen V Michel. 1980. 'Extra-terrestrial Cause for the Cretaceous-Tertiary Extinction', *Science* 208: 1095-108.

Anonymous. 1757. *An Account of the Remarkable Comet whose Appearance Is Expected at the End of this Present Year 1757, or at the Beginning of 1758* (London: n.p.).

Asher, David J., Mark E. Bailey, Vacheslav V. Emel'yanenko, and Bill Napier. 2005. 'Earth in the Cosmic Shooting Gallery', *Observatory* 125: 319-22.

Bailey, Mark E., S. Victor M. Clube, and William M Napier. 1990. *The Origin of Comets* (Oxford: Pergamon Press).

Bailey, Mark E., D.J. Markham, S. Massai and J.E. Scriven. 1995. 'The 1930 August 13 "Brazilian Tunguska" Event', *The Observatory* 115: 250-53.

Biot, Jean-Baptiste. 1810. *Traité Élémentaire d'Astronomie Physique* (Paris: J. Kloster-mann).

Boslough, Mark B.E. and D.A. Crawford. 2008. 'Low-altitude Airbursts and the Impact Threat: Hypervelocity Impact', *Proceedings of the 2007 Symposium - HVIS 2007, International Journal of Impact Engineering* 35: 1441-48.

Brown, Peter. 2002. 'The Flux of Small Near-Earth Objects Colliding with the Earth', *Nature* 420: 294-96.

Burbine, Thomas H., Timothy J. McCoy, Anders Meibom, Brett Gladman, and Klaus Keil. 2002. 'Meteoritic Parent Bodies: Their Number and Identification', in eds., *Asteroids* 3: 653-67 (Tucson: University of Arizona).

Bury, R.G., trans. 1929. *Plato*, Volume VII: *Timaeus, Critias, Cleitophon, Menexenus and Epistles*, Loeb Classical Library (London: Heinemann)

Buxton, Richard. 1994. *Imaginary Greece: The Context of Mythology* (Cambridge: Cambridge University Press).

Calder, Nigel. 1980. *The Comet Is Coming! The Feverish Legacy of Mr. Halley* (London: British Broadcasting Corporation).

Campbell, Joseph.1975 [1949]. *The Hero with a Thousand Faces* (New York: Bollingen Foundation, 1949; repr. London: Abacus, Sphere Books, 1975).

Cary, Earnest, trans. 1968 [1918]. *Dio's Roman History*, Loeb Classical Library, 9 vols. (London: Heinemann; New York: Macmillan, 1914–27), vol. 8 (1918; repr. London: Heinemann; Cambridge, MA: Harvard University Press, 1927, 1968).

Clarke, John, trans. 1910. *Physical Science in the Time of Nero, Being a Translation of the Quaestiones Naturales of Seneca* (London: Macmillan).

Clube, Victor, and Bill Napier. 1982. *The Cosmic Serpent: A Catastrophist View of Earth History* (London: Faber & Faber).

———. 1990. *The Cosmic Winter* (Oxford: Blackwells).

Cohen, I. Bernard, and Anne Whitman, eds. 1999. *Isaac Newton, the Principia: Mathematical Principles of Natural Philosophy* (Berkeley/Los Angeles: University of California Press).

Cox, George William. 1870. *The Mythology of the Aryan Nations*, Part I (London: Longmans, Green).

Crawford, D.A., M.B. Boslough, T.G. Trucano, and A.C. Robinson. 1995. 'The Impact of Periodic Comet Shoemaker-Levy 9 on Jupiter', *International Journal of Impact Engineering* 17.1–3: 253-62.

Dall'Olmo, Umberto. 1980. 'Latin Terminology Relating to Aurorae, Comets, Meteors and Novae', *Journal for the History of Astronomy* 11: 10-27.

Dharma, Krishna, trans. 2000. *Ramayana: India's Immortal Tale of Adventure, Love, and Wisdom* (Badger, CA: Torchlight Publishing).

Dumézil, Georges. 1958. *L'idéologie Tripartite des Indo-Européens* (Bruxelles: Berchem Latomus).

Earth Impact Database. 2009. Online: http://www.unb.ca/passc/ImpactDatabase/ (May 2009). Developed and Maintained by the Planetary and Space Science Centre, University of New Brunswick, Canada.

Einstein, Albert. 1946. Letter to Immanuel Velikovsky, 8 July 1946, The Immanuel Velikovsky Archive, 1999 by Shulamit V. Kogan and Ruth V. Sharon. Online: http://www.varchive.org/cor/einstein/460708ev.htm.

Eliade, Mircea. 1958. *Patterns in Comparative Religion* (London: Sheed & Ward).

Evelyn-White, Hugh, trans. 1977. *The Homeric Poems and Homerica*, Loeb Classical Library, 57 (Cambridge, MA: Harvard University Press; London: Heinemann).

Fernández, Yanga R. 2009. 'That's the way the comet crumbles': Splitting Jupiter-family Comets', *Planetary and Space Science* 57.10: 1218-27.

Frazer, James George. 1922. *The Golden Bough: A Study in Magic and Religion*, abr. ed. (New York: Macmillan).

Freud, Sigmund. 1960. *Totem and Taboo: Some Points of Agreement between the Mental Lives of Savages and Neurotics*, trans. James Strachey (London: Routledge & Kegan Paul).

Gadbury, John. 1665. *De Cometis: Or a Discourse of the Natures and Effects of Comets... Historically and Astrologically Considered* (London: Printed for L. Chapman).

Giles, John Allen. 1900. 'Geoffrey of Monmouth, "History of the Kings of Britain" (1138)', in *Six Old English Chronicles*, ed. J.A. Giles (London: George Bell & Sons): 87-292.

Grant, Michael, trans. 1996 [1956]. *Tacitus, The Annals of Imperial Rome* (London: Penguin Books, 1956; rev. ed. 1996).

Graves, Robert. 1961 [1948]. *The White Goddess: A Historical Grammar of Poetic Myth*, amended and enlarged ed. (London: Faber & Faber).

Graves, Robert, and Michael Grant. 2003 [1957]. *Suetonius, The Twelve Caesars*, trans. Robert Graves (1957; rev. ed. Michael Grant, London: Penguin Books).

Gregory, Lady Augusta. 1905. *Gods and Fighting Men: The Story of the Tuatha de Danaan and of the Fiana of Ireland* (London: John Murray).

Guillemin, Amédée. 1875. *Les Comètes* (Paris: Hachette)

Halley, Edmond. 1724. 'Some Considerations about the Cause of the Universal Deluge, Laid before the Royal Society, on the 12th of December 1694', *Philosophical Transactions* 33: 118-23.

Hamacher, Duane W., and Ray P. Norris. 2010. 'Australian Aboriginal Geomythology: Eyewitness Accounts of Cosmic Impacts?', *Preprint: Archaeoastronomy— The Journal of Astronomy in Culture*: 1-51. Online: http://arxiv.org/pdf/1009 .4251v1.pdf.

Hellmann, C. Doris. 1944. *The Comet of 1577: Its Place in the History of Astronomy* (New York: Columbia University Press).

Heyerdahl, Thor. 1950. *The Kon-Tiki Expedition: By Raft across the South Seas*, trans. F.H. Lyon (London: Allen & Unwin)

———. 1978. *Early Man and the Ocean* (London: George Allen & Unwin).

Jakiel, Richard. 2008. 'How Comets Shaped History', *Astronomy* 36.2: 22-27.

James, E.O. 1963. *The Worship of the Sky-God: A Comparative Study in Semitic and Indo-European Religion*, Jordan Lectures 1962 (London: University of London/ Athlone Press).

Jones, D.C.H., and E.V. Rieu, trans. 2003. *Homer, The Iliad* (London: Penguin Classics).

Jung, Carl Gustav. 1964. *Man and his Symbols* (London: Aldus Books).

Kiang, T., trans. 1984. 'The Cometary Atlas in the Silk Book of the Han Tomb at Mawangdui', *Chinese Astronomy and Astrophysics* 8: 1-7 [translation of article by Ze-zong Xi, *Kejishi Wenjie* 1: 39-43].

Koch, John T., ed. in collaboration with John Carey. 2000. *The Celtic Heroic Age: Literary Sources for Ancient Celtic Europe & Early Ireland & Wales*, 3rd ed. (Oakville, CO and Aberystwyth: Celtic Studies Publications).

Kronk, Gary W. 1999–2009. *Cometography: A Catalogue of Comets*, 4 vols. (Cambridge: Cambridge University Press), vol. I (1999): *Ancient–1799*; vol. II (2003a): *1800–1899*; vol. III (2003b): *1900–1932*; vol. IV (2009): *1933–1959*.

Kulik, Leonid. 1927. 'The Problem of the Impact Area of the Tunguska Meteorite of 1908', *Doklady Akad. Nauk SSSR* 23: 399-402, trans. John W. Atwell, in *The Fire Came By: The Riddle of the Great Siberian Explosion*, ed. John Baxter and Thomas Atkins (London: Futura, 1977): 154-57.

Levy, David H. 1998. *Comets: Creators and Destroyers* (New York: Touchstone, Simon & Schuster).

———. 2003. *David Levy's Guide to Observing and Discovering Comets* (Cambridge: Cambridge University Press).

Lévi-Strauss, Claude. 1970, *The Raw and the Cooked: Introduction to a Science of Mythology*, trans. John and Doreen Weightman (London: Jonathan Cape). French original, *Le Cru et le Cuit* (1964).

Littleton, C. Scott. 2002. *Mythology. The Illustrated Anthology of World Myth and Storytelling* (London: Duncan Baird Publishers).

Mac Airt, Seán, and Gearóid Mac Niocaill, eds. 1983. *The Annals of Ulster* (Dublin: Dublin Institute for Advanced Studies).

McCafferty, Patrick. 2007. 'Cult in Cometary Context', in *Cult in Context: Reconsidering Ritual in Archaeology*, ed. David Barrowclough and Caroline Malone (Oxford: Oxbow Books): 229-33.

———. 2011. 'The Cometary Paradigm and Irish Myths: Medieval Writings in their Celestial Context' (PhD diss., Queens University Belfast).

McCafferty, Patrick, and Mike Baillie. 2005. *The Celtic Gods: Comets in Irish Mythology* (Stroud: Tempus).

Mackay, Christopher S. 2004. *Ancient Rome: A Military and Political History* (Cambridge: Cambridge University Press).

Malik, Tariq. 2013. 'Russian Meteor Blast Bigger Than Thought, NASA Says', Space.com, 16 February 2013. Online: http://www.space.com/19838-russian-meteor-blast-bigger-size.html (accessed August 2014).

Mallory, J.P. 1989. *In Search of the Indo-Europeans* (London: Thames & Hudson).

Mallory, J.P., and D.Q. Adams, eds. 1997. *Encyclopedia of Indo-European Culture* (London and Chicago: Fitzroy Dearborn).

Martin, Benjamin. 1757. *The Theory of Comets, Illustrated, in Four Parts... The Whole Adapted to, and Exemplified in the Orbit of the Comet of the Year 1682, Whose Return Is Now Near at Hand* (London: [n.p.]).

Milne, David. 1828. *Essay on Comets: Which Gained the First of Dr. Fellowes's Prizes, Proposed to Those Who Had Attended the University of Edinburgh within the Last Twelve Years* (Edinburgh: Adam Black).

Minford, John, and Joseph S.M. Lau, eds. 2000. *Classical Chinese Literature: An Anthology of Translations* (Hong Kong: Chinese University Press; New York: Columbia University Press, 2000).

Monroe, Jean Guard, and Ray A. Williamson. 1987. *They Dance in the Sky: Native American Star Myths* (Boston: Houghton Mifflin Co.).

Müller, F. Max. 1899. *Natural Religion: The Gifford Lectures Delivered before the University of Glasgow in 1888*, Collected Works of The Right Hon. F. Max Müller, vol. 1 (London: Longmans, Green).

NASA Near Earth Object Program. 2014. 'Near Earth Asteroid Discovery Statistics'. Online: http://neo.jpl.nasa.gov/stats/ (accessed July 2014).

Nutt, Alfred. 1895. 'The Happy Otherworld in the Mythico-Romantic Literature of the Irish: The Celtic Ddoctrine of Re-birth', in *The Voyage of Bran, Son of Febal*, ed. Kuno Meyer (London: David Nutt): 101-331.

O'Curry, Eugene. 1863. 'The "Trí Thruaighe na Scealaigheachta" (The "Three Most Sorrowful Tales") of Erinn', *The Atlantis: Or Register of Literature and Science of the Catholic University of Ireland* 4: 113-240 (London: Longman, Brown, Green, Longmans & Roberts, 1863).

Oxford Dictionaries Online. 2014. (Oxford: Oxford University Press). Online: http://www.oxforddictionaries.com/definition/english/myth; http://www.oxforddictionaries.com/definition/english-thesaurus/myth.

Potter, David. 2007. *Emperors of Rome: The Story of Imperial Rome from Julius Caesar to the Last Emperor* (London: Quercus).

Rackham, H., trans. 1949. *Pliny: Natural History*, 10 vols., Loeb Classical Library (London: Heinemann; Cambridge, MA: Harvard University Press, 1938–63), vol. I.
———. trans. 1956 [1933]. *Cicero, De Natura Deorum; Academica*, The Loeb Classical Library (London: Heinemann; Cambridge, MA: Harvard University Press, 1933; rev. ed. 1956).

Reed, Alexander Wyclif. 2004. *Reed Book of Maori Mythology* (Auckland: Reed).

Sagan, Carl, and Ann Druyan. 1985. *Comet* (London: Guild Publishing).

Sandars, N.K., trans. 1960. *The Epic of Gilgamesh* (Harmondsworth: Penguin Books).

Schaaf, Fred. 1997. *Comet of the Century: From Halley to Hale-Bopp* (New York: Springer).

Schechner-Genuth, Sara. 1997. *Comets, Popular Culture, and the Birth of Modern Cosmology* (Princeton, NJ: Princeton University Press).

Schiaparelli, G.V. 1867. 'Sur la relation qui existe entre les comes et les étoiles filantes', *Astronomische Nachrichten* 68: 331.

Scott-Kilvert, Ian, trans. 1987. *Cassius Dio: The Reign of Augustus* (London: Penguin Classics, 1987).

Shakespeare, William. 1599. *Julius Caesar*, ed. Michael Macmillan, *The Tragedy of Julius Caesar*, The Arden Shakespeare (London: Methuen, 1902).

Smith, William. 1913. *A Smaller History of Rome from the Earliest Times to the Death of Trajan*, new ed. (London: John Murray).

Steel, Duncan I. 1995. *Rogue Asteroids and Doomsday Comets: The Search for the Million Megaton Menace That Threatens Life on Earth* (New York etc.: John Wiley).

Sykes, Mark V. et al. 1986. 'The Discovery of Dust Trails in the Orbits of Periodic Comets'. *Science* 232: 1115-17.

Tashak, Elena. 2004. 'In the Beginning There Were Only Legends', in *The Phenomenon of Baikal* (Moscow: Greenpeace): 31-48.

Terry, Milton S., trans. 1899. *The Sibylline Oracles: Translated from the Greek into English Blank Verse* (New York: Eaton & Mains; Cincinnati: Curts & Jennings).

Velikovsky, Immanuel. 1950. *Worlds in Collision* (London: Victor Gollancz).

von Däniken, Erich. 1968. *Erinnerungen an die Zukunft* (Dusseldorf: Econ-Verlag). ET, *Chariots of the Gods? Unsolved Mysteries of the Past* (London: Corgi Books).

Whiston, William. 1708. *A New Theory of the Earth* (Cambridge: Printed at the University-press; for Benj. Tooke).

Wilde, Oscar. 1917 [1893]. *Lady Windermere's Fan* (London: Methuen).

IMAGERY AND NARRATIVE IN AN ANCIENT HOROSCOPE: P.LOND. 130 (*GREEK HOROSCOPES* NO. 81)

Roger Beck

University of Toronto Mississauga, Department of Historical Studies,
3359 Mississauga Road N., Mississauga, ON L5L 1C6, Canada
roger.beck@utoronto.ca

Abstract

In a Greek papyrus horoscope from the first century CE, highly elaborate descriptions of planetary journeyings have replaced the usual matter-of- fact listing of celestial longitudes. An analysis of the horoscope's language and narrative form demonstrates how ancient astrologers understood the stars and planets as agents that communicate by their appearances, configurations, and motions.

Keywords

Horoscopes, ancient astrology, narrative, poetic astronomy, narratology.

Extant Greek horoscopes fall into two categories in the terminology of Neugebauer and van Hoesen: 'original documents' and 'literary horoscopes' (1987: vii, 14, 76). The former were composed, with few exceptions, on scraps of papyrus. For the most part, a horoscope of this sort gives simply the date and hour of birth, followed by a list of the seven planets and the *Horoscopos* (Ascendant) together with the sign of the zodiac occupied by each. In contrast, the 'literary horoscopes' are preserved in ancient astrological treatises—their richest reservoir by far being the *Anthologies* of Vettius Valens from the second century CE— where they serve as examples and test cases. They tend to be somewhat fuller in astronomical data, and they are coupled with actual life outcomes known to the authors and compilers.

All horoscopes tell a story—a story about the heavens—and horoscopes of the ancient 'literary' type tell two stories, a celestial and a terrestrial. The celestial story is about the stars, their motions, and their relationships; the terrestrial story is the biography of the so-called 'native', the subject of the horoscope. The function of this double story-telling in the ancient astrological treatises was to explore entailments: what was it precisely in the celestial story that entailed such-and-such a feature of the terrestrial story? Whether, in this context, 'entailed' means 'determined the outcome' or 'indicated the outcome' does not concern me here; what does is the story-telling itself—questions of narrative and narration.

Among the non-literary horoscopes—the 'original documents'—is preserved a handful of what Alexander Jones, in his edition of the astronomical and astrological papyri from Oxyrhynchus (Jones 1999: xi), calls 'deluxe' horoscopes. In their astronomical data, these horoscopes are much more detailed and informative than the run-of-the-mill sort that offer a bare list of the planets plus the *Horoscopos* and the signs occupied at birth. This is a straightforward market-place matter: the more you pay, the more you expect to get.

Neither deluxe horoscopes nor their run-of-the-mill relatives offer predictions. Quite probably, purchasers of both sorts of horoscopes would bring them in, not necessarily to the original astrologers, for subsequent paid consultations. The question asked would be along the lines of the following: 'Given this horoscope and today's configurations, should I close the deal?' Otherwise, like all luxury goods always, deluxe horoscopes were for display, for demonstrating one's stature both to oneself and others. It is not the mass or specificity of the details in the deluxe horoscopes that concerns us here so much as the way these details are marshalled into a story and, in particular, the appeal to the visual imagination in the telling of the story. The astrologer invites his client not merely to *hear* his story but to *visualise* it.

And so to the celestial story of *Greek Horoscopes* No. 81 (Neugebauer and van Hoesen 1987: 21-28). As its number indicates, the birth occurred in the year 81 of the Common Era, in fact on 31 March at about 9:00 pm. The astrologer gives the month and the day in three calendar formats: Alexandrian, Roman, and Egyptian. The year is specified as 'the third of the God Titus'. That the emperor Titus is called a 'god' means that he was already dead and deified when the horoscope was cast. In fact, Titus died in this same third regnal year, a mere six months after the subject's birth. It is worth noting that, narratologically, the dating belongs more to the terrestrial and human story than to the celestial. Ultimately, of

course, 'the motion of the seven gods', as the astrologer terms it, determines earthly time. But the precise day of the month, the month's name,
and who was then on the throne are human, not divine, contingencies.

The Horoscope No. 81 opens with a prologue that belongs neither to a
celestial nor to a terrestrial narrative, but instead to a meta-history, the
story of astrology:

> The Egyptian men of old who had faithfully studied the heavenly bodies
> and had learned the motions of the seven gods, compiled and arranged
> everything in perpetual tables and generously left to us their knowledge
> of these things. From these I have accurately calculated and arranged for
> each one (of the seven gods) according to degree and minute [of longi-
> tude], aspect and phase, and, simply, not to waste time in enumerating
> each item, whatever concerns its investigation. For thus the way of
> astrological prediction is made straight, unambiguous, that is, consistent.
> Farewell, dearest Hermon (Neugebauer and van Hoesen 1987: 23, Cols. I
> and II).

This appeal to a high tradition and the self-location of a narrator within
that tradition is a commonplace of ancient story-telling. It was a medi-
ating device, linking narrator to audience—in this instance, an astrologer
to his client—and both to the matter of the story. The name of the client,
who is the primary audience of the impending narrative, is Hermon. The
name of the intrusive storyteller, Titus Pitenius, the reader does not
discover until the end, when it is determined that he is the astrologer
himself, as shown in the clause in which he signs off: 'I, Titus Pitenius,
made the calculations' (Neugebauer and van Hoesen 1987: 24, Col.
VIII).

The threefold dating follows this prologue. Next one might expect the
place of birth to be specified since, in order to calculate horoscopes,
location is the necessary complement to date and time. Location belongs
to the terrestrial story—but not entirely, for without location there can be
no linking of the events in the heavens to a *particular* human story. In
genethlialogy (divination of the destinies of the newly born), location
determines the all-important *Horoscopos* or Ascendant, the point where
the ecliptic and the local horizon intersect at the moment of birth. In fact,
the astrologer does specify the location but he does so right at the end of
the document. The place is Hermopolis, some 400 kilometres up the Nile
valley from the sea where, the astrologer/narrator says, 'the horizon has
the ratio seven to five' (Neugebauer and van Hoesen 1987: 26, Col.
IX)—such was a normal Greek way of expressing geographic latitude, in
terms of zones (*klimata*) in which the ratio of the longest to the shortest

day within the same zone was the same. By explicitly locating Hermopolis in the zone (*klima*) of Lower Egypt, the narrator demonstrates that he knew what he was talking about when he positioned the Ascendant in the eighteenth degree of Scorpio.

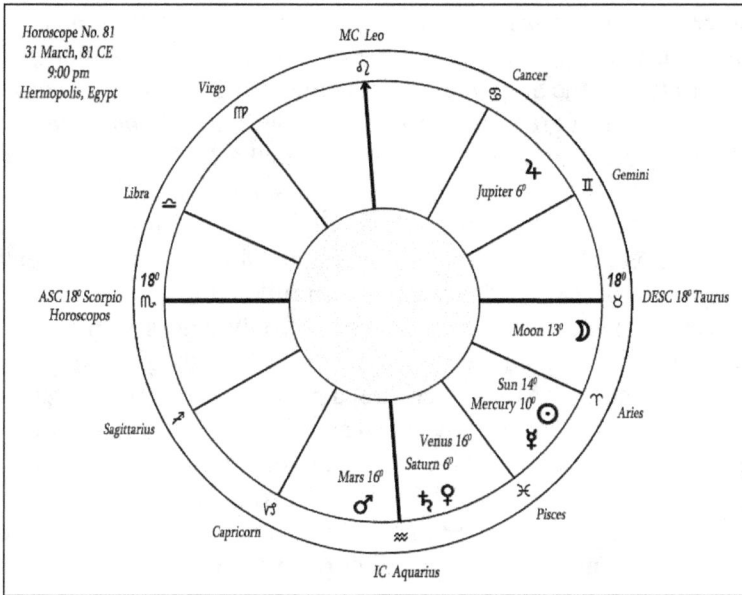

Figure 1. Diagram of Horoscope no. 81.

After the prologue and the temporal definitions, the astrologer/narrator tells what each of the 'seven gods' was then doing (see Fig. 1). That narrative makes up the bulk of the horoscope. Each of the gods is vividly described, and in the way it is written—the sense of the flow of the narrative—adjectives and verbs matter. The narrator speaks of the planets as agents *doing things* over and above occupying specific locations, as can be seen from this example of the Moon:

> And the divine and light-bringing Moon, waxing in crescent, had advanced in Taurus thirteen degrees, and a thousandth part of a degree; in the sign of Venus; in her own exaltation; in the terms of Mercury; in a female and solid sign; like gold; mounting the Back of Taurus; in the second decan called Aroth; her dodekatemorion again was shining on about the same place in Scorpio (Neugebauer and van Hoesen 1987: 23, Col. IV).[1]

---

1. Author has replaced 'its' with 'her'.

Much of the vividness rides on the language of astrology itself. That, of course, is the point. If one is going to go into detail, one must, at least in the ancient world, speak, for example, of places of 'exaltation' and 'humiliation', and of gendered signs.

What one notices first is the verbs, and through the verbs, the *actions* of the celestial bodies. The Moon is not merely *at* a certain position in longitude. Literally it—or rather, *she*—'*had run*' thirteen-plus degrees of Taurus. Likewise the Sun, '*moving* from the spring equinox, had *attained* in Aries fourteen degrees and six minutes'. Saturn 'had *completed* [literally, "*filled*"] six degrees in Pisces less a sixtieth'. Jupiter, '*running up* its exaltation [Cancer] had *attained* six degrees and ten thirds'. Mars 'had *ascended* sixteen degrees and a twentieth of Aquarius'. Venus 'had *completed* [again "*filled*"] sixteen degrees and four minutes'. Seventh of the planets, Mercury, 'had *run across* ten full degrees of Aries'.

However, the seven planets are not the only actors in the celestial field. Strangely (from a modern perspective), both the *Horoscopos* (the Ascendant) and the Midheaven are described in the same terms as the planets, and so must be envisaged as behaving in the same way. The *Horoscopos* 'had *cut off* eighteen degrees of Scorpio', while the Midheaven 'had *struck* the back of the Lion'. Hearing or reading this, what is one supposed to *see* with the mind's eye? As the heavens turn, a reified point moving to and fro on the local horizon to the east *cuts* the ecliptic at the eighteenth degree of Scorpio, while another reified point moving up and down the local meridian *strikes* Leo on the back. That is certainly what the astrologer *says* is going on.

In turning from verbs to adjectives, one can observe how the narrator describes his cast of celestial agents, particularly those whom he has characterised in his prologue as 'the seven gods'. In each of the seven passages which constitute the bulk of the narrative, a subject phrase ('the divine and light-bringing Moon') precedes a verb phrase ('had advanced in Taurus thirteen degrees and a thousandth part of a degree'), sometimes with a participial phrase in between ('waxing in crescent'). Here for each planet in order are (a) the subject phrase, and (b) the participial phrase:

1 (a) The Sun, the mightiest and ruler of all, (b) moving from the spring equinox...
2 (a) The divine and light-bringing Moon, (b) waxing in crescent...
3 (a) Phainon, the star of Kronos (i.e. Saturn)...
4 (a) Phaithon, the star of Zeus (i.e. Jupiter), (b) running across his exaltation (i.e. Cancer)...

5 (a) Pyroeis, the star of Ares (i.e. Mars)…
6 (a) Phosphoros, the star of Aphrodite (i.e. Venus)…
7 (a) Stilbon, the star of Hermes (i.e. Mercury)…

Those familiar with Hellenistic astrology will notice the use of the alternative nomenclature for the five naked-eye planets (in the modern sense of that term). Since the more common divine names (in their Greek forms) are also given, the primary purpose here in the narrative is descriptive rather than indicative: Phainon/Saturn is 'the Shining One'; Phaithon/Jupiter is 'the Brilliant one'; Pyroeis/Mars is 'the Fiery One'; Phosphoros/Venus is 'the Light-Bringer'; Stilbon/Mercury is 'the Glittering one'. Four of these refer to appearance, to what one *sees*. The fifth refers to function: Venus, as the Morning Star, heralds the dawn. But that too is an *appearance*: when one sees Venus in the east, one sees—or will soon see—the light of dawn spreading upwards and outwards from the horizon in that direction.

Here I draw attention to the way the astrologer added an eighth and a ninth actor to his cast of celestial characters: the *Horoscopos* or Ascendant and the Midheaven. The Ascendant is introduced as 'the *rudder* of them all, the *Horoscopos*'. It might seem strange to describe the Ascendant as a 'rudder' or 'steering oar'. But in point of fact, 'the steering oar' as an epithet for the Ascendant, though not common, does occur in other astrological texts, including a deluxe horoscope from Oxyrhynchus (Jones 1999: 420-21). In the Oxyrhynchus horoscope the astrologer calls the Ascendant 'the steersman'. From a narrator's perspective, promoting the Ascendant from instrument to agent was a smart choice. Parity with the planetary gods is thereby conferred.

Though vividly described in its action (*'striking* the back of the Lion'), the Midheaven is less vividly introduced than the Ascendant. It is called simply 'the meridian at right angles to it', 'it' being the Ascendant. 'The meridian' serves, *totum pro parte*, as shorthand for 'the point on the meridian at which the ecliptic intersects it'.

The final location to be specified is that of the Lot of Fortune 'in the sign and triangle of Jupiter', meaning Sagittarius. Interestingly, Titus Pitenius uses the blandest of verb phrases: 'will be into'. Here, towards the end, he seems to be tiring of his narrator's mode. The professional astrologer reasserts himself with the comment that only 'ignorance' would put the Lot of Fortune in Libra.[2]

---

2. Editor's note: The Lot of Fortune was the angle of separation between the Sun and Moon applied to the Ascendant. However, the reason that Titus Pitenius would suggest ignorance lies in the two ways the Lot of Fortune is calculated: for daytime

Returning to the 'seven gods', each passage after the verb phrase expressing the longitude attained contains a string of phrases conveying further data. For the Moon this was as follows: in the sign of Venus; in its own exaltation; in the terms of Mercury; in a female and solid sign; like gold; mounting the back of Taurus; in the second decan called Aroth; its *dodekatemorion* was shining on about the same place in Scorpio. What concerns us is not the astronomical and astrological information in itself but the way in which that data is presented: First, notice the verbs. The Moon *mounts* the back of Taurus; her *dodeka-temorion* (a type of proxy or surrogate) *shines* on a particular spot. Both verbs imply—indeed they emphasise—*agency*. Secondly, notice *appearance*. The Moon is like *gold*. Likewise, Venus is said to be 'like *crystal*'. Both of these words ignore that on the occasion in question neither imputed quality was observable. Both planets have already set. What you get is what you *do not* see, though you are led to imagine it, despite explicit data to the contrary.

Third, and in many ways the most interesting point, is the astrologer/ narrator's introduction of constellations and even stars, over and above signs and degrees, to describe where in the sky each planet has reached. Again, notice the actions implied by the verbs. The Moon is '*mounting the back of Taurus*'. The reader is to envisage a goddess climbing onto a bull's back, much like the icon of the 'Bull-sacrificing Victory' or indeed of the tauroctonous Mithras. It is worth setting out all seven of these phrases:

Sun:	shining upon the flank of Aries
Moon:	mounting the Back of Taurus
Saturn:	descending from the Swallow-Fish
Jupiter:	two fingers from the more northerly bright star on the back (sc. of Cancer)
Mars:	(by?) the Star in the Cloak called Ganymede, homonymous with the whole constellation, far to the east
Venus:	at the Southern Fish…distant two lunar diameters from the bright star in the connecting cords
Mercury:	(nothing said)

(diurnal) births, when the sun is above the horizon, the astrologer measures the angle of separation between the Sun and the Moon and applies that angle clockwise from Ascendant; for nighttime (nocturnal) births, when the sun is below the horizon, the astrologer measures the angle from the Moon to the Sun and applies that angle anticlockwise to the Ascendant. Thus only an 'ignorant' astrologer would apply a diurnal formula for the Lot of Fortune to a nocturnal chart.

The 'seven gods' encounter new and exotic beings in their travels, not just those familiar markers of longitude, the twelve signs, each with its thirty degrees. Saturn descends from a Swallow-Fish, a Babylonian name for the Northern Fish of Pisces. Jupiter is two fingers' width away from a particular star in Cancer. Mars is near a star in the Cloak. The Cloak is actually the cloak of Aquarius, but the astrologer transforms this item of apparel into a distinct sub-constellation—as well as the individual star— which he calls Ganymede. He thus equates Aquarius—as others did too—with the wine steward of the Olympians. Finally, Venus is in the Southern Fish of the constellation of Pisces, two lunar diameters from a bright star in the cord that links the two Fishes together. In summary, making their appearance in these snippets of the celestial story are the following novel features: one immortalised human, Ganymede; one hybrid animal, the Swallow-Fish; and two artefacts, a cloak and a piece of string.

Most horoscopes in their planetary stories send their seven heroes forward and sometimes backward along a single path, or more precisely along what, for narrative purposes, is *treated* as a single path. Put astronomically, ancient horoscopes give longitudes, very seldom latitudes. The astrologers knew, of course, that the planets, with the exception of the Sun, wandered off to the north and south of the ecliptic. The point is that astrologically these divergences in latitude were of little or no consequence for the terrestrial stories of human beings. They are therefore normally omitted from the celestial stories of horoscopes. On the principal that if you have paid good money you are entitled to a good story, however, Titus Pitenius enriches the celestial story by personalising the adventures of the seven, each along his or her own path. He does this not as an astronomer would do by specifying latitude as well as longitude, but by introducing stars and parts of constellations near which or through which the planets pass. The function of these details, then, is to enrich the celestial story; they are not just proxies for latitude. In fact, they are not proxies for latitude at all, and were not intended as such. That they have been mistaken for such is understandable, since the astrologer/narrator uses language, which, in a different context, would indeed refer to latitude.

Consider the following two phrases: the Moon '*mounting* the back of Taurus'; Saturn '*descending* from the Swallow-Fish'. Visually this suggests that the Moon is *going up* and Saturn *going down*. If one thinks of 'north' as 'up' and 'south' as 'down', and if that fundamental cognitive metaphor, current then as now, holds for the heavens as for the earth, then it is understandable that one would here envisage the Moon moving northward and Saturn southward. So we can say that, in context, the 'mounting' and 'descending' phrases would have *evoked* motion north- ward and southward respectively, as they still do now. *Evoked*—yes, but the verbs indicated, signified, intended, and meant are not deployed. How can I be so sure that Titus Pitenius, in saying that the Moon was 'mounting the back of Taurus', did not *mean* that she was then moving to the north of the ecliptic or ascending in latitude? Quite simply, because she was not doing so. The Moon was then almost five degrees to the south of the ecliptic and still descending in latitude. Since the astrologer is reasonably correct with his longitudes, why suppose him to be other- wise about latitude, especially when the supposition is unnecessary? This becomes clear when one realises that Titus Pitenius is telling Hermon a story about significant planetary adventures. He is asking Hermon to *imagine* the Moon climbing onto the back of the Bull of heaven.

It is worth a closer look at the actual verb translated as 'mounting' in the participial phrase 'mounting the back of the Bull'. The verb used is *anabibazein*, which is primarily a *causative* verb meaning 'to make go up' or, more succinctly, 'to send up'. It usually requires a direct object. What, then, is it that the Moon makes or causes to go up on to the Bull's back? The reader is never told. So one must default to a different image. Instead of imagining the Moon putting someone or something up onto the Bull's back, one imagines the Moon herself ascending there. Linguistically, in the absence of a direct object, one is compelled to construe the participle *anabibazousa* as intransitive, as the functional equivalent of the intransitive, non-causative *anabainousa*.

This is not, however, the end of the story. There is an answer to the obvious question: 'Why has the astrologer/narrator chosen a verb which he must deploy in an unusual way?' The answer lies in astrology's technical vocabulary. The participle of *anabibazein* in the masculine form *anabibazôn* (rather than the feminine *anabibazousa*) is the technical term for the ascending node of the lunar orbit, the noun *syndesmos* ('node') being understood. The ascending node is the point on the ecliptic where the Moon crosses from south to north. The complementary point where she crosses back again from north to south is the descending node, the Greek technical term for which is *katabibazôn* (the Greek for 'down' being *kata*, as the Greek for 'up' is *ana*). The causative verbs are used because the Greek astronomers and astrologers thought of the nodes as agents, at least potentially. Thus the ascending node was conceptual- ised via language as the being who *sends* the Moon up north across the ecliptic, and the descending node is the being who sends her back again,

across from north to south. Because the nodes exhibit motion in longitude (regressing westwards around the ecliptic in a period of eighteen
and two-thirds years), in later Greek astrology they were treated as
planets for horoscopal purposes (Bouché-Leclercq 1963 [1899]: 122-23).

The best evidence for the attribution of agency to the nodes comes,
however, not from an astrological source but from the Christian apologist
Tertullian. In his *Against Marcion* (1.18), which was written little more
than a century after this analyzed horoscope, Tertullian says sarcastically
of the failure of Marcion's beneficent God to arrive in the world
expeditiously: 'Perhaps Anabibazon stood in his way (*obstabat*), or some
malefics (sc. *stellae*, "stars"), Saturn in quadrature or Mars in trine'.

To sum up, in order to enhance his description of the Moon on the
back of the Bull, the astrologer/narrator has chosen a verb that does not
quite do the lexical job required—for it does not say what it generally
means—but which is nevertheless highly appropriate to the lunar subject.
Appropriate, yes; but not accurate. As has been seen, there is a serious
suggestio falsi, for the Moon at the time was not 'ascending' in the technical sense evoked; she was far 'below' the ecliptic and still 'descending'. The narrator applies the same manoeuvre to Saturn. Saturn is said
to be 'descending from the Swallow-Fish', and the word used is again
the causative *katabibazôn*, which should mean, but does not in this
context, that Saturn is sending someone or something down from the
Swallow-Fish.

In an ancient horoscope of the 'deluxe' type, the astrologer can
become the author-narrator of a celestial story. To transform celestial
data usually presented as a bald set of planetary and other longitudes into
a compelling story, the astrologer Titus Pitenius, as I have demonstrated,
adopts the following narrative stratagems: (a) he represents the planets as
travellers on a journey, emphasising their agency, especially in his
choice of verbs; (b) he depicts a richer and more exotic landscape for
their travels, primarily by taking celestial latitude into account and so
introducing constellations other than the routine twelve which constitute
the signs of the zodiac; and (c) he intensifies the visual imagery, stressing
brilliance and colour and, in particular, preferring the rarer descriptive
names (e.g., Pyroeis, the 'Fiery One') over the standard divine names
(e.g., Mars) for the seven planets.

As an author, Titus Pitenius belongs with the historians and before
them with the tellers of received tales, not with the writers of pure
fiction. The celestial events of 81 CE that he relates are a given. He could
no more have invented them than Thucydides could have invented the

Peloponnesian War or Homer the Trojan War; likewise the celestial players. The artistry lies wholly in the narration, based on the contemporary astronomy and astrology that inform and constrain it—a narration that presented an ensouled sky that was alive, engaged, and wholly informative to that audience.

References

Bouché-Leclercq, A. 1963 [1899]. *L'astrologie Grecque* (Brussels: Culture et Civilisation).

Jones, Alexander, ed. 1999. *Astronomical Papyri from Oxyrhynchus (P. Oxy. 4133–4300a)*, vols. 1 and 2 (Philadelphia: American Philosophical Society).

Neugebauer, O., and H.B. van Hoesen. 1987. *Greek Horoscopes*, Memoirs of the American Philosophical Society, 48 (Philadelphia: American Philosophical Society).

REFLECTIONS ON THE FARNESE *ATLAS*: EXPLORING THE SCIENTIFIC, LITERARY AND PICTORIAL ANTECEDENTS OF THE CONSTELLATIONS ON A GRAECO-ROMAN GLOBE*

Kristen Lippincott

3 Mount Vernon, London NW3 6QS, UK

Abstract

In exploring the figures of the constellations on the celestial globe held by the so-called 'Farnese *Atlas*', this article reflects upon Ptolemy's comment that '…in many cases our descriptions [of the constellations] are different because they seem to be more natural and to give a better proportioned outline to the figures described' (*Syntaxis Mathematica/ Almagest* VII, 4). It suggests that, whereas most scholars writing on the history of constellation imagery tend to focus on two areas to support their findings—scientific data gleaned from early descriptions and depictions of the stars and iconographical details derived from Graeco-Roman mythology—more attention should be paid to the largely independent pictorial tradition that also helped to shape the heavens. By examining a wide range of visual sources, such as Greek vase painting, coins and sculptural reliefs, one can conclude that, in many cases, the role of the artist is neither as an inventor nor as a scientific draughtsman, but as a torch-bearer for the continuity of a specific set of widely accepted pictorial formulae. Working from this, I tentatively propose a new avenue of exploration for the mysterious grid-like figure on the Farnese Globe, often misidentified as the 'Throne of Caesar'.

Keywords

Farnese Globe, Ptolemy, constellational imagery, Graeco-Roman mythology, iconography.

* This essay is dedicated to the memory of my dear friend, Professor Henk van Bueren (1925–2012), astronomer, humanist and poète extraordinaire.

The so-called 'Farnese *Atlas*', currently located in the Museo Archeo-logico Nazionale in Naples, is a Roman statue of a crouching male figure supporting a celestial globe, decorated with *bas-relief* figures of the constellations, on his back (Fig. 1). Despite the wealth of scholarly literature on this figure and its globe, the current state of research on the date of the statue and, more importantly, the date of the putative Greek model upon which it was based has not progressed significantly since the study published by Georg Thiele in 1898. In his study, Thiele proposed that the statue was a Roman copy of a Hellenistic original. He argued that both the iconography and the positioning of the constellations relative to the celestial circles showed that the globe was taken from a Hipparchan astronomical model that recorded an epoch of 128 BCE, whereas the style in which the figures were executed pointed to the kinds of artistic adjustments often made by Hellenophile Roman artisans (Thiele 1898: 27-42). More specifically, he believed that the *Atlas* was a Hadrianic copy of a Greek original and, therefore, could be dated to sometime between 117 and 138 CE.

Figure 1. *Atlas* holding the celestial sphere (Farnese Globe) on his shoulders, marble, full height 191 cm, diameter of the sphere 66 cm. Inv. No. 6374, Museo Archeologico Nazionale, Naples. Photo: I.Sh, Creative Commons.

In her study of the construction and iconography of the globe, Elly Dekker has shown that Thiele's instincts concerning the dating of the Farnese Globe and its putative model are largely correct, though she cautioned that it would be wrong to insist on a set of precise dates for either the model or its copy for a number of reasons (Dekker 2013: 84-102 and 111-15). First, it is impossible to use the location of the equinoxes (the points of intersection between the vernal colure, the ecliptic and the equator) with respect to the stars to determine the epoch for which the globe was created, since the three celestial circles delineated on the globe do not meet at a single point, so there is no definitive zero-point from which to measure (Fig. 2). Faced with this reality, some scholars writing on the topic have assumed this lack of precision was intentional on the part of the globe-maker and that it provided a key to the date either of the model or its copy by recording precession data. Working through all the possible combinations proposed, however, Dekker clearly showed that none of the previous attempts to prove a hypothetical date or to tie the globe specifically to the Hipparchan or Ptolemaic epoch by astronomical means is scientifically robust. Moreover, the statistical attempts to analyse a larger body of 'data' collected from the globe in the hope of demonstrating that it was based on the legendary lost star-catalogue of Hipparchus were fundamentally flawed. In particular, the method and the conclusions employed by Bradley Schaefer (2005) have been well-refuted by Dennis Duke (2006) and Dekker herself (2013: 94-98).

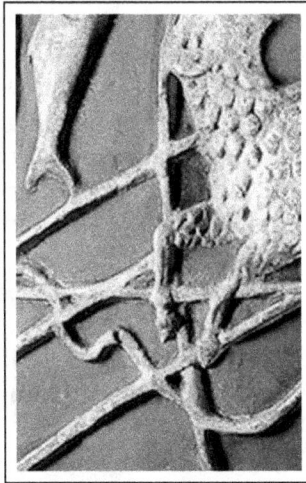

Figure 2. Detail of a copy of the Farnese Globe showing the intersections of the equinoctial colure, the celestial equator and the ecliptic. Roman, early twentieth century. Museo della Civiltà Romana, Rome. Photo: Creative Commons.

Ancillary to the argument that the astronomy of the globe itself does not provide the information required to determine an exact date for its construction, is the warning, as Dekker has raised elsewhere (Dekker 2005), that a certain degree of caution should always be exercised when dating any scientific instrument to a particular epoch since it seems often to have been accepted practice for the makers of globes, armillary spheres, celestial maps, star tables and other scientific instruments, such as astrolabes, to rely on old, outdated astronomical data when construct-ing their otherwise new creations. The use of astronomical information without any supporting corollaries—signatures, materials, techniques of manufacture or stylistic analysis—can really only provide a reasonable *terminus post quem* as a dating tool.

From an art historical point of view, neither iconography nor the style in which the constellation figures have been carved offer any significant clues to a more definitive dating. It is worth pointing out that, whereas the forms of the constellations depicted on the Farnese Globe may have echoes of earlier Hipparchan elements, the details of several of the figures themselves are definitely Roman. For example, in the depiction of the Argo, the addition of a female figure on the prow of the ship could be an allusion to the figurehead identified as the 'daughter of the speak-ing oak of Dodona' through which Athena spoke to Jason several times during his journey, but its placement on the side of the hull is definitely a Roman invention (Lehmann and Lehmann 1973: 180-235; Casson 1971: 344-60 and figs. 125-27, 130, 132, 144, 146). Dekker (2013: 97) listed the major deviations in the details of thirteen figures on the globe from what one is able to establish as a 'Hipparchan form' from a close reading of Hipparchus's *In Arati et Eudoxi Phaenomena Commentariorum* (Hipparchus 1894). She concluded that the differences neither deny nor confirm an Hipparchan original, proposing that the best one can argue at this stage is that the original model for the Farnese Globe postdates 138 BCE. For, as she observed (Dekker 2013: 97), once a globe leaves the strict confines of a mathematical instrument and enters into the world of an 'artistic' production, variation in the forms of the constellations becomes endemic, for:

> Artists do not always follow faithfully the sources they are supposed to copy but create their own pictorial language and use traditions outside the astronomical context.

Indeed, as more critical research is carried out on the forms of the constellations in antiquity, it is becoming increasingly clear how large and varied the corpus of illustrations of the individual constellations available to artists working from the fourth century BCE onwards must have been (Dekker 2013: 97-102; Lippincott 2009). As Dekker (2013: 101) pointed out, Ptolemy himself testified to the fluidity of the tradition (Ptolemy, VII, 4 [H 37], 1998 [1984]: 340):

> ...the descriptions which we have applied to the individual stars as parts of the constellation are not in every case the same as those of our predecessors (just as their descriptions differ from their predecessors).

Following on from the above, he went on to cite what we might call 'stylistic criteria' as the reason for many of these changes:

> ...in many cases our descriptions are different because they seem to be more natural and to give a better proportioned outline to the figures described.

Ptolemy's admission to having altered 'many' of the forms of the constellation figures in accordance with the stylistic conventions of 'naturalism' and 'better proportion' should be much more disconcerting to historians of science than it seems to have been to date. For, in essence, it somewhat subverts Pierre Duhem's theoretical construct of 'saving the phaenomena' (σῴζειν τὰ φαινόμενα/*sōzein ta phenomena*) (Duhem 1908/1969) in favour of E.H. Gombrich's observation (Gombrich 1956: 3-25) that artists often tend to draw what they 'know', rather than what they 'see', with a nod to Michael Baxandall's socio-anthropological formulation of the 'period eye' (Baxandall 1972: 29-109). It also decisively moves the crux of the discussions about the early forms of the constellations away from the purely mathematical or scientific realm into the much less quantitatively prescriptive world of art history.

From the earliest known antique images of constellation figures onwards, three external influences regularly effect their depictions. The first is the mythological stories associated with each constellation, which can influence the way a constellation itself is depicted to such an extent that its form no longer bears any discernible relationship to the pattern of stars with which it was originally associated. As I have discussed elsewhere (Lippincott 2009), whereas the constellation of Eridanus is clearly described by all the early astronomical sources as the 'segment of a river', it had already become pictorially transfigured into the figure of a river god or a depiction of the falling Phaethon by the first century CE.

One aspect of the on-going dialogue between texts and pictures often discussed by scholars of Hellenistic art is the extent to which contemporary theatrical productions may have influenced the development of

narrative painting and sculpture during the period (Engelmann 1900;
Peters 1904; Séchan 1926: 256-57; Woodward 1957; Schauenburg 1960;
Phillips 1968; Green 1991: 42; Green and Hadley 1995: 39-40). It has
been argued, for example, that the sudden popularity of depictions of the
story of Perseus and Andromeda on Sicilian and South Italian ('Italiote')
vases painted during the middle years of the fourth century BCE is
directly related to the appearance of at least two new plays dating to the
period, both of which were entitled 'Andromeda': one by Sophocles
(dating to c. 430 BCE) and the other by Euripides (first performed in
412 BCE). Both plays are now lost and exist only in fragmentary form
(Nauck 1899: 392; Collard, Cropp and Lee 2004; Klimek-Winter 1993,
which also includes fragments from the Latin Andromeda-plays by
Livius Andronicus, Q. Ennius and L. Accius). The opening scenes of
Euripides's 'Andromeda' are known from Aristophanes's parody of it
in the *Thesmophoriazusae*, which was produced either a year after
Euripides's play, or in 412 BCE. Furthermore, whereas some scholars have maintained a more sceptical view of the ability to tie these
images directly to the plays and/or argued that it was actually a development in the taste for multi-scene renderings of literary tales that
prompted this sudden proliferation of imagery (Moret 1975; Small
2003), it is surely worth noting that the development of the multi-scene
pictorial narrative coincided with the earliest-known Greek description
of the heavens by Eudoxus. Given the fact that Sophocles's 'Andromeda'
is mentioned in relation to the catasterism of Cassiopeia in the writings
of ps-Eratosthenes (*Catasterismi* 16; Pearson 1917: 78-96), and references to both Sophocles and Euripides appear in Hyginus (*De Astronomia*
II. 10; Viré 1992: 36-37), it does raise the question as to how an author
of the period might have visualised the individual figures of the eternal
celestial drama. The reader is repeatedly asked to 'imagine' the figure of
Perseus, Andromeda, Hercules or Cassiopeia, but what exactly is it that
we are being asked to imagine?

Ptolemy reminded us that the pictorial formulae used to represent a
constellation figure evolved over time and he implied that the figures he
described did not necessarily resemble those of previous generations
owing to an increased interest and the presumed (by him) improved
ability of artists to render figures more 'naturally' in his lifetime. If the
pictorial formulae used to represent these figures do develop over time,
how does this effect what one assumes to have been originally a close
correspondence between the positions of the stars and the outline of a
specific figure? With his use of the comparators of 'better' and 'more
natural', Ptolemy's answer seems to have been that his formulations

are to be preferred—not because he was the superior astronomer, but because *his* placement of the stars within the figures that *he* imagines populating the heavens represented a pictorial improvement over those of the past.

One solace to this somewhat disconcerting admission is the third factor that should be taken into account when trying to uncover the imagined shapes of the early constellations. Throughout the Graeco-Roman period, there tended to be a certain consistency in the depiction of a wide range of figural types. Dolphins, bears, dogs, centaurs, hare, geese, crabs and eagles each developed characteristic forms very early on. These were widely reproduced and circulated through 'portable' media, such as ceramics (both finely painted vases and stamped terracotta vessels), coins, engraved jewels and mosaics, which were usually composed locally according to designs that circulated through model books (Figs. 3 and 4). There were also several sets of canonical postures for humans, such as the lunging male and the seated figure, and certain accepted conventions for representing a number of fantastic beings, such as sea monsters (Fig. 5), bearded snakes, the *protome* of a horse, a centaur and the winged horse, Pegasus. That is not to say that there was not ample scope for pictorial invention in antiquity, only that the majority of the images that would have been most widely available tended to rely on being recognisable—legible, if you like—by following certain pictorial formulae.

Figure 3. Wine-pouring vessel in the shape of a dolphin, from Eretria (Euboea), 33–310 BCE. Munich, Staatliche Antikensammlungen. Photo: Christa Koppermann.

Figure 4. Detail from a decorative border from Villa Selene, second century CE. Libya, nr. Leptis Magna. Photo: Kristen Lippincott.

Figure 5. Detail of a Neireid riding Cetus on the cover of the Projecta Casket, from Rome, c. 380. London, British Museum. Photo: © Trustees of the British Museum.

To take one test case in which all these pictorial elements have the potential to play a role, the fourth- and third-century BCE artistic render-ings of the main protagonists of the story of Perseus and Andromeda (Perseus, Andromeda, Pegasus and Cetus) regularly bear a resemblance to depictions of these figures as constellations on the surviving globes from the first and third centuries CE, as well as in much later early-medieval manuscripts. The stylistic details may change, but the figures themselves seem to have settled into a relatively consistent type. This is not the case, however, for the minor *dramatis personae* of the story: Cepheus and Cassiopeia. In the case of Cassiopeia, the main difference between the literary, 'artistic' Cassiopeia and the astronomical Cassiopeia is that the former is generally artistically rendered exhibiting one of three dramatic postures.

The first posture is holding the edge of her *himation*, as in the Apulian *oenichoe* from the second half of the fourth century in the Museo Nazionale in Naples (inv. no. Stg. 318), in which Cassiopeia is depicted in the lower right, facing towards the central scene. She is seated in profile and holds her *himation* with her right hand as if to draw it closer, while her left hand rests on the invisible seat of her chair (Engelmann 1900: 73; Séchan 1926: 263, fig. 83; Phillips 1968: 9 and pl. 9, fig. 21).

The second posture is the act of mourning, using the formulaic gesture of resting her cheek on her hand. Sometimes Cassiopeia is seated alone and other times she is accompanied by a female attendant. The Apulian *lutrophotos* in the Collezione Costantini in Fiesole is attributed to the Baltimore Painter and depicts Cepheus with a sceptre and Phrygian cap seated to the right and Cassiopeia to the left of a bound Andromeda set within a cave. Cassiopeia sits facing to the right and inclines her head so that it rests on her left hand, displaying the canonical 'mourning' posture. She is surrounded by the wedding/funeral gifts, including a *cistus* near her head, and attended to by a female figure holding an open jewellery box (Schmidt, Trendall and Cambitoglu 1976: 56 n. 5; Saladino 1979: 104 and figs. 7-9; and *Corpus vasorum antiquorum* 1988: 19-20 and pls. 20.2 and 21.1-3).

In the *loutrophoros* by the Darius Painter from Canosa (third quarter of the fourth century BCE; Naples, Museo Nazionale, inv. no. H. 3225), Cassiopeia is placed to the left of the central scene of Andromeda, seated in profile, and attended by a female slave, who holds a sun parasol over the queen's head. Cassiopeia is depicted slumped forward with her head resting on her right hand, again demonstrating the 'mourning' posture (Séchan 1926: 259, pl. VI; Rocco 1953: esp. pp. 173ff., and pls. 81-82; Schauenburg 1960: 59 n. 396 and pl. 24, fig. 2; Phillips 1968: 10 and pl. 10, fig. 24).

Cassiopeia exhibits a similar posture in the fragments from an Apulian amphora from Ruvo in the University Museum of Halle, which is also by the Darius Painter and dates to the third quarter of the fourth century. They show Cassiopeia in a slight variant of the 'mourning' posture, holding her right hand to her cheek. She is seated on a wooden throne, with her legs crossed at the ankle (Engelmann 1900: 143-51 and pl. 9;

Séchan 1926: 260-61 and fig. 79; Phillips 1968: 12 and pl. 12, figs. 34-36). The upper part of her female attendant is lost, but she may have been holding a parasol or fan.

A third example of a sun-shaded Cassiopeia appears on the *pelike* now in the Museo Nazionale in Naples (inv. no. Sant'Angelo 708). Originally from Arentum, it has been attributed to a follower of the Darius Painter and dates to the third quarter of the fourth century BCE. Here, the shaded Cassiopeia looks upwards towards her maid. Her hand has just dropped from her cheek, while her left forearm rests on the back of her wooden throne (Séchan 1926: 259-60 and fig. 77; Schauenburg 1960: 59 n. 397 and pl. 23; Phillips 1968: 10 and pl. 10, fig. 25 and pl. 11, fig. 26). Cassiopeia's third posture is pleading with Andromeda to forgive her.

The red-figure *pelike* attributed to the Darius Painter in the Getty Museum in Malibu (inv. no. 87. AE) was painted c. 340–330 BCE. It depicts a mature woman on her knees with the outstretched arm of a supplicant. Her hair is covered as befits her matronly status. The seated figure, to whom she is appealing, wears a crown and appears, from her hair style, to be younger. She sits in right profile in a wooden chair and holds her left hand up to her chin—as if considering a proposition. The otherwise unusual postures of these two figures would make them difficult to identify, but luckily the painter has labelled them: the suppliant is labelled 'ΚΑΣΣΙΕΠΕΙΑ', and the seated, younger woman is 'ΑΝΔΡΟΜΕΔΑ' (Acquisitions 1987: 144, no. 8 [ill.]; Trendall and Cambitoglou 1991, no. 18/69a).

The astronomical Cassiopeia follows none of these models. Although Louis Séchan and J.R. Green have discussed the different emotional responses expressed by Cassiopeia (Séchan 1926: 258-72; and Green 1994: 22-26), it is difficult to determine from the surviving fragments in Hipparchus's commentary how Eudoxus envisioned Cassiopeia (Hipparchus 1894: 16-17, 54-57, 112-13, 166-69, 170-71 [I, ii, 15; I, v, 2-3; I xi, 1; II, iii, 4 and II, iii, 10]). Nevertheless Aratus (408–355 BCE) (Aratus 1997: 120-21, vv. 653-58,) was clear in his description of her. He stated that she was seated in a chair and noted that she sat with her feet pointing to the zenith and her head towards the horizon:

> Also, sorrowful Cassiepeia [*sic*] herself hurries after the image of her daughter; but the part of her seen in the chair, feet and knees uppermost, is no longer comely: she goes down head first like a tumbler, having her own share of trouble, for she had no hope of being a rival to Doris and Panope without severe penalty.

Not only is Cassiopeia seated, but Aratus (1997: 86-87, vv. 190-93) summoned a particularly potent simile when describing the structure of her posture:

> only a few zig-zagging stars adorn her, giving her all over a distinct outline. Like to a key with which men attacking a double door barred on the inside knock back the bolts,...

This description of the pattern of Cassiopeia's stars marking a shape of a key has regularly misled scholars unaware of the intricacies of Greek clavology and, perhaps, overly reliant on the modern convention in which Cassiopeia's stars are seen as forming a distinctive 'W' or 'M' in the night sky (Fig. 6) (Aratus 1997: 252-54). For example, Jean Martin translated the passage as: *Semblables à la clé dont on heurte une porte à deux battants, verrouillée de l'intérieur, pour tirer les barres, ainsi apparaissent, isolées, ses étoiles* (Aratus 1998: 12 and 240-42). He also suggested that there were six stars used by Aratus to define the constellation (α, β, γ, x, δ and ε), while noting that the two dimmer stars of this group (x and ε) would certainly not be visible when the Moon was full. Both Victor Buescu (Cicero 1966: 188-89) and Jean Soubiran (Cicero 1972: 202) repeat the idea that Cassiopeia's stars are '*en forme de W*' in the night sky in their notes to Cicero's Latin translation of the *Phaenomena*.

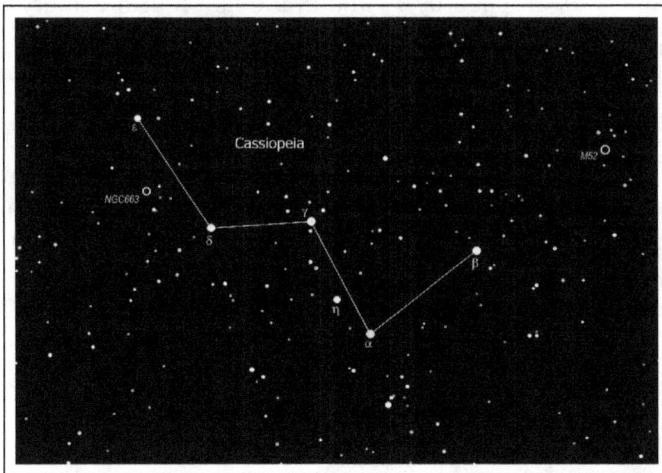

Figure 6. Modern sky mapping of the stars of Cassiopeia. Image: Creative Commons.

This confusion regarding the shape of Cassiopeia may also stem from the fact the classical sources do not appear to be entirely consistent in their description of the stars forming the constellation. In his Commentary on the *Phaenomena*, Hipparchus cited six stars—five of which formed a zig-zag not unlike the one described by Aratus resembling a Greek 'temple key' (Hipparchus 1894: 114-15, 192-93, 202-203, 204-205, 208-209, 228-29, 230-31, 278-79 [I, xi, 1; II, v, 9; II, vi, 2; II, vi, 4; II vi, 9; III, i, 12; III, i, 13 and III, v, 17]). As Hipparchus's nineteenth-century editor, Karl Manitius, noted, there is a slight problem in the consistency of Hipparchus's description of the star in the 'seat of the throne', which he first describes as 'small', but later says is 'bright' and is the first star of *Cassiopeia* to rise. Manitius suggested the $\varkappa$ Cas could be the small one Hipparchus saw 'in the seat' of the throne, but the identification of the 'bright' star in the seat with β Cas was unlikely as it is not the first star in the constellation to rise. The use of 'bright' in this second instance probably reflects an early scribal error.

As was amply demonstrated by Hermann Diels in 1897, Aratus's original reference to a 'key' ($\dot{\eta}$ $\varkappa\lambda\varepsilon\dot{\iota}\varsigma$) would have most likely indicated a so-called 'temple key' ($\dot{\eta}$ $\varkappa\lambda\eta\ddot{\iota}\delta$' $\varepsilon\dot{\upsilon}\varkappa\alpha\mu\pi\dot{\varepsilon}\alpha$), which has a very distinctive shape. Citing more than a dozen examples provided in early vase paintings and carved reliefs, Diels (1897: 123-35 and 1914/1920: 39-46) showed how the structure of an early Greek temple key formed a zig-zag pattern with two bends (Figs. 7 and 8). To this list, one might also add the key that was dropped by Pythia in the late fourth-century Apulian volute-krater from Ruvo in the Museo Archeologico in Naples (Carpenter 1991: fig. 356; Waldstein 1905: II, pl. 133, no. 2722; and Kunze and Schleif 1944: 166, pl. 72b). Furthermore, as was first pointed out by Albert Schott and Robert Böker (1958: 61), and more recently by Kidd (Aratus 1997: 252-54), the zig-zag line that links the four stars of α, γ, δ and ε Cas exactly mimics this shape. Drawing attention to the antiquity of Aratus's simile, Kidd (Aratus 1997: 253-54) notes the clear echo of Homer and his description of Penelope using a 'temple key' to knock back the interior bolts holding closed the two wings of a door (*Odyssey*, ϕ [XXII], vv. 47-50).

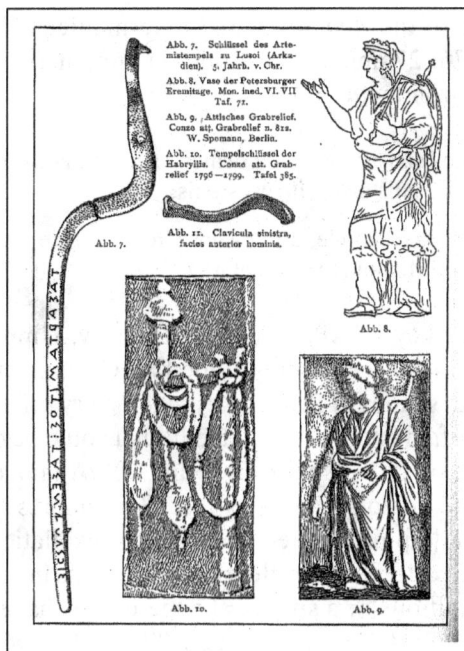

Figure 7. Hermann Diels's 1897 drawing showing how the structure of an early Greek temple key formed a zig-zag pattern with two bends. Image: Diels 1914: 40, figs. 7-10.

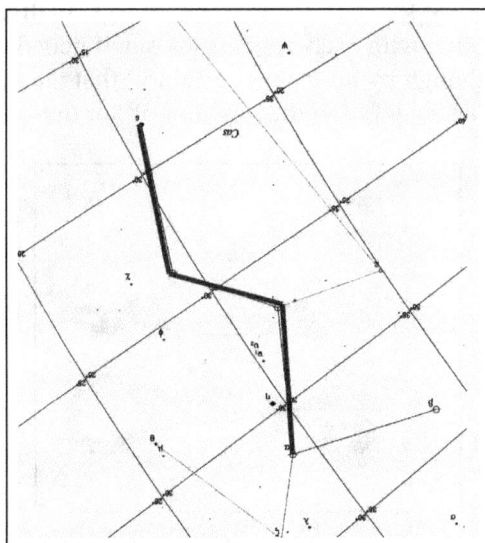

Figure 8. Sky map of the figure of Cassiopeia, with one possible position for her arms. Image: Kristen Lippincott.

In his translation of the *Aratea*, though, Germanicus (15 BCE–19 CE) (Germanicus 1976: 27 and 58, vv. 196-97) imagined a very differently shaped key with iron teeth:

> …qualis ferratos subicit clavicula dentes / succutit et foribus praeducti vincula claustri, / talis disposita est stellis.
>
> ('Their disposition resembles a key whose iron teeth are placed under the bar before a pair of doors to remove it'.)

The Greek temple key of Aratus and, apparently, Hipparchus does not have 'teeth', but the description provided by Germanicus does seem to reflect the fact that shapes of Roman keys were very different from Greek ones in that they often had extended 'teeth' that could be described as forming either a 'W' or 'M' shape (Figs. 9 and 10). Again, one is presented with a puzzle: the analogy suggests that Germanicus 'sees' a slightly different shape underpinning the form of the constellation of Cassiopeia. But do these small differences reflect developments in astronomy, literature, pictorial traditions or a simple change in the shape of a household object? Finally, Aratus (Aratus 1997: 86-87, vv. 195-96) mentions that:

> She extends her outstretched arms just from her small shoulders: you would say she was grieving over her daughter.

From this, it is easy for the reader to begin to visualise the form of a seated female figure, with each of her arms outstretched to the side, with the possibility (though by no means certainty) that the stars θ and β Cas could be imagined as defining the position of her outstretched arms.

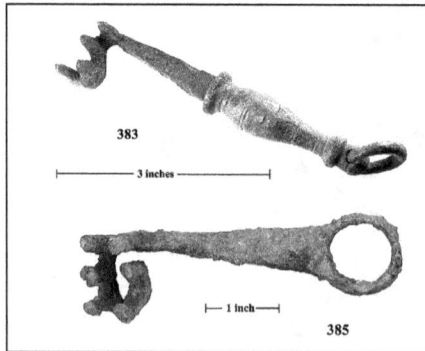

Figure 9. Roman keys with raised teeth. From http://romanlocks. com/Keys [Long keys, Pin Tumbler images, nos. 383 and 385]. Photo: © Don Jackson, 2014.

Figure 10. Roman keys with 'W'-shaped teeth. From http://romanlocks.
com/Keys [Long keys, Pin Tumbler images, nos. 268, 197 and 264].
Photo: © Don Jackson, 2014.

One would hope that this outline would coincide with contemporary depictions of the 'sorrowful' mother; but, after a relatively thorough study of images of Cassiopeia created between the fourth century BCE and the second century CE, I have found only one image of a female figure featured in a rendering of the Perseus and Andromeda story that comes close to the figure described by astronomers and depicted on antique globes, such as that held by the Farnese *Atlas* or the Mainz or Kugel globes (Figs. 12 and 13). In the red-figure *hydria* from Campania datable to the second quarter of the fourth century BCE and now in Staatliche Museen, Berlin (inv. no. 3238) (Fig. 11), there is a central depiction of Andromeda framed by a seated male figure on the left and a seated female on the right. The female figure sits in profile, faces to the left and raises both hands to her face as if about to cover her eyes. Somewhat frustratingly, however, a number of scholars have argued that this figure does not represent Cassiopeia; and even if she did, it must be admitted that she does not, strictly speaking, hold her arms 'out-stretched...just from her small shoulders...grieving over her daughter' as Aratus prescribed. Numerous scholars have discussed the identity of the figures on this vase at length (Brommer 1955: pl. 2; Séchan 1926: 260 and fig. 78: 'qui est vraisemblable Cassiopé, malgré son air de jeunnese'; Phillips 1968: 12 and pl. 13, fig. 37; and Trendall 1967: I, 227-28; II, 89, figs. 1-6). Most have identified the male figure as Cepheus and the corresponding female figure as Cassiopeia. Some, however, have suggested one of the other elderly male characters in the story, the sea-gods Poseidon or Nereus—though one would expect these to hold a trident as an attribute were that the case. If the male figure were a marine deity, then the female deity might be Doris, mother of the Nereids. As a possible comparator for this alternate identification, one could cite the third-quarter of the fourth century BCE calyx-krater by the Darius Painter in the Matera Museum (Phillips 1968: 10 n. 73 and pl. 10, fig. 27 and pl. 11, figs. 28-29).

Figure 11. Detail of the figure of Cassiopeia (?) from the Perseus and Andromeda scene from a red-figure Campanian *hydria*, mid-fourth century BCE. Berlin, Staatliche Museen.

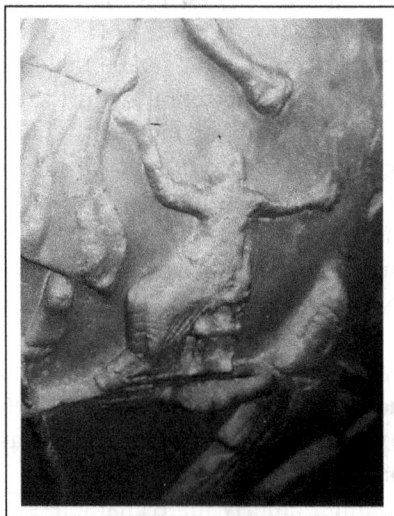

Figure 12. Detail of Cassiopeia on the Farnese *Atlas*. Museo Nazionale Archeologico, Naples. Photo: Kristen Lippincott.

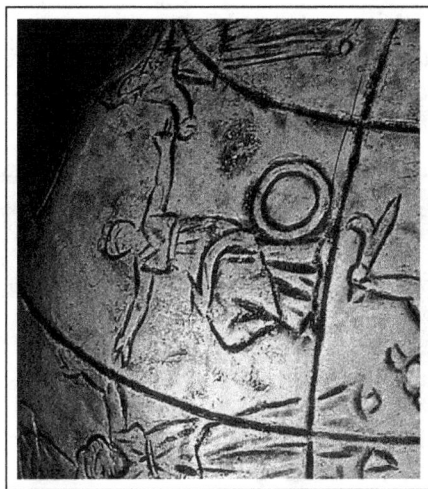

Figure 13. Detail of Cassiopeia from the Kugel Globe. Photo: Galerie J. Kugel, Paris.

The fact that the astronomical form of Cassiopeia seems not to reflect contemporary iconographic models edges one towards the hypothesis that her original form in the skies was based on a more generic, early pictorial formula of a woman seated in a chair with her arms extended, rather than with the specific actions allotted to the Ethiopian queen. In the same way that the dolphins, sea-monsters, bears, dogs, and so on, represent transmissions through a well-known and widely shared pictorial vocabulary, so one is able to find numerous examples of seated women with their arms extended in all the major and minor arts. And although none of these can be associated with the mythological figure of Cassiopeia, each depicts a variant of the predominant artistic convention for representing any seated figure in early Greek art: showing the figure with his or her hips presented in profile and, often, with the lower legs crossed at the ankle or one foot slightly in advance of the other. From the mid-torso upwards, the figure appears to twist so that the shoulders are presented parallel to the picture plane. Both shoulders are usually visible, as is the entire length of both arms. The head is then most often twisted back either to the right or left to a full or three-quarters profile view, usually facing the same direction as the legs. Anatomically difficult, the postures displayed by these figures demonstrate a form of artistic rendering in which each of the individual body parts is depicted in what Gombrich has described as 'its most characteristic angle' (Gombrich 1978 [1950]: 34-36, esp. 35). Heads and legs are seen in profile; the torso and shoulders are presented straight-on. The line defining the overall posture of such a seated figure is a zig-zag: formed (starting with the head) by a vertical line, which bends nearly at right angles at the hips, and then bends again towards the vertical at the knee. This final line runs straight to the feet.

Figure 14. Detail of *The Apotheosis of Homer*, signed by Archelaos of Priene, c. 225–205 BCE. London, British Museum. Photo: © Trustees of the British Museum.

To cite just three examples representing different media: in the marble relief of *The Apotheosis of Homer*, signed by Archelaos of Priene and dating to 225–205 BCE, now in the British Museum (inv. no. 1819.0812.1) (Fig. 14), the first and fourth Muses—possibly Clio and Erato (Robertson 1975: 562-65)—are seated with one of more of their arms raised in a manner that is notably close to the depictions of Cassiopeia on the Farnese and Kugel globes (Figs. 12 and 13). There is also the fragmentary, but still intriguing, figure of Cassiopeia, which echoes this posture in the sculptural grouping of Perseus and Andromeda in the Capitoline Museum in Rome. In vase paintings, the numerous figures representing gift-bearing female funeral attendants or ladies at their toilet provide suitable analogues—for example, the seated female figures along the bottom of the body of the late-classical Apulian terracotta, red-figure volute-krater attributed to the 'Group of New

York', c. 340–320 BCE (New York, Metropolitan Museum of Art, inv. no. 17.210.240) and the seated female figure between youths in the Apulian column-krater of 360–340 (New York, Metropolitan Museum of Art, inv. no. 06. 1021.215) (Fig. 15).

Figure 15. A seated female figure between youths in the Apulian column-krater of 360–340. New York, Metropolitan Museum of Art. Photo: Kristen Lippincott.

In coins and gems, several depictions of female allegorical figures, such as Victory, Plenty or Concord, show a seated female with one hand extended and the other raised to hold the back of her throne. This last example foreshadows the numerous medieval manuscript illustrations of Cassiopeia stemming from the Arabic translations of Ptolemy's *Syntaxis mathematica/Amagest* and continued in the various Latin versions and adaptations of the so-called 'Sufi latinus' (Fig. 16). Again, all these examples show that the astronomical rendering of Cassiopeia is not derived from iconographic sources tied to literary descriptions of the queen, but from a simple pictorial formula of a 'seated female figure'. In this case, 'type', as it were, overrides her identification specifically as Cassiopeia.

Figure 16. Cassiopeia from Gotha, Forschungsbibliothek, Membr. II. 141, fol. 12r (*Sufi latinus*). Image: Creative Commons.

Figure 17. Detail of Hercules from Bentley-Foulkes map. Marcus Manilius, *Astronomica*, ed. R. Bentley, London, 1739. Photo: Kristen Lippincott.

A similar disjunction occurs when one compares the astronomical figure of Hercules with contemporary artistic representations of the demi-god. The identification of the constellation which Hipparchus, Aratus, Germanicus and Cicero call 'the Kneeler' (Ἐν γόνασιν, *Engonasin, Nixus/ Nisus, nisus genu species* and *innixus*) (LeBoeuffle 1977: 100-102) is clearly depicted as kneeling on the Farnese Globe (Fig. 17). His iden- tification as 'Hercules' first appears in the mythographic writings of ps-Eratosthenes (Ps-Eratosthenes, *Castaterismi* IV) and, later, in those of Hyginus (*De astronomia* II.6).

When one surveys Greek, Roman and even early Christian repre- sentations of the many episodes of Hercules's life and twelve heroic deeds, however, he is almost never depicted kneeling. He is often shown lunging, with his leading knee slightly bent or, sometimes, he rests one knee on the back of the Ceryneian Hind. One could cite, for example, the depiction of the twelve labours of Hercules on the third-century sarcophagus panel from the Ludovisi Collection in the Museo Nazionale di Roma (Palazzo Altemps, inv. 8642), the version in the Museo delle Terme in Rome, or the depiction in the early third-century mosaic from Liria (Valencia) in the Museo Arqueológico in Madrid (inv. 38.315). He also sometimes leans on the back of the back of the Cretan Bull, as in the depiction of Hercules and the Bull in the mosaics in Volubilis or on the coils of the Lernian Hydra, such as on the panels in the aforementioned depiction in the Museo Arqueológico in Madrid, while holding the other leg outstretched (Fig. 18). There are remarkably few examples, however, in which the hero actually sinks to his knees. One is where Hercules battles almost head-to-head with the Nemean Lion, such as one sees on the Attic black-figure lip cup attributed to the Workshop of the Phrynos Painter, c. 550 BCE in the Getty Museum (inv. no. 96. AE. 91), the Attic terracotta water jar attributed to the Aegisthus painter, c. 470 BCE, in the Getty Museum (inv.no. 86. AE. 230) (Fig. 19), and the similar Attic red-figure *stamnos*, attributed to the Kleophrades painter, c. 140 BCE, in the University of Pennsylvania Museum, Philadelphia. Another is the figure of Hercules watching the Stymphalian Birds (Weitzmann 1947: fig. 11); and a third example is the figure of Hercules, identifiable by his lion-skin cap, in the late Archaic, eastern pediment from the Temple of Aphaia II (510–470 BCE) from Aigina, now in the Glyptothek in Munich (Boardman 1993: 51-53, no. 38).

Figure 18. Detail of Hercules on the coils of the Lernian Hydra from the *Twelve Labours of Hercules*, Roman, third century CE. Madrid, Museo Arqueológico. Photo: Kristen Lippincott.

Figure 19. Hercules and the Nemean Lion, Attic terracotta water jar attributed to the Aegisthus painter, c. 470 BCE. Malibu, CA, The J. Paul Getty Museum (inv.no. 86. AE. 230). Digital image courtesy of the Getty's Open Content Program.

In the vast majority of the images of the hero, though, he is depicted as standing. Again, one is tempted to argue that the visual model for the figure we now call 'Hercules' was based on a generic formula for a kneeling man (such as one sees in the figure of a warrior on the Athenian *kylix* seen from the back, attributed to Cavias and found in the Agora at Athens, c. 510 BCE, now held in the Allard Pierson Museum in Amsterdam [inv. no. 591]). Despite the fact that the 'Kneeler' is specifically identified as Hercules by later mythographers, the pictorial tradition of a kneeling man is maintained over a text-derived (or iconographic) one associated with the hero. This may be one of the reasons why the astronomically nonsensical addition of the serpent curled in the tree is added to the constellation in later manuscript images of it, since, even if 'a kneeling man' were to hold a lion's pelt and a club, there would be nothing in his posture to identify him specifically as Hercules. Aside from those narrative elements that are used to signal the identification of a male figure as Hercules, the only attribute that seems unique to him in the early classical depictions of the demi-god is his wearing of the Nemean Lion's head as a kind of hood, with the front paws wrapped around his neck and shoulders like a scarf. Intriguingly, though, the image of Hercules wearing the Lion's head seems never to appear in astronomical imagery prior to early Renaissance manuscript depictions of the hero.

If nothing else, this marked disparity between the 'iconographic' representation of characters from the Greek and Roman myths and the shapes and postures of the surviving classical descriptions and depictions of the constellation figures should serve as an alert, if not a warning. It suggests two things: first, that it is quite easy for academics in all disciplines to overlook the fact that most practising artists rely on existing pictorial models, conventions and styles as the basis for their own artistic creations. Those periods in the history of art—or, as Gombrich would say, in the 'history of artists'—in which a truly new way of looking at the world emerges are exceedingly rare. Pictorial formulae are so well engrained in the artist's training and experience that it can often take generations to accommodate or absorb new iconographic models or, even, the sorts of mathematical constructs demanded by the rigours of incorporating astronomical co-ordinates or single-point perspective. Second, when any author evokes a visual metaphor, it is prudent for the modern scholar to question the extent to which the imagery itself may have been conditioned by what the author 'knew', rather than what we might 'see'. As with the case of the Greek temple key, our assumption that we share an innate understanding of the details of daily life with our predecessors can be surprisingly misleading.

In pursuing this idea that the pictorial language of the past can be somewhat exclusive, one might reconsider one other detail of the Farnese Globe. In her study of the globe, Dekker (2013: 88-91), citing the previous literature and arguments, succeeded in putting to rest the suggestion that one could date the Farnese Globe by identifying the grid-shaped object, which appears to the north of Cancer, as the 'Throne of Caesar', and/or connect it to the well-known appearance of a comet at the funeral games of Julius Caesar in 44 BCE (Figs. 20 and 21). As Dekker pointed out, it is astronomically impossible that a comet could have been observed in that part of the sky in either March (the date of Caesar's death) or in July 44 BCE (the date of the funeral games).

Figure 20. Detail of the grid-like object on the Farnese Globe. Museo Nazionale Archeologico, Naples. Photo: Kristen Lippincott.

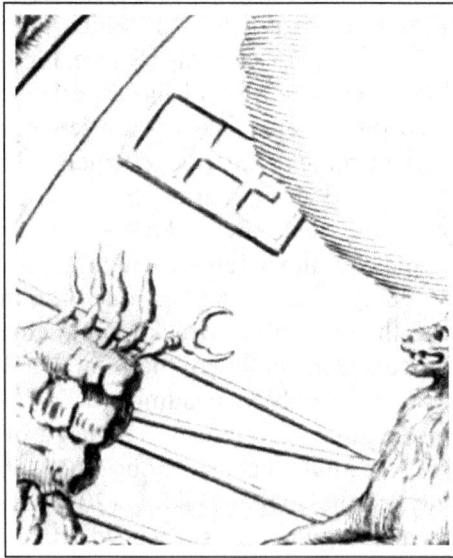

Figure 21. Detail of the grid-like object from the Bentley-Foulkes map. Marcus Manilius, *Astronomica*, ed. R. Bentley, London, 1739. Photo: Kristen Lippincott.

Pictorially, the grid does not resemble any known depiction of a comet or asterism. Thiele (1898: 41) was the first to suggest, tentatively, that the grid might represent either a Greek or a Roman throne, but the truth of the matter is that it does not look like a throne either. Nor do the arguments that it represents a curule seat (*sella curulis*) (Kunzl, Fecht, and Greff 2000: 535) bear much weight, as the two major identifying features of the seat—its characteristic X-shaped frame and curved legs— are lacking (Fig. 22).

Figure 22. Sella curulis. Museo nazionale di Villa Guinigi, Lucca. Photo: Kristen Lippincott.

If one considers the object from a pictorial point of view, it most closely resembles the sculptural rendering of a window, door or gate, such as depictions on the reverse of Roman Imperial coins showing the closed door to the temple of Janus or the *Ara Providentiae* Augustae in Rome or, as in Figure 23, the door to the House of Augustus. It also recalls the false doors or so-called 'gates to eternity', common on Roman sarcophagi in Asia Minor; or, even, surviving examples of Roman folding doors, such as the false doors from a Roman sarcophagus in the Kütahya Museum of Archaeology in Turkey or the fossilised wooden folding doors from the first century CE taken from the Villa of Mysteries in Pompeii.

Figure 23. Reverse of an aureus celebrating Augustus, showing the door of Augustus' house between laurel trees, with the *corona civica* above. Lucius Caninius Gallus, moneyer, mint of Rome, 12 BCE. London, British Museum. Photo: © Trustees of the British Museum.

One other close visual similarity is with the mysterious gate-like object known as the δόκανα (*dokana*), the precise significance of which remains the subject of debate, though its connection to doors, tomb entrances and gates seems fairly widely accepted (Fig. 24). Plutarch (*Moralia* VI, 478A; 1939: 246-47) relates in his *De fraterno amore* that:

> The ancient representations of the Dioscuri are called by the Spartans 'beam-figures' (δόκανα): they consist of two parallel wooden beams joined by two other transverse beams placed across them; and this common and indivisible character of the offering appears entirely suitable to the brotherly love of these gods.

Figure 24. Votive relief of Argenidas in Verona, second century BCE. Verona, Musei Maffeiano. Image: Waites 1919: 1, fig. 1, from Maffei 1749: fig. 7.

Beyond this, however, the *dokana* seems to have some connection to the cult of the Dioscuri that was specifically associated with death, perhaps in connection with the Twins' role as *psychopompi*, or 'guardians between the two worlds, protectors of the living, companions also of the dead' (Waites 1919; Nilsson 1940: 68-69; Pipili 1987; and *LIMC*, 'Dioscuri: A (*dokana*)', 1986: III, 586-87). There are also a number of portable lead amulets or talismans of the *dokana* that have survived (Fig. 25), and aspects of the cult appear to have spread fairly widely throughout the Mediterranean.[1]

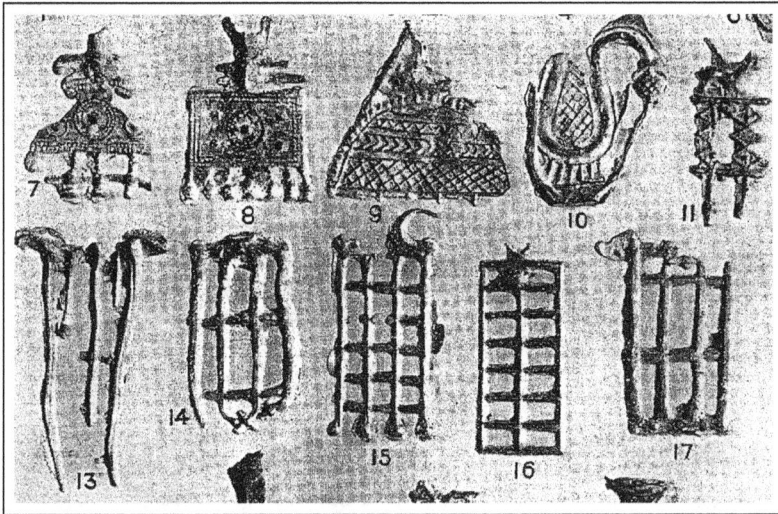

Figure 25. Various lead *dokana* amulets. Image: Artemis Orthia 1929: pl. CLXXXV.

If the grid-like object of the Farnese Globe is a door, a gateway or is even somehow related to the cult image of the *dokana*, it does still not explain why any of these would appear on a celestial globe or why such a portal might appear near the zodiacal constellation of Cancer. Astronomically, this portion of the sky is relatively empty and, as Dekker has pointed out, it provides a convenient space where ancillary information, such as magnitude tables or dedication cartouches, can be and often are placed by the artists of later western celestial globes.[2] The most likely explanation is that the grid-like object is the remnant of some non-astronomical insertion. Having said that, if this grid is intended to

1. I thank David Hibler for his conversations with me on this subject.
2. Personal correspondence, 18 August 2013.

represent a portal, then one might mention the well-known astrological formulation of Cancer and Capricorn as the gates of birth and death. Allegedly developed from the positions of these two zodiacal constellations defining the summer and winter solstices, the notion traces its textual authority to Pythagoras and to Plato's 'Cave of the Nymphs'. What this myth meant to the early Greeks is not clear, but to later commentators on Plato's text, such as the third-century CE neo-Platonist, Porphyry, in his *On the Cave of the Nymphs* (Porphyry 1917: 27-29), the astrological aspect of the trope comes to the fore:

> Theologists therefore assert, that these two gates are Cancer and Capricorn; but Plato calls them entrances. And of these, theologists say, that Cancer is the gate through which souls descend; but Capricorn that through which they ascend. Cancer is indeed northern, and adapted to descent; but Capricorn is southern, and adapted to ascent. The northern parts, likewise, pertain to souls descending into generation. And the gates of the cavern which are turned to the north are rightly said to be pervious to the descent of men; but the southern gates are not the avenues of the Gods, but of souls ascending to the Gods. On this account, the poet does not say that they are the avenues of the Gods, but of immortals; this appellation being also common to our souls, which are *per se*, or essentially, immortal. It is said that Parmenides mentions these two gates in his treatise 'On the Nature of Things', as likewise that they are not unknown to the Romans and Egyptians.
>
> ...with the Egyptians, the beginning of the year is not Aquarius, as with the Romans, but Cancer. For the star Sothis, which the Greeks call the Dog, is near to Cancer. And the rising of Sothis is the new moon with them, this being the principle of generation to the world. On this account, the gates of the Homeric cavern are not dedicated to the east and west, nor to the equinoctial signs, Aries and Libra, but to the north and south, and to those celestial signs which towards the south are most southerly, and, towards the north are most northerly; because this cave was sacred to souls and aquatic nymphs.

In his notes to the passage, Thomas Taylor (Porphyry 1917: 27-29) cited similar descriptions in the *Commentarii in Somnium Scipionis* of Macrobius (I, xii, 3-8):

> Pythagoras thought that the empire of Pluto began downwards from the milky way, because souls falling from thence appear to have already receded from the Gods. Hence he asserts that the nutriment of milk is first offered to infants, because their first motion commences from the galaxy, when they begin to fall into terrene bodies. On this account, since those who are about to descend are yet in *Cancer*, and have not left the milky way, they rank in the order of the Gods. But when, by falling, they arrive

at the *Lion*, in this constellation they enter on the exordium of their future condition. And because, in the *Lion*, the rudiments of birth and certain primary exercises of human nature, commence;

...As soon, therefore, as the soul gravitates towards body in this first production of herself, she begins to experience a material tumult, that is, matter flowing into her essence. And this is what Plato remarks in the *Phædo*, that the soul is drawn into body staggering with recent intoxication; signifying by this the new drink of matter's impetuous flood, through which the soul, becoming defiled and heavy, is drawn into a terrene situation. But the starry *cup* placed between Cancer and the Lion is a symbol of this mystic truth, signifying that descending soul's first experience intoxication in that part of the heavens through the influx of matter.

The formulae can also be found in Macrobius's *Saturnalia* (I, xvii, 63) and in Helpericus of Auxerre's *De computo* (Migne, *PL*, CXXXVII, 25, ch. II). It is certainly unwise to insist that the neo-Platonic interpretation of an early Greek myth has any bearing on the iconography of a Graeco-Roman globe, but it may well be worth considering this option amongst the many potential non-astronomical sources yet to be explored.

In conclusion, most scholars writing on the history of constellation imagery tend to focus on two areas to support their findings: scientific data gleaned from early descriptions and depictions of the stars and iconographical details derived from Graeco-Roman mythology. It is hoped that this study has shown the extent to which a largely independent pictorial tradition also helped to shape the heavens, and, in this process, how the role of the artist is not as an inventor, but as a torch-bearer for continuity with the past.

References

Acquisitions. 1987. 'Acquisitions/1987', *The Getty Museum Journal* 16 (1988): 144, no. 8 (ill.).

Aratus. 1997. *Phaenomena*, ed. and trans. D.A. Kidd (Cambridge: Cambridge University Press).

———. 1998. *Phénomènes*, ed. and French trans. Jean Martin (Paris).

Artemis Orthia. 1929. *The Sanctuary of Artemis Orthia at Sparta: Excavated and Described by Members of the British School at Athens, 1906–1910*, ed. R.M. Dawkins (London: British Council/Macmillan).

Baxandall, Michael. 1972. *Painting and Experience in Fifteenth-century Italy* (Oxford: Oxford University Press).

Boardman, John. 1993. *The Oxford History of Classical Art* (Oxford: Oxford University Press).

Brommer, Frank. 1955. 'Die Königstochter und das Ungeheuer', *Marburger Winckelmann-Programm*: 3-15.

Carpenter, T.H. 1991. *Art and Myth in Ancient Greece* (London: Thames & Hudson).

Casson, Lionel. 1971. *Ships and Seamanship in the Ancient World* (Princeton: Princeton University Press).

Cicero, Marcus Tullius. 1966. *Cicéron. Les Aratea*, ed. and French trans. V. Buescu (Hildesheim: Georg Olms).

———. 1972. *Cicéron. Aratea fragments poétiques*, ed. and French trans. J. Soubiran (Paris: Les Belles Lettres).

Corpus vasorum. 1988. *Corpus vasorum antiquorum. Italia. Fiesole. Collezione Costantini*, ed. G. Camporeale and V. Saladino (Rome: L'Erma di Bretschneider).

Dekker, Elly. 2005. 'Exploring the Retes of Astrolabes', in *Astrolabes at Greenwich: A Catalogue of the Astrolabes in the National Maritime Museum, Greenwich*, ed. K. van Cleempoel (London and Oxford: National Maritime Museum and Oxford University Press): 47-71.

———. 2013. *Illustrating the Phaenomena: Celestial Cartography in Antiquity and the Middle Ages* (Oxford: Oxford University Press).

Diels, Hermann. 1897. *Parmenides Lehrgedicht* (Berlin: G. Reiner).

———. 1914 [3rd ed. 1920]. *Antike Technik* (Leipzig and Berlin: B.G. Teubner).

Duhem, Pierre. 1908. *Sōzein ta phainomena: essai sur la notion de théorie physique de Platon à Galilée* (Paris: A. Hermann).

———. 1964. *To Save the Phenomena: An Essay on the Idea of Physical Theory from Plato to Galileo*, trans. E. Doland and C. Maschler (Chicago: University of Chicago Press).

Duke, Dennis. 2006. 'Analysis of the Farnese Globe', *Journal for the History of Astronomy* 37: 87-100.

Engelmann, Richard. 1900. *Archäologische Studien zu den Tragikern* (Berlin: Weidmann).

Euripides. 2004. *Euripides: Selected Fragmentary Plays*, ed. and trans. C. Collard, M. Cropp and K.H. Lee (Warminster: Aris & Phillips): II, 133-68.

Germanicus. 1976. *The Aratus Ascribed to Germanicus Caesar*, ed. and trans. D.B. Gain (London: Athlone Press).

Gombrich, E.H. 1978 [1950]. *The Story of Art* (London: Phaidon).

———. 1956. *Art and Illusion: A Study in the Psychology of Pictorial Representation* (London: Phaidon).

Green, J.R. 1991. 'On Seeing and Depicting Theatre in Classical Athens', *Greek, Roman and Byzantine Studies* 32.1: 15-50.

———. 1994. *Theatre in Ancient Greek Society* (London and New York: Routledge).

Green, J.R., and Eric Handley. 1995. *Images of the Greek Theatre* (London: British Museum Press).

Hipparchus. 1894. *Hipparchi in Arati et Eudoxi Phaenomena commentariorum, libri tres*, ed. and German trans. K. Manutius (Leipzig: Teubner).

Hyginus 1992. *Hygini De astronomia*, ed. Ghislaine Viré (Stuttgart and Leipzig: Teubner).

Klimek-Winter, Rainer. 1993. *Andromedatragödien. Sophokles. Euripedes. Livius Andronikos. Ennius. Accius. Text, Einleitung und Kommentar*, Beiträge zur Altertumskunde, 21 (Stuttgart: Teubner).

Kunze, E., and H. Schleif. 1944. *Atlas zu Olympische Forschungen*, I (Berlin: Gruyter).

Künzl, Ernst, M. Fecht, and S. Greff. 2000. 'Ein römischer Himmelsglobus der mittleren Kaiserzeit. Studien zur römischen Astral-ikonografie', *Jahrbuch der Römisch-Germanischen Zentralmuseums Mainz* 47: 495-94.

Le Boeuffle, Andre. 1977. *Les noms latins d'astres et de constellations* (Paris: Les Belles Lettres).

Lehmann, P.W., and K. Lehmann, 1973. *Samothracian Reflections. Aspects of the Revival of the Antique*, Bollingen Series, 17 (Princeton: Princeton University Press).

LIMC (Lexicon Iconographicum Mythologiae Classicae). 1981-99. (Zurich and Munich: Artemis Verlag).

Lippincott, Kristen. 2009. 'The Problem with Being a Minor Deity: The Story of Eridanus', in *Images of the Gods: Papers of a Conference in Memory of Jean Seznec* (3-4 December 2004), ed. R. Duits and F. Quiviger, Warburg Institute Colloquia, 14 (London: The Warburg Institute): 43-96.

Maffei, Scipione. 1749. *Museum veronense: hoc est Antiquarum inscriptionum atque anaglyphorum collectio cui taurinensis adiungitur et vindobonensis* (Verona: Typis Seminarii).

Moret, Jean-Marc. 1975. *L'Ilioupersis dans céramique italiote. Les myths et leur expression figure au IVe siècle*, Bibliotheca Helvetica Romana, 14 (Rome: Institut suisse de Rome).

Nauck, August. 1856 [repr. 1899, 1926, 1964 and 1971-2004). *Tragicorum graecorum fragmenta* (Leipzig: Teubner). Repr. Leipzig: Teubner (1899); Leipzig: Teubner (1926); Hildesheim: B. Snell (1964) and Göttingen: Vandenhoeck & Ruprecht (1971-2004).

Nilsson, M.P. 1940. *Greek Popular Religion* (New York: Columbia University Press).

Pearson, A.C. 1917. *The Fragments of Sophocles* (Cambridge: Cambridge University Press).

Peters, E. 1904. 'Andromeda', *Journal of Hellenic Studies* 34: 99-112 and plate V.

Phillips, Kyle M. 1968. 'Perseus and Andromeda', *American Journal of Archaeology* 72: 1-23.

Pipili, Maria. 1987. *Iconography of the Sixth Century BC*, Oxford University Committee for Archaeology, 12 (Oxford: Oxford University Press).

Plutarch. 1939. *Moralia*, trans. W.C. Helmbold, Loeb Classical Library (London: Heinemann; Cambridge, MA: Harvard University Press).

Porphyry. 1917. *On the Caves of the Nymphs in the Thirteenth Book of the Odyssey. From the Greek of Porphyry*, trans. Thomas Taylor (London: J.M. Watkins).

Ptolemy. 1998. *Ptolemy's Almagest*, trans. G.J. Toomer (Princeton: Princeton University Press).

Robertson, Martin. 1975. *A History of Greek Art* (Cambridge: Cambridge University Press).

Rocco, Anna. 1953. *Corpus vasorum antiquorum Italia* (Rome: Libreria dello Stato).

Saladino, Vincenzo. 1979. 'Nuovi vasi apuli con temi Euripidei (Alcesti, Crisippo, Andromeda)', *Prometheus* 5: 97-116.

Schaefer, B.E. 2005. 'The Epoch of Constellations on the Farnese Atlas and their Origin on Hipparchus's Lost Catalogue', *Journal for the History of Astronomy* 36: 167-95.

Schauenburg, Konrad. 1960. *Perseus in der Kunst der Altertums*, Antiquitas, 3 (Bonn: R. Habelt).

Schmidt, Margot, A.D. Trendall, and Alexander Cambitoglu. 1976. *Eine Gruppe Apulischer Grabvasen in Basel* (Basel: Archäologischer Verlag/Philipp von Zabern [Mainz]).

Schott, Albert, and Robert Böker. 1958. *Aratos. Sternbilder und Wetterzeichen* (Munich: M. Hueber).

Séchan, Louis. 1926. *Études sur la tragédie grecque dans ses rapports avec la céramique* (Paris: Champion).

Small, Jocelyn Penny. 2003. *The Parallel Worlds of Classical Art and Text* (Cambridge and New York: Cambridge University Press).

Thiele, Georg. 1898. *Antike Himmelsbilder, mit Forschungen zu Hipparchos, Aratos und seinen Fortsetzern und Beiträge zur Kunstgeschichte des Sternhimmels* (Berlin: Weidmannsche Buchhandlung).

Trendall, A.D. 1967. *The Red-figure Vases of Lucania, Campania and Sicily* (Oxford: Clarendon Press).

Waites, M.C. 1919. 'The Meaning of the "Dokana"', *The American Journal of Archaeology* 32.1: 1-18.

Waldstein, Charles. 1905. *The Argive Heraeum* (Boston and New York: The Archaeological Institute of America /School of Classical Studies at Athens).

Weitzmann, Kurt. 1947. *Illustrations in Roll and Codex: A Study of the Origin and Method of Text Illustration*, Princeton Studies in Manuscript Illumination, 9 (Princeton: Princeton University Press).

Woodward, Jocelyn M. 1957. *Perseus: A Study in Greek Art and Legend* (Cambridge: Cambridge University Press).

GIOTTO'S SKY: THE FRESCO PAINTINGS OF THE FIRST FLOOR SALONE OF THE PALAZZO DELLA RAGIONE, PADUA, ITALY

Darrelyn Gunzburg

University of Wales Trinity Saint David
Sophia Centre for the Study of Cosmology in Culture
School of Archaeology, History and Anthropology
Lampeter, Ceredigion SA48 7ED, Wales, UK
d.gunzburg@uwtsd.ac.uk

Abstract

Giotto's frescos in the Salone of the Palazzo della Ragione, Padua, were painted across three registers. The upper register contains celestial astronomical imagery that few scholars have been able fully to understand. Using two sections of this upper register as case studies, I reconstructed the skies over Padua in the medieval period using astronomical and astrological software, together with the knowledge of poetic astronomy and naked eye astronomy. This approach showed that, rather than being simple decorations, these images are instead reflective of the constellations that dictated the seasons and the cycle of the year as seen over Padua c. 1309. Furthermore, they reveal a night sky that was populated with a constellational iconography that, I argue, was part of an ensouled cosmology.

Keywords

Art history, cosmology, medieval period, cultural astrology, Padua, Pietro d'Abano, constellational imagery.

Introduction

There is often an assumption that documents constitute what is written and that textual documents alone give us primary information about the way people thought about their world. Yet non-textual documents, such as images, can and should also influence how we understand a period or culture. This becomes extremely important in the area of art history, for which primary source materials consist not only of manuscripts but also buildings, frescoes, stained glass, mosaics, and sculpture (the arts of carving and casting).

There is another type of primary source material, however, that provides us with visual information, often ignored yet universally consistent, and that is the sky. Indeed, it is possible to argue that the sky can be utilised as a primary source for other areas of the humanities, not just art history. As Matthew Fox (2004) reconstructed the skies of the first century CE and offered a different perspective on Ovid's (43 BCE– c. 17 CE) *Fasti*, and Arthur Beer (1967) reconstructed the skies of the seventh century to understand the cupola of the Qusayr'Amra, so too sky maps reconstructed for the fourteenth century in Padua, linked with naked eye astronomy, have become one of the primary documents of my research and a language that can be used to help correlate and understand images.

I will illustrate the value of such methodology by focusing attention on the upper register of the fresco scheme of the first floor Salone of the Palazzo della Ragione, or Palace of Reason—the law courts—in Padua, Italy. Scholars from as far back as the sixteenth century have approached this imagery by correlating them with horoscopic images found in a book published some 200 years after the fresco scheme was first painted. I contend that these particular images are descriptive of the medieval view of the sky and, moreover, that it is possible to consider the images in this medieval building as exemplifying the way the medieval sky was seen and imbued with meaning—as constellation patterns, rather than as disconnected images in a book. This approach, I argue, allows us to connect more closely with a culture that once connected directly with the sky, making the medieval view of the sky vivid to us in ways that our contemporary society may have lost. Indeed, the top register of the painted fresco scheme opens up a wonder-filled case study on the medieval view of the sky.

History

The history of the Palazzo della Ragione is well documented. It was originally begun in 1172 and finished in 1218–19 as three large halls where the judges held court. In 1306–1309, the Commune entrusted Fra Giovanni degli Eremitani (active in Padua 1289–1318) to create one large hall and build a new wooden roof that resembled the keel of an upturned ship. In order to do this he increased the outer walls in height from 16 to 24 metres and constructed walls that curved in towards the top to reduce the span of the wooden vault (Figs. 1, 3) (Cunningham 1995: 51). The Commune then commissioned Giotto di Bondone (c. 1267–1337) to implement a three-tiered cycle of paintings at the top of these newly heightened bare walls of this first-floor Salone (Fig. 3).

Figure 1. Exterior Palazzo della Ragione, south face.
Photo: D. Gunzburg.

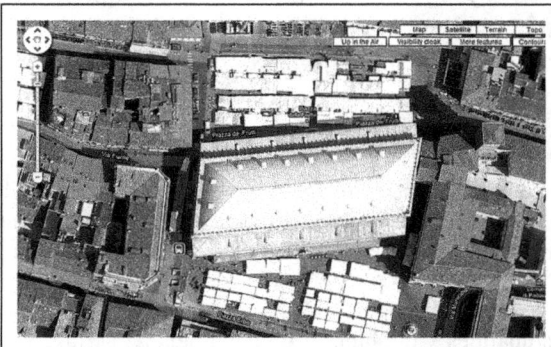

Figure 2. The Palazzo della Ragione from Google Earth.

Figure 3. Interior first floor Salone, Palazzo della Ragione, showing the whaleback wooden vault and the top three registers located at the upper part of the walls of the room right beneath the wooden ceiling. Photo: D. Gunzburg.

The scheme was—and still is— filled with astronomical and astrological imagery, said to be influenced by Pietro d'Abano (c. 1250–c. 1316), who was teaching medicine, philosophy, and astrology at Padua University at the time. The original meaning of the scheme, contained within a careful arrangement of sky images and symbols, all faithfully maintained over the centuries, has continued to puzzle art historians, modern icono-graphers, and scholars such as Antonio Barzon (1924), Pier Luigi Fantelli and Franca Pellegrini (2000), Dieter Blume (2000), M. Beatrice Rigobello and Francesco Autizi (2008), and Giordana Mariani Canova (2011). With the lack of original commissioning documents for 1306–1309, the primary source that describes the Palazzo della Ragione is that of an eyewitness of the time, Giovanni da Nono (c. 1275–1346), who worked as a judge at the Palazzo della Ragione in the first two decades of the fourteenth century and witnessed the reconstruction. His Paduan chronicle, *Visio Egidij Regis Patavie*, which describes the interior decoration of the Salone, is bare and circumspect (da Nono 1934–39: 20):

> Duodecim celestia signa et septem planete cum suis proprietatibus in hac cohopertura, fulgebunt, a Zotho summo pictorum mirilce laborata, et alia sidera aurea cum speculis et alie figurationes similiter fulgebunt interius.

> The twelve heavenly signs and seven planets with their respective properties/qualities will shine in this complete covering, wonderfully worked by the topmost painter Giotto, and further inside with mirrors will shine other golden constellations and other forms (trans. Gunzburg).

On 2 February 1420, the roof of the Salone was destroyed by fire and much of the scheme was badly damaged. Padua had succumbed to Venetian rule in 1405, and whilst there was unanimous agreement by the Venetian Senate that restoration of the internal fresco scheme was to take place, all that survives from the minutes of the meeting on 6 February 1420 was the vague directive to return the Salone to *ut prius erat*, 'how it was before' (Verdi 2008: 75). Giovanni Michele Savonarola (1385–1468), an eye-witness of the time, noted that the extensive repainting of the astrological scheme, undertaken by Nicolò Miretto (c. 1375–c. 1450) and Stefano da Ferrara (active fifteenth century) from 1425 to 1440, followed the original iconographical program. On 17 August 1756, a hurricane tore off the vault and once more, in 1759, the fresco scheme was repainted by Francesco Zannoni (active eighteenth century) in the period 1762–70, matching the previous scheme but omitting the stars painted on the ceiling (Fantelli and Pellegrini 2000: 16). This known history recognises that, although the scheme has suffered impairment since its original construction, the Commune kept commissioning a repainting of the same themes, rather than painting something new. One can suggest that this was due to the importance of the individual images and their meanings for the medieval viewer, and thus there was the desire to have them faithfully maintained. In addition, unlike so many frescoes in such buildings of the medieval period that have disintegrated, been broken up, smashed apart, sold off, or destroyed, these images are still with us today. Therefore, although the scheme can really only be approached through what Guido Giglioni (2008: 94) terms 'a series of interpretative refractions', with the images apparently being reproduced through the different levels of restoration it is still possible to explore some of the original thinking behind the scheme.

The Fresco Scheme and the People Who Brought It into Manifestation

The Palazzo della Ragione is a trapezium in shape and specifically a parallelogram where opposite sides of the figure are parallel (Fig. 2). The fresco scheme on the first floor Salone is located on the upper part of the walls of the room right beneath its wooden ceiling and the 319 compartments form a painted arrangement on three horizontal registers and along all four walls (Fig. 3). These are the earlier registers of frescoes, as distinct from the register visible beneath this that was painted at a later stage by Giusto de' Menabuoi and with which I will not be dealing. Each scene is created either within a square, within a Romanesque arch, within a trefoil-cusped arch, or, as with some saints, within doorways with square lintels, and the background of each depiction is blue (Fig. 4). Each column is visually articulated by fictive pilasters with Corinthian capitals, giving a three-dimensional appearance. These pilasters, painted to look like terracotta, white, and green marble, mediate between the represented scenes vertically. The terracotta frieze of acanthus leaves carries horizontally across the registers but does not run underneath the signs of the zodiac, nor under the scenes that appear to represent the months. This *trompe l'oeil* effect serves both to separate one scene from another and to integrate the scheme into a decorative whole. As can be seen in Figure 4, the horizontal registers are also divided into columns so that scenes assemble one upon another. It is this separation into individual *quadrata* that, I shall argue later, has captured and segued an understanding of this scheme. The top register of horizontal scenes running around all four walls closest to the ceiling depicts stars and constellations, amongst other images. The imagery of the middle and lower registers contains the signs of the zodiac, the seven major pagan deities, Luna, Mercury, Venus, Sol, Mars, Jupiter, and Saturn, a rich assembly of Christian saints, labours associated with each month and season, trades and skills exemplified by the Paduan workforce, images that depict the latitude bands, and theological and liturgical themes.

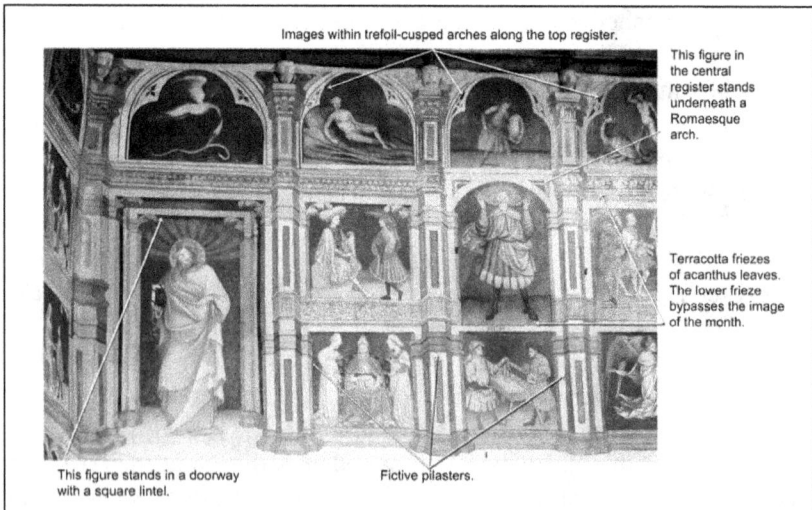

Images within trefoil-cusped arches along the top register.

This figure in the central register stands underneath a Romaesque arch.

Terracotta friezes of acanthus leaves. The lower frieze bypasses the image of the month.

This figure stands in a doorway with a square lintel.

Fictive pilasters.

Figure 4. Images from the earlier top three registers along the south wall. Photo: D. Gunzburg.

Fra Giovanni degli Eremitani was the engineer/architect/town planner who designed and created the Salone roof, the shape of which appears to be the oldest example of its kind in Italy. He was highly praised by his contemporaries in the mendicant orders as a monk with an exceptional wealth of technical knowledge, and, as a well-travelled man, was said to have been inspired by what he had seen in far-away lands (Dellwing 1969: 152). When the 1420 fire destroyed the roof, Guglielmo de Paolo Ongarello's 1441 chronicle noted that the keel arch ceiling was rebuilt in its original form (Dellwing 1969: 146 n. 7).[1] Therefore not only were the images being reproduced but also the architecture of the roof. It was, however, the interaction between Pietro d'Abano and Giotto di Bondone that allowed the imagery of the fresco scheme to come to life.

Pietro d'Abano—the Astrological Advisor

Pietro d'Abano, or Peter of Padua as he was also known, was one of the most influential men of learning during the last years of the thirteenth and the early years of the fourteenth century, writing on medicine, philosophy, and astrology. His career incorporated teaching positions at the *studium generale* of Paris and later at Padua University. Nancy Siraisi (1970: 322) regards this as 'a link between the dialectical and philosophical achievement of Paris in the thirteenth century and the burgeoning scientific interests of fourteenth-century Padua'. Antonio Favaro (1880: 7) named d'Abano as the first professor definitely known to have taught astrology at Padua. In his will d'Abano described himself as 'artis medicine philosophie et astrologie professor'.[2] D'Abano's reputation as a respected authority on medicine and natural science extended well beyond Padua and continued into the sixteenth century (Siraisi 1970: 322). Michele Savonarola declared he was regarded as a second Aristotle and called 'the great Lombard' (Thorndike 1923–58: 887). Three of his books, all dated to 1310, *The Conciliator*, *The Lucidator*, and *De motu octave spere*, contain his astrological writings. Many of these works are extant, yet only a few parts of them have been translated into English. Federici Vescovini (1987: 38, 39) argues that d'Abano combined 'Aristotelian philosophy and other doctrinal, medical

1.   Ognarello's chronicle is held in the Bibiloteca Civica di Padova 1121,1.
2.   'Master professor of medicine, philosophy and astrology'. The will is printed in *Atti della R. Accademia dei Lincei*, Series 3, *Memorie delle Classi di Scienze Morali, Storiche, Filologiche*, vol. 11 (1877–78): 548-50 and cited in Favaro 1880: 8 and Siraisi 1970: 322.

and astronomical traditions' derived from Byzantine and Islamic scholars, 'separated it [astrology] from demonic magic, and reinstated it
between astronomy and mathematics whence certain philosophers and
theologians had removed it' and, drawing on the work of Bruno Nardi,
concludes that d'Abano should be recognised as an advocate of 'the
independence of secular medical, philosophical, and astronomical
thinking from theological interference'.

In 1293 whilst he was teaching at the University of Paris, d'Abano
collected and translated into Latin a number of works by the Jewish-
Spanish astrologer and polymath Abraham Ibn Ezra (1089–1164). As a
result, Ibn Ezra's ideas about astrology gained wide currency in the Latin
West (Thorndike 1944: 293-94). Among his works were *The Beginning
of Wisdom* (1148), a basic textbook of astrology, *The Book of Reasons*, a
commentary and additional material for *The Beginning of Wisdom*, and
The Book of Nativities and Revolutions, all three of which created an
integrated textbook of basic astrological doctrine. These remained
popular and influential until the Renaissance.

Giotto di Bondone—the Painter

Documents and sources describe Giotto di Bondone as enthusiastic and
diligent in his desire to build a career, and a widely travelled young man
whose sound business skills allowed him to participate in artistic projects
all over Italy (Derbes and Sandona 2004: 6). By c. 1313 he had been
noticed by chronicler Riccobaldo Ferrarese (c. 1246–died after 1314)
(Murray 1953: 59-60):

> Zottus pictor eximius, Florentinus, agnoscitur qualis in arte fuerit,
> testantur opera facta per eum in Ecclesiis Minorum Assisii, Arimini,
> Padue, ac per ea que pinxit Palatio Comitis (deve dire Communis) Padue
> et in Ecclesia Arena Padue.

> Giotto is an excellent Florentine painter. The quality of his art is attested
> in his works in the Franciscan churches at Assisi, Rimini, Padua, and in
> those works that he painted in the Palace of Judgements (that is to say of
> the Commune) of Padua and in the Arena church at Padua (quoted in
> Murray 1953: 59-60, trans. Gunzburg).

Francesco da Barberino (1264–1348), in his *Documenti D'Amore*
c. 1308–12, praised Giotto's *Envy* in the Arena Chapel (Stubblebine
1969: 109):

Inimica: inimicatur enim patientibus eam unde Invidiosus invidia comburitur intus et extra hanc padue in arena optime pinsit Giottus.

Animosity: it suffers this, indeed, with endurance, as where Envy is consumed with envy inside and out, this Giotto painted excellently in the Arena at Padua (trans. Gunzburg).

In 1315, Dante (c. 1265–1321) in his *Purgatorio* XI, 94-96, cited Giotto's having eclipsed the fame of Cimabue as an example of the transience of temporal fame (Alighieri 1995: 266):

Credette Cimabue ne la pittura
tener lo campo, e ora ha Giotto il grido,
sì che la fama di colui è scura.

Cimabue believed that in painting he led the field,
and now it is Giotto's turn,
So the fame of the former is darkened (trans. Gunzburg).

When he painted the frescoes in the Arena Chapel, Giotto was not yet forty, yet his status stood on secure foundations. As Anne Derbes and Mark Sandona (2004: 2) note, 'The startling freshness of his observations, the economy and empathy of his narratives, the profound dignity and humanity of his figures all set Giotto apart from his contemporaries'.

Although da Nono does not mention Pietro d'Abano, Jean-Michel Massing (1987: 171) suggests that 'it is not to be ruled out that' he was the man who advised Giotto, or his commissioner, Enrico Scrovegni, on the representation of the comet in 'The Adoration of the Magi' scene in the Arena Chapel. Yet Olson and Pasachoff (2002: 1564) argue that d'Abano did not return to Padua from Paris until 1306 and thus could not have advised Giotto on the comet. Furthermore, there is the suggestion that Giotto, a great observer of natural phenomena, had observed Halley's comet of 1301 himself, noted it in his sketchbook, and incorporated it when he frescoed the Arena Chapel between 1303 and 1305, thus becoming the first painter to represent the Star of Bethlehem as a comet in painting (Olson and Pasachoff 2002: 1564). It is plausible, however, that when Giotto went on to be employed by the Commune to work on the cycle of paintings in the first floor Salone of the Palazzo della Ragione, given the amount of sky phenomena included in the frescoes, he would have been advised on the nature of this material and that advice would, in all likelihood, have come from Pietro d'Abano; he would also have brought his own innovative techniques and thinking to the scheme, as he did with the comet and The Star of Bethlehem.

There is another possible connecting link between the two men. D'Abano completed his *Expositio problematum Aristotelis* in Padua in 1310. Siraisi (1970: 321) has identified the *Expositio* as conceivably being the principal work in this genre and of this period that sought to integrate Greek *problemata* literature with the natural scientific knowledge that was understood by medieval scholars in the West at this time. The question d'Abano was answering in Book xxxvi, 1. §3 was 'Why do (men) make images of the face?' (Thomann 1991: 240). J. Thomann (1991: 240-41) points out that d'Abano offered a theory of visual art as his commentary on the problem and cited Giotto, and Giotto alone, as his example, whereas an anonymous scholar of the same period approached the same problem in an entirely different way and with no reference to visual theory. Thomann thus proposes that d'Abano's choice of subject matter—painting—and painter—Giotto— may have implied a personal connection.

The 'Astrolabium Planum'

When writing about the scheme, scholars have recognised this connection between Giotto and Pietro d'Abano. As noted earlier, contemporary chroniclers and writers da Nono and Michele Savonarola wrote of how the scheme was informed by the astrological ideas of Pietro d'Abano, yet neither of these writers attempted to decipher the scheme. One could argue that this may have been because it was so culturally familiar that they did not feel the need to describe it. Additionally, I argue that, as scholars moved further away in time from the cosmology that shaped the original images of the Salone fresco scheme—the medieval worldview that was astrologically underpinned—so they understood the meaning of the scheme less and less. The key moment occurred, I contend, in 1560 when Bernardino Scardeone (1478–1574) in his book *Historiae de urbis Patavii antiquitatea* (1560) equated the images of the Salone fresco scheme with Pietro d'Abano's *Astrolabium Planum* (Scardeone 1560: 201-202), a book in which d'Abano was said to have correlated astrological images with each degree of the zodiac as it rose over the horizon. This theory of degree symbolism is known as *Myriogenesis*, forecasting from individual degrees (Firmicus Maternus 1975: 272-300), and *Monomoriai*, planetary rulers of individual degrees (Greenbaum 2001: 2-14, 66-70, 135, 136, 138-45).

From the sixteenth century onwards, then, up to the work of Rigobello and Autizi (2008) and to a certain extent the work of Giordana Mariani Canova (1998, 2011), the arguments of scholars rested on seeking a correlation between d'Abano's *Astrolabium Planum* and the Salone fresco images. One of the predicaments they encountered was that d'Abano's work was apparently no longer extant. As a result, scholars turned to a work that was said to be based on that of d'Abano and was readily available, namely, Johannes Engel's *Astrolabium Planum*, published by Erhard Ratdolt in Augsburg in 1488, in order to derive meaning for the images in the Salone. The difficulty with this inter-textual methodology—the shaping of a text's meanings by other texts—is that the actual nature of an *Astrolabium Planum* has not been questioned. The full title of the *Astrolabium Planum* by Johannes Engel is as follows:

> Astrolabium planum in tabulis Ascendens continens qualibet hora atque minuto. Equationes domorum celi. Moram nati in utero matris cum quodam tractatu nativitatum utili ac ornato. Necnon horas inequales pro quolibet climate mundi.

> Plane astrolabe in Tables (or a list) containing the Ascendant in Each Hour and Minute; the Calculated Positions for the Houses of Heaven; the Length of Time of the Native/Unborn Child in the Mother's Womb along with a Certain Useful and Splendid Treatise on Nativities; and also the unequal hours for Each Clime of the World (trans. Hand).

So what is an 'Astrolabium Planum' and how might it be related to the Salone? An Astrolabium Planum is a flat astrolabe, a set of tables created by using an astrolabe (Greek: *astrolabes*, 'star-taker'). The astrolabe itself, also known as a planispheric astrolabe since it projects the celestial sphere onto the plane of the equator, contains layers of rotating instru-mentation. It was considered to be the precision tool of the age, the new high-tech computer, a mathematical *tour de force* that 'placed an image of the heavens in human hands' (Evans 1998: 157). As a two-dimen-sional version of a celestial globe, the astrolabe was a working model of the heavens, enabling medieval astronomers to calculate the positions of the sun and prominent stars with respect to both the horizon and the meridian, indicating how the sky looked at a specific place at a given time. The front of a European astrolabe is made up of a mater divided into 24 hours, latitude plates (its terrestrial features), a rete that contains the zodiac belt and the fixed stars (its heavenly features), and a ruler. The rete and the ruler move so that risings and settings of planets and stars can be easily ascertained. By using the sighting device on the back of the instrument, the altitude of the sun or a given star can be determined. One then either sets the mark for the sun on the ecliptic, or the selected star-pointer on the rete over the appropriate altitude mark on the plate (King 2011: I, 146). Its most important use was for time-finding and thus time-telling, for day and also night, and it was an essential tool for constructing horoscopes. The astrolabe, a time-finder, was used to construct horoscopes, a time-marker (Ackerman 2005: 73). The user can see at a glance the instantaneous configuration of the ecliptic relative to the local horizon and meridian by which astrological houses are defined.

An *Astrolabium Planum* then laid out this information in tabular format for ease of access. It is fair to assume that Pietro d'Abano, as a professor at the University of Padua, would have been familiar with and would have used astrolabes to construct horoscopes and thus created a set of tables—the *Astrolabium Planum*—for his own use. The astrolabe is the instrument; the *Astrolabium Planum* is the set of tables created from the instrument.

Johannes Engel's *Astrolabium Planum* consists of four parts. Part 1— 'the Calculated Positions for the Houses of Heaven'—is a table of houses. A table of houses allows an astrologer to mathematically construct part of a horoscope. Part 2—'the Ascendant in Each Hour and Minute'— contains images. In this part of the book Engel connected each ascending degree with an image that denoted the nature and quality of a person. Once a horoscope was cast, this was one way of considering a person's profession. For example, Figure 5 is the image drawn for seven degrees of Scorpio as it rises in the east. The image that was associated with this degree was described as, 'A man sits with purse in his right hand and a golden bowl in his left hand. This man will be a rich merchant' and was placed in the centre of the square chart. Part 3— *Moram nati in utero matris*, 'the Length of Time of the Native/Unborn Child in the Mother's Womb along with a Certain Useful and Splendid Treatise on Nativities'—is devoted to finding the best time for conceiving a child so that a child of the required sex was born at the proper time. '*Moram*' in the title of the document is the accusative of the word '*mora*' which means a span of time or delay and is the word regularly used for length of the gestational period found routinely in connection with the Trutine of Hermes or *Trutina Hermetis*, attributed to Hermes Trismegistus, and which forms the 51st aphorism of Ptolemy's *Centiloquium* (Ptolemy 1969 [1917]: 229-30). Part 4—'and also the unequal hours for Each Clime of the World'—includes a table defining the length of an hour depending on the season and latitude. In the medieval world not all hours were equal.

Since part 2 of Engel's *Astrolabium Planum* contained images connected with each individual degree of the zodiac, there was a natural disposition for scholars to try to correlate these images with the images in the Salone as follows: the methodology of these scholars was to look at the images surrounding each zodiac sign, for example Scorpio (Fig. 6) and then seek to correlate those images with any of the 30 images for that sign in part 2 of Engel's *Astrolabium Planum* (Fig. 5).

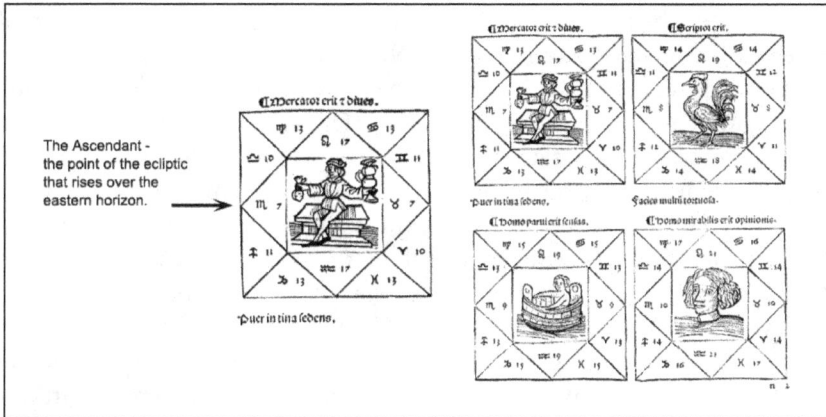

Figure 5. Four of thirty different images associated with the degrees of the zodiac that are rising whilst the Sun is in the sign of Scorpio. From *Astrolabium Planum* by Johannes Engel. BSB-Ink E-63 - GW 1900. Augsburg 1488 'Vigesimoseptimo kalendas Nouembris' 4 Inc. ca. 555. Image: Bayerische Staatsbibliothek.

Figure 6. North wall, Salone, Palazzo della Ragione. The sign of Scorpio is outlined in black. Photo: D. Gunzburg.

There are multiple difficulties with this approach. If the images on the walls of the Salone were to be a direct correlation with each of the images of the *Astrolabium Planum*, then there would be 360 images in the top three registers of the Salone. However, there are only 319 images. Additionally, the images in part 2 of the *Astrolabium Planum* relate to the calculation of a single horoscope—a particular moment, a date, and a time of day—and thus scholars were in effect suggesting that the Salone images were representative of precise moments in time. A number of extant horoscopic ceilings survive from when such was the intention by artists and commissioners: the Old Sacristy of San Lorenzo, whose fresco represents a horoscope dated to 6 July 1439 at about 12 noon (Beck 1989); the decoration of the vault of the Camera dello Zodiaco of Federico Il Gonzaga (Lippincott and Signorini 1991); Giovanni Antonio Vanosino da Varese's ceiling (Hess 1967); and the horoscope tile in the Sala Bologna, Vatican Palace, 1575 (Urban 2013). Scholars have recreated these ceilings astronomically and astrologically and understand that they reflect the skies at particular times and dates. Other ceilings, such as that in the Villa Farnese at Caprarola (Partridge 1995) and that in the Sala Bologna, Vatican Palace, depict a sky map frescoed within a large central oval projecting the complete celestial sphere. This does not, however, seem to be how the images of the Salone are being deployed. Indeed, this methodology has not revealed significant correlations and many of the images of the Salone still remain undeciphered. Furthermore, the actual document on which the Salone frescoes are meant to be based *does* exist but appears to have been unknown to earlier scholars, thus they used Engel, since he cited d'Abano's 'lost' work. Pietro d'Abano's *Astrolabium Planum* is held in the *Bayerische Staatsbibliothek* in Munich (CLM22048) and is catalogued as:

> De signis celestibus eorumque signilcatione et potestate, cum multis tabulis astronomicis.

> On the heavenly signs or images which have significance and potential, with many astronomical tables (trans. Gunzburg).

It also appears to contain four parts, including tables, but it does not contain the images found in the later copies (such as in Engel's version some 150 years later), only written descriptions of them. Federici Vescovini (1987: 36) translated these written descriptions in the 1980s but she appears to have only focused on the third of the four sections of the complete document.

The opening text of the first section is headed *'Canon Tabule de moris infantum'* ('Rule of the table of the period of infants'). Here once again is a section of the document connected with the length of the gestational period connected with the Trutine of Hermes. The manuscript also contains completed and blank charts, indicating that perhaps this is the workbook of a working, consulting astrologer. What is more, one can argue from the palaeography that this text is a copy made to be read and worked with only by the person who wrote or copied it. Despite the weak correlations, and ignoring the exact date issues (described earlier) and that the images did not exist in Pietro d'Abano's *Astrolabium Planum*, with no other solution to understanding Giotto's images, scholars have persisted with employing Engel's *Astrolabium Planum* as the key to the images of the Salone. This flawed assessment has become a standard discourse, reproduced as recently as 2008 (Rigobello and Autizi) and to a certain extent in 2011 (Mariani Canova 2011: 125-29).

Putting this historical argument to one side, any questions asked about the Salone must include questions concerning the whole of d'Abano's text, how d'Abano would have used it, and how it might have contributed to the fresco images of the Salone. Furthermore, by understanding the astrolabe, additional questions can be asked of the images of the Salone. Given the nature and power of the astrolabe as a calendrical, time-keeping device with an ability to recreate a skymap for any date, it seems a more valid approach to consider that the images of the fresco scheme may have been informed by the astrolabe, by reproducing the sky on the walls for any given month, rather than looking at the astrological part of d'Abano's text, which is devoted to an individual's unique horoscope. For the Palazzo della Ragione was a public place, not a private chapel commissioned for one individual.

A Different Perspective

Having reviewed this past work on the scheme, I decided to take a fresh approach starting from Giovanni da Nono's statement that the Salone images contained 'the twelve heavenly signs and seven planets with their respective qualities' (da Nono 1934–39). (These relate to the twelve horoscope signs still used in astrology today.) The twelve zodiac signs are clearly identifiable in the middle register of the walls (Fig. 6). Beginning along the south wall in calendar order, it can be seen that the scheme moves in a clockwise or sunwise direction around the Salone.

Using the sky as a primary document, with the help of astronomical software,[3] I recreated the night sky for Padua in 1309 for each of the

---

3. Starlight is a virtuoso astronomical software program created by Bernadette Brady with mathematician Sarah Ashton. It contains a planetarium especially designed for astrologers so they can learn about, find, and name the stars in the sky

months. The actual position of the sun amongst the stars can be determined by observing (i) the stars rising or setting before the sun rises,
(ii) the stars rising or setting after the sun sets, or (iii) the stars culminating at midnight when the sun is on the nadir (Ptolemy 1998: 407-
13). Accordingly, I constructed the night sky for these three different
views for each of the twelve months at the moment when the sun moves
into each zodiac sign, and then looked at the sky patterns. This provided
a set of constellation images that could then be compared with the
images along the top register of the Salone situated near each appropriate
zodiac sign in the middle register. The iconography of the constellations
is well established from Aratus (c. 315–240 BCE) in his *Phaenomena*
onwards and described in detail by Ptolemy (c. 90–168) in his *Almagest*,
articulating the exact positions of the parts that form the images of the
constellations.

Sky Maps on the Salone Walls: The Zodiac Sign of Aries

My own examination of the Salone walls agrees with previous scholars
that the section of the scheme describing the month of March along
the South Wall for when the sun enters the zodiac sign of Aries is
recognisable by the image of the Ram of Aries (Fig. 7). Barzon (1924),
Fantelli and Pellegrini (2000), and Rigobello and Autizi (2008) have
correlated the images along the top register above the saint, using
Barzon's numbering system as follows: a heron (1A); a woman of the
underworld or a woman of misdeed or wrongdoing (2A), since she is a
naked and lying on her back with her legs apart; a warrior (3A); the
constellation Hercules (4A); and a woman reading or imprudent love
(5A) (Table 1).

through images, myths, and constellations. Based on the Yale Bright Star Catalogue,
it includes all of Ptolemy's 1100 stars, as well as substantial additions from Richard
Hinckley Allen's masterwork on star names, every named star (over 350), as well as
every star visible to the naked eye—over 9000 stars in all. It also takes into account
precession, which is defined as follows: the ecliptic crosses the celestial equator at
two points. The sun reaches these two crossing points at the time of the equinoxes.
Precession, also known as the 'Precession of the Equinoxes', is the movement of
these crossing points along the equator at the rate of 50.25 seconds of longitudinal
arc per year. Thus the first point of the tropical zodiac, Aries, which is defined by the
equinox, seems to move in a retrograde fashion against the backdrop of the fixed star
constellations.

Figure 7. The section of the scheme depicting the month of March along the south wall for when the sun enters the zodiac sign of Aries (outlined in black). Photo: D. Gunzburg.

Table 1. Comparison of historical argument for the images with the revised meanings for the sky map for the sun moving into the tropical zodiac sign of Aries, Padua, c. 1309.

Barzon number	Historical argument	Revised meanings
1A	A heron	The constellation Cygnus the Swan
2A	A woman of wrongdoing	The constellation Andromeda the Maiden
3A	A warrior	The constellation Perseus the Warrior
4A	The constellation Hercules	The constellation Hercules the Hero
5A	A woman reading/ imprudent love	The constellation Cassiopeia the Queen

Using the software to reconstruct the sky for Padua 1309 when the sun ingressed into the zodiac sign of Aries, I looked to see what were the constellations in the night sky after the sun had set, at midnight, and predawn. The constellations visible in the predawn sky, which would have been easily calculated by Pietro d'Abano using an astrolabe and easily seen on a clear night in Padua (Fig. 8), revealed the following: the constellation Perseus the Warrior, Andromeda's suitor, young, masculine, and full of male energy (correlating with the image in the top register of the Salone at 3A), is clearly visible along the northeast horizon.

The Imagined Sky

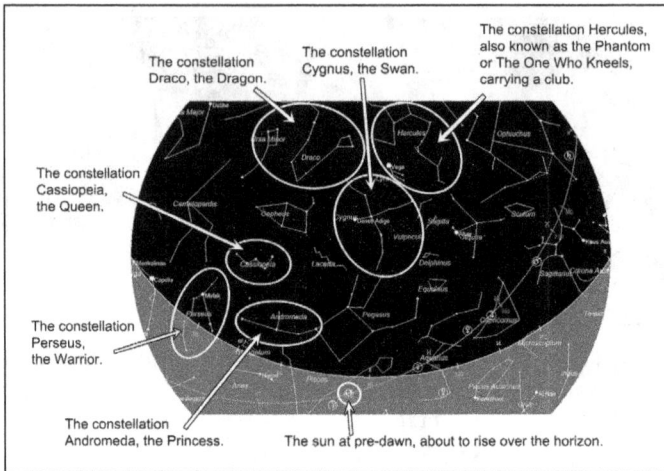

Figure 8. Sky map for pre-dawn Aries Ingress 13 March 1309 (Old Style calendar), LMT, Padua, Italy, showing the constellations that are visible in the night sky (black). Constellations below the horizon (grey) have not yet risen and hence are not visible.

Figure 9. Sky map for pre-dawn Aries Ingress 13 March 1309 (Old Style calendar), LMT, Padua, Italy, showing the artist's impression of the sky and their correct orientation of Perseus the Hero (3A), Cassiopeia the Queen (5A), Andromeda the Princess (2A), Hercules and Draco (4A), and Cygnus the Swan (1A).

Next to him in the sky is the constellation Andromeda, the Princess, the young, fertile virgin, the marriageable daughter waiting for suitors in a position of willing receptiveness (correlating with the image in the top register of the Salone at 2A). Above her is the distinctive 'W' of Cassiopeia the Queen, a noble woman (correlating with the image in the top register of the Salone at 5A). Next to her is Cygnus the Swan, situated at the point above the horizon where the sun would rise due east (correlating with the image in the top register of the Salone at 1A). On the zenith, the point directly above one's head, is Hercules, also known as the Phantom or The One who Kneels (correlating with the image in the top register of the Salone at 4A).

In Greek literature Hercules carries a club in his right hand and the double-headed Cerberus in his left hand. In the image at 4A (Fig. 7), Hercules holds a club in his raised right arm and stands with his right foot on the tail of a dragon or serpent, representing the constellation Draco the dragon or serpent. Damage has, however, obliterated any object in his left hand. Images from medieval bestiaries show how the serpent/dragon was perceived with wings and legs. The serpent was said to flee from a naked man but attack a clothed man, which may account for why Hercules is depicted in the image at 4A as nearly naked. This methodology of seeing this upper register informed by the astrolabe offers an extremely different interpretation of these images, as summarised in Table 1, suggesting that the images reveal what the sky actually looked like as a seasonal marker with this narrative of constellations (Fig. 9). Whilst the sequencing of images along the top register of the Salone is not exact, the collection of the five images forming this set are indeed the images of the five constellations for that month seen before the rising sun.

Sky Maps on the Salone Walls: The Zodiac Sign of Gemini

The section of the scheme describing the month of May along the South Wall, when the sun enters the zodiac sign of Gemini, is recognisable by the image of the Twins of Gemini (Fig. 10). In the same way as scholars described the images of the top register of Aries, so they also described a man with a crossbow (30A), a man with a stick (31A), the constellation of the Little Horse (32A), and the constellation of The Plough (33A).

Figure 10. The section of the scheme depicting the month of June along the south wall for when the sun enters the zodiac sign of Gemini. The image of The Twins is clearly identifiable along the middle register on the right hand side. Photo: D. Gunzburg.

Table 2. Comparison of historical argument for the images with the revised meanings for the sky map for the sun moving into the tropical zodiac sign of Gemini, Padua, c. 1309.

Barzon number	Historical argument	Revised meanings
30A	A man with a crossbow	The constellation Sagittarius the Archer
31A	A man with a stick	The constellation Perseus the Warrior
32A	The constellation of the Little Horse	The constellations of Pegasus, and Equuleus the Little Horse
33A	The constellation of The Plough	The constellations of the Great and Little Bears, Ursa Major and Ursa Minor

'A man with a crossbow'…is possibly the constellation of Sagittarius the Archer. The image depicts as a swarthy man with short dark hair and a beard holding a crossbow. He wears a brown sack hat on his head and is dressed in a square-necked, waisted tunic that falls just below his knees, with long, close-fitting sleeves and cream hose. Whilst this may differ from the recognised wild satyr constellation of half man, half beast, said to have been derived from the Sumerian Enkidu created to destroy Gilgamesh (Jobes 1964: 236-37), the constellational emphasis was always on the bow and the destruction that the archer could cause through using his sharp eyesight in conjunction with the bow, allowing him to kill a man from afar, rather than through hand-to-hand combat with a sword. Aratus described the constellation Sagittarius the Archer simply as 'Bow and Archer' (2010: 13). In considering the sky at sunset, midnight, and predawn for Padua at the Gemini Ingress (when the sun moves into the sign of Gemini), at predawn—exactly the same time of the day as the previous example—the constellation of Sagittarius (Fig. 11) and the narrative he depicts (Fig. 12) is setting in the west.

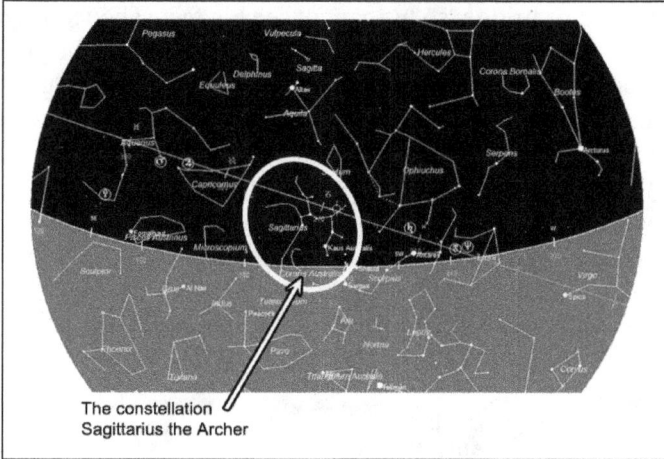

Figure 11. Sky map for pre-dawn Gemini Ingress 13 May 1309 (Old Style calendar), LMT, Padua, Italy, showing the constellation Sagittarius the Archer setting on the horizon in the west.

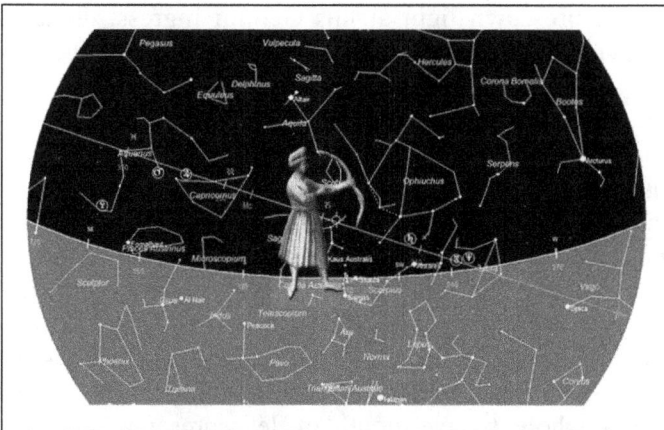

Figure 12. Sky map for pre-dawn Gemini Ingress 13 May 1309 (Old Style calendar), LMT, Padua, Italy, showing the artist's impression of the sky of the constellation Sagittarius the Archer setting on the horizon in the west.

In the east, before the sun rises, there are three images from the top register of the Salone (Fig. 10) that correlate with the three other constellations that are visible in the sky at this latitude. 'A man with a stick' is possibly the constellation Perseus the Warrior. The image at 31A depicts a swarthy man with a baton held in his right arm in readiness to take action. He is painted above the arch of the window as if keeping watch on a battlement or bridge, so we cannot see his feet. The iconography of the image is in keeping with the constellation of Perseus, the young warrior, the champion, holding a weapon in readiness. The image at 31A is contiguous with the image of the two horses in the Salone at 32A, and the two horses of Pegasus and Equuleus the Little Horse lie near Perseus in the sky. Completing this run of sky images is the image of a wagon covered with a red cloth with four large cartwheels. To the left can be seen the back two wheels of a second wagon. This image is what scholars call 'Plaustrum', The Plough, also known as The Wain or Wagon, and they are the Great and Little Bears, Ursa Major and Ursa Minor. These were called Wagons or Wains by Aratus (2010: 1; Allen 1963: 420, 426):

> Two Bears surround this pole
> (Which are at times called Wagons since they roll
> Like wagon-wheels).

As northern constellations situated around the North Pole, the Bears never set. In the sky map (Fig. 13) all four constellations are clearly visible in the pre-dawn light at this Gemini Ingress, depicted in the Salone as a vivid sky alive with imagery (Fig. 14). Again the sequencing is not exact but the collection of the four images forming this set are indeed the images of the four constellations for that month seen before the morning light—one setting in the west and three rising in the east, as summarised in Table 2.

One might ask why the constellation Sagittarius was chosen and not, for example, Pisces, as another major constellation on the sun's ecliptic. The answer may be that Pisces is an extremely faint and hard to see constellation, whereas Sagittarius is bright and striking. The other issue to consider is that not all astrolabes have all the constellations, and we do not have the instrument used by d'Abano. Although these are just two months of a whole twelve-month cycle represented in the Salone, nevertheless, it appears that the top register of this three-tiered scheme is reflective of a twelve-month cycle of constellational images.[4]

---

4. My continuing research is also examining the images and their connections along all three registers.

The cosmological implications of this research are far-reaching. The scheme was painted at a time when Scholastic thought—the joining of faith to reason—was flourishing in the Latin West (Pieper 2001) and, like other visual schemes of the time that included astrological imagery, such as the Fontana Maggiore, a fountain located in the centre of Perugia in Umbria in central Italy, built in 1278 and sculpted by Nicola and Giovanni Pisano (Gunzburg 2013), indicated that astrology was embraced and understood as the physics of the day, the way the world worked. Thomas Aquinas (c. 1225–1274) followed Albertus Magnus (1193–1280) when he crystallised the orthodox view of astrology and Christianity (Aquinas, *SCG* 3.85, 89, 91, 92). Astrology, a belief in an ensouled sky, provided information and a rationale for medicine and meteorology. The spirit/soul, however, as Aquinas qualified, was 'controlled immediately by God' (Aquinas, *SCG* 3.91.2).

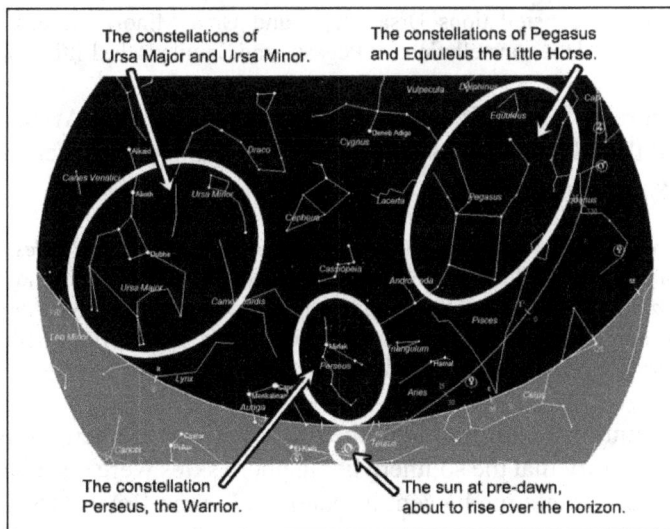

Figure 13. Sky map for pre-dawn Gemini Ingress 13 May 1309 (Old Style calendar), LMT, Padua, Italy, showing the showing the constellations that are visible in the night sky (black). Constellations below the horizon (grey) have not yet risen and hence are not visible.

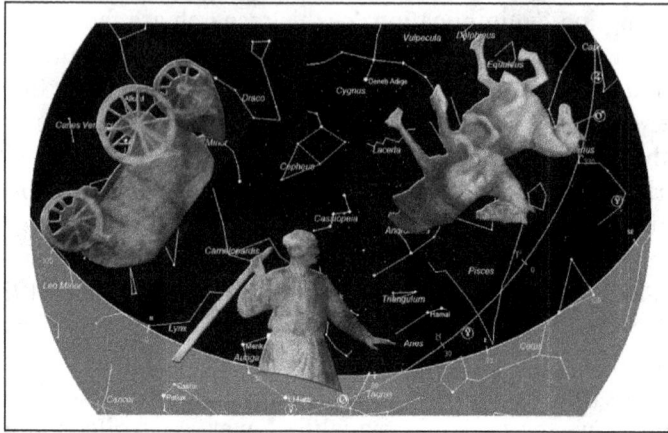

Figure 14. Sky map for pre-dawn Gemini Ingress 13 May 1309 (Old Style calendar), LMT, Padua, Italy, showing the artist's impression of the sky of the constellations Ursa Major and Ursa Minor, Perseus the Warrior, and the constellations of Pegasus and Equuleus the Little Horse.

Furthermore, in terms of constellation iconography, since Aratus the sky images of the 48 named constellations have remained consistent. Richard Hinckley Allen (1963: 12) noted:

> From Ptolemy's time, with the exception of the *Alfonsine Tables*, no advance was made in astronomical science for 1300 years, and the *Syntaxis* continued to be the standard of the world's astronomy, a sort of astronomical Bible from which nothing was taken, and to which nothing material in principal was added.

It was not until the exploration of the New World at the beginning of the sixteenth century that the southern hemisphere skies were discovered and then formally catalogued a century later by Johann Bayer (1572–1625) (Allen 1963: 13-14). The new images were added, bringing the total number of constellations to 88, but the original 48 were left unaltered. Consequently, the constellation of Cassiopeia today (as argued by Brady in this volume) was also the constellation of Cassiopeia that rose over Padua in the fourteenth century. This change in the sky occurred at the same time as Platonic cosmology and Aristotelian physics fell from grace under the influence of Copernicus, Kepler, and Galileo (Kuhn 1990 [1957]: 1-2), giving the scholars of the seventeenth century a different worldview from the artists of the thirteenth century.

Conclusion

For at least three centuries, the upper register of the three-tiered fresco scheme of the first moor Salone, with its depiction of heavenly constellations informed by the extensive astrological knowledge of Pietro d'Abano, and the artistic innovation of Giotto, visually reminded the judges who worked in this building of the cosmology in which they lived. By the sixteenth century, however, the scheme's meaning had been lost to the observer who stood in a different cosmology from the first painters and advisors. Scholars from Scardeone (1560) to Mariani Canova (1998, 2011) all acknowledged that there were constellation images contained within this top register, yet they looked for meaning from the *Astrolabium Planum* of Johannes Engel of 1488, rather than turning their eyes to the actual sky. My work has been to reconstruct the skies over Padua in the medieval period using astronomical and astro-logical software. This approach reveals a night sky that was populated with a constellational iconography which, I argue, was part of an ensouled cosmology reflective of the constellations that dictated the seasons and the cycle of the year as seen over Padua c. 1309.

Acknowledgments

For their help in the preparation of this essay I would like to thank Beth Williamson, Ronald Hutton, Bernadette Brady, and Bron Taylor. I am indebted to Dorian Greenbaum and Amy Kilby for their translations from German into English of Massing's (1987) and Dellwing's (1969) papers respectively. My thanks to Rob Hand for applying his astrological eye to the Latin in CLM22048 and offering his valuable academic insights. Grateful thanks also to Davide Banzato, Direttore Musei e Biblioteche del Comune di Padova, for permission to photograph the Salone images.

References

Ackermann, Silke. 2005. 'Astrological Scales on the National Maritime Museum Astrolabes', in *Astrolabes at Greenwich*, ed. Koenraad van Clempoel (Oxford: Oxford Univerity Press): 73-89.

Alighieri, Dante. 1995. *The Divine Comedy*, trans. Allen Mandelbaum, Everyman's Library, 183 (New York: Alfred A. Knopf). Online: http://dante.ilt.columbia.edu/comedy/.

Allen, Richard Hinckley. 1963. *Star Names: Their Lore and Meaning* (New York: Dover Publications).

Aquinas, Thomas. 1975. *Summa Contra Gentiles, Book Three: Providence Part II*, trans. Vernon J. Bourke (London: University of Notre Dame Press).

Aratus. *Phaenomena*. 2010. Trans. Aaron Poochigian (Baltimore: Johns Hopkins University Press).

Barzon, Antonio. 1924. *Gli affreschi del Salone in Padova* (Padua: Libreria Gregoriana).

Beck, James. 1989. 'Leon Battista Alberti and the "Night Sky" at San Lorenzo', *Artibus et Historiae* 10.19: 9-35.

Beer, Arthur. 1967. 'Astronomical Dating of Works of Art', *Vistas in Astronomy* 9: 177-223.

Blume, Dieter. 2000. *Regenten des Himmels. Astrologische Bilder in Mittelalter und Renaissance*, Studien aus dem Warburg-Haus (Berlin: Akademie Verlag).

Cunningham, Colin. 1995. 'For the Honour and Beauty of the City: The Design of Town Halls', in *Siena, Florence and Padua: Art, Society and Religion 1280-1400*. Vol. II, *Case Studies*, ed. Diana Norman (New Haven and London: Yale University Press in association with the Open University): 52-53.

da Nono, Giovanni. 1934–39. 'Visio Egidij Regis Patavie', *Bollettino del Museo Civico di Padova* NS X-XI [XXVII-XXVIII] and XIII-XVII: 1-20.

Dellwing, Herbert. 1969. 'Zur Wölbung des Paduaner "Salone"', *Mitteilungen des Kunsthistorischen Institutes in Florenz* 14.2: 145-60.

Derbes, Anne, and Mark Sandona, eds. 2004. *The Cambridge Companion to Giotto* (Cambridge: Cambridge University Press).

Evans, James. 1998. *The History and Practice of Ancient Astronomy* (Oxford: Oxford University Press).

Fantelli, Pier Luigi, and Franca Pellegrini, eds. 2000. *Il Palazzo Della Ragione in Padova* (Verona: Cierre Edizioni).

Favaro, Antonio. 1880. *Le Matematiche nella Studio di Padova dal Principio del Secolo 14 Alla Fine del 16* (Padova: Tipografia, G.B. Randi).

Federici Vescovini, Graziella. 1987. 'Peter of Abano and Astrology', in *Astrology, Science and Society: Historical Essays*, ed. Patrick Curry (Suffolk: The Boydell Press): 19-39.

Firmicus Maternus, Julius. 1975. *Ancient Astrology Theory and Practice: Matheseos Libri VIII*, trans. Jean Rhys Bram, Noyes Classical Studies (Park Ridge, NJ: Noyes Press), Book 8.

Fox, Matthew. 2004. 'Stars in the *Fasti*: Ideler (1825) and Ovid's Astronomy Revisited', *American Journal of Philology* 125: 91-133.

Greenbaum, Dorian Gieseler. 2001. *Late Classical Astrology: Paulus Alexandrinus and Olympiodorus*, ed. Robert Hand (Reston: ARHAT).

Giglioni, Guido. 2008. 'Nature and Demons, Girolamo Cardano Interpreter of Pietro d'Abano', in *Continuities and Disruptions between the Middle Ages and the Renaissance*, ed. Jacqueline Hamesse, F.I.D.E.M, Textes et Etudes du Moyen Age (Turnhout: Brepols): 89-112.

Gunzburg, Darrelyn. 2013. 'The Perugia Fountain: An Encyclopaedia of Sky, Culture and Society', in *Sky and Symbol*, ed. Nicholas Campion and Liz Greene (Ceredigion: Sophia Centre Press, University of Wales Trinity Saint David): 103-18.

Hess, Jacob. 1967. 'On Some Celestial Maps and Globes of the Sixteenth Century', *Journal of the Warburg and Courtauld Institutes* 30: 406-409.

Jobes, Gertrude, and James Jobes. 1964. *Outer Space: Myths, Name Meanings, Calendars from the Emergence of History to the Present Day* (New York: Scarecrow Press).

King, David A. 2011. *Astrolabes from Medieval Europe* (Farnham: Ashgate Variorum).

Kuhn, Thomas S. 1990 [1957]. *The Copernican Revolution: Planetary Astronomy in the Development of Western Thought* (Cambridge, MA: Harvard University Press).

Lippincott, Kristen, and Rodolfo Signorini. 1991. 'The Camera Dello Zodiaco of Federico Il Gonzaga', *Journal of the Warburg and Courtauld Institutes* 54: 244-47.

Mariani Canova, Giordana. 1998. '*Duodecim Celestia Signa et Septem Planete Cum Suis Proprietatibus:* L'immagine Astrologica nella Cultura Figurativa e Nell'illustrazione Libraria a Padova Tra Trecento E Quattrocento', in *Il Palazzo della Ragione di Padova* (Treviso: Ministero per I Beni Culturali e Ambientali): 23-61.

———. 2011. 'Padua and the Stars: Medieval Painting and Illuminated Manuscripts', in *Padua and the Stars: Medieval Painting and Illuminated Manuscripts*, ed. Enrico Maria Corsini (San Francisco: Astronomical Society of the Pacific): 111–29.

Massing, J.M. 1987. 'Der Stern des Giotto', in *Die Kunst und das Studium der Natur vom 14. zum 16. Jahrhundert*, ed. W. Prinz and A. Beyer (Weinheim: Acta Humaniora VCH): 159-79.

Murray, Peter. 1953. 'Notes on Some Early Giotto Sources', *Journal of the Warburg and Courtauld Institutes* 16.1 and 2: 58-80.

Olson, R.J.M., and J.M. Pasachoff. 2002. 'Comets, Meteors and Eclipses: Art and Science in Early Renaissance Italy', *Meteorites & Planetary Science* 37: 1563-78.

Partridge, Loren. 1995.'The Room of Maps at Caprarola, 1573–75', *The Art Bulletin* 77.3: 413-44.

Pieper, Josef. 2001. *Scholasticism*, trans. Richard and Clara Winston (South Bend, IN: St Augustine's Press).

Ptolemy. *Tetrabiblos.* 1969 [1917], ed. J.M. Ashmand (Mokelumne Hill, CA: Health Research).

Ptolemy. *Ptolemy's Almagest.* 1998, translated by G. J. Toome (New Jersey: Princeton University Press, 1998).

Rigobello, M. Beatrice, and Francesco Autizi. 2008. *Palazzo della Ragione di Padova. Simbologie Degli Astri e Rappresentazioni del Governo* (Padova: Il Poligrafo).

Scardeone, Bernardino. 1560. *De Antiquitate Urbis Patavii Et Claris Ciuibus Patauinis Libri Tres, in Quindecim Classes Distincti. Eiusdem Appendix De Sepulchris Insignibus Exterorum Patavii Iacentium* (Basel: Nicolaum Episcopium iuniorem).

Siraisi, Nancy. 1970. 'The Expositio Problematum Aristotelis of Peter of Abano', *Isis* 61.3: 321-39.

Stubblebine, James H. 1969. *Giotto: The Arena Chapel Frescoes* (London: Thames & Hudson).

Thomann, J. 1991. 'Pietro d'Abano on Giotto', *Journal of the Warburg and Courtauld Institutes* 54: 238-44.

Thorndike, Lynn. 1923–58. *A History of Magic and Experimental Sciences* (8 vols.; New York: Columbia University Press).

———. 1944. 'The Latin Translations of the Astrological Tracts of Abraham Avenezra', *Isis* 35.4: 293-302.

Urban, Emily. 2013. 'The Sala Bologna in the Vatican Palace: Art and Astronomy in Counter Reformation Rome' (PhD diss., Rutgers University).

Verdi, Adriano Verdi. 2008. 'Il Monumento attraverso documenti e disegni storici', in *Il Palazzo della Ragione di Padova, La storia, l'architettura, il restauro*, ed. Ettore Vio (Padova: Signum Padova Editrice): 75-98.

ASTROLOGY AS A SOCIAL FRAMEWORK: THE 'CHILDREN OF PLANETS', 1400–1600

Geoffrey Shamos

RedLine Contemporary Art Center, 2350 Arapahoe Street, Denver, CO, 80205, USA
geoffrey.shamos@gmail.com

Abstract

During the Early Modern period, many believed that the seven planets— Mercury, Venus, Mars, Jupiter, Saturn, the Sun, and the Moon—affected the course of terrestrial events and determined the temperament, complexion, profession, and even the manner of death of individuals. Such concepts were depicted by artists in a series of images commonly referred to as the 'Children of the Planets'. By merging scientific knowledge and popular imagery, the convention helped to shape the contemporary understanding of the cosmos. Astrology is often described in terms of the correspondence between the macrocosm and the microcosm or the universe and the individual, but by linking diverse individuals according to mutual planetary affiliations, the 'Children of the Planets' also offered a system for categorizing corporate identity and defining social relations.

Keywords

'Children of the Planets', cultural astrology, Mercury, Antwerp, Early Modern and/or Renaissance, Engraving, Abu Ma'shar.

Introduction

Giovanni Michele Savonarola (1385–1468), a physician and humanist from Padua, observed that 'everything here below is subjected, in its actions and its properties, to the influx and government of stars, and above all of planets, which are the noblest among the celestial bodies' (*De balneis* 1485: BN 7357 102r, translated in Jacquart 1990: 150).

Savonarola, like many of his contemporaries, believed that the seven planets—Mercury, Venus, Mars, Jupiter, Saturn, the Sun, and the Moon—affected the course of terrestrial events and determined the temperament, complexion, profession, and even the manner of death of individuals. Such concepts were depicted by late medieval and Renaissance artists in a series of seven images commonly referred to in scholarly literature as the 'Children of the Planets' (Hauber 1916; Blume 2000: 158-90). This pictorial convention typically shows the personified planets ruling over groups of earthly figures arranged according to their susceptibility to particular planetary influences. Enjoyed by a variety of audiences and employed in diverse contexts, the series appeared in manuscripts, prints, paintings, and tapestries throughout central and Western Europe for nearly two centuries (1400–1600).

As a union of scientific knowledge and popular imagery, the 'Children of the Planets' helped shape a general understanding of the cosmos for a wide range of society in Renaissance Europe. Such imagery precluded elaborate astrological calculations by reducing celestial forces to the dominance of a single planet in the formation of an individual's disposition and constitution. In depicting the planets' influence over humankind, the convention offered a visual distillation of the complex correspondences between the macrocosm and microcosm. As several scholars have noted, the 'Children of the Planets' played an important role in the popularization of astrology. Few, however, have discussed the convention's equally significant role in linking astrological concepts to contemporary social conditions.

In addition to elucidating the origins of personal identity, the 'Children of the Planets' also served as a means of defining societal relations. The series grouped diverse figures according to mutual planetary affiliations, parsing individuals based on their common behaviours and characteristics. In establishing correlations between various classes, ranks, and professions, depictions of the planets' children offered a system for categorizing corporate identity. By reflecting and affirming contemporary social attitudes, the convention illustrates the broad cultural applications of astrological thought during the fifteenth and sixteenth centuries.

The Origins of the Convention

Rooted in medieval astrology, the 'Children of the Planets' situated humanity in relation to the cosmos. The 'Children of the Planets' was thought to represent the revival of a dormant classical tradition (Saxl 1918–19; 1938; Saxl and Panofsky 1933). More recently, however,

Blume (2000: 159) has identified the convention as a late medieval invention influenced primarily by the astrological works of Abu Ma'shar (787–886). In the twelfth century, Latin translations of the *Almagest* and *Tetrabiblos* written by Ptolemy (c. 90 CE–c. 168 CE) spurred a revival of classical astrology in the West. Abu Ma'shar's *Kitab*, written in 849–850 and translated into Latin by John of Seville in 1133 and by Herman of Carinthia in 1140 as the *Introductorium in Astronomiam*, likewise provided a wealth of information related to zodiacal and planetary influences in the natural world (Burnett, Yamamoto, and Yano 1994: 1-2). Such works promoted a belief in the sympathetic correspondence between the universe and humanity predicated on their metaphorical and physical association. As a microcosmic recapitulation of the macrocosmic universe, the ideal human body exhibited proportions akin to the regularity displayed in the harmonic movement of the heavenly bodies (Heninger Jr 1974; Barkan 1975).

This structural parallelism was augmented by the material cohesion of the entire cosmos based on the concept of the four elements: earth, water, air, and fire. These existed as pure forms in the celestial spheres and as raw materials in the concrete world, where a mixture of the elements was thought to comprise all physical reality, including humankind. Within the human body the elements took the form of the four humors: black bile (earth), phlegm (water), blood (air), and yellow bile (fire) (Klibansky, Panofsky, and Saxl 1964; Filipczak 1987). The accommodation of elements to humors established the physical compatibility of the universe and humanity and reinforced their analogical congruence. With macrocosm and microcosm linked through form and substance, the movements of the celestial bodies were thought to act upon human bodies and influence the course of terrestrial events.

Introduced around 1400, the 'Children of the Planets' reduced the complexity of astrological influences by proposing simple, genealogical relationships between particular planets and those under their sway (Blume 2004). Each of the planets was paired with particular signs of the zodiac representing the planetary 'houses'. Although most of the planets ruled two houses, one for daytime and one for night, the Sun (Sol) and Moon (Luna) ruled only one each (Veldman 1980: 164). A cursory examination of the zodiacal division of the monthly calendar allowed one to ascertain planetary identification based one's date of birth. More often, however, planetary filiation was simply determined—albeit somewhat retroactively—by considering which planet possessed qualities most closely associated with one's profession or personality. The convention possessed limited prognostic value, but unlike horoscopes or genitures, the 'Children of the Planets' did not require the interpretation of a skilled specialist. As 'astrology for the layman', the pictorial series provided easily legible information concerning an individual's physical constitution and behavioural inclinations (Blume 2004: 553).

The various traits ascribed to each of the planetary deities were consistent with the qualities described in mythological narratives about the Olympian gods of the same name. These attributes were then passed on to the planets' earthly progeny. Regarded as destructive, devouring, and tyrannical, Saturn was associated with the Melancholic temperament inspired by a predominance of black bile. His afflicted children were typically described as traitorous, greedy, lame, toiling, and condemned to die in sorrow. They included criminals, cripples, farmers, and the destitute. As king of the gods, Jupiter was considered regal, sturdy, and mature. His wards, including judges, courtiers, and scholars, were thought to be modest, virtuous, fortunate, just, wise, well mannered, and well clothed. Mars, the belligerent god of war, presided over soldiers, smiths, butchers, and others who were bellicose, angry, haughty, and proud. The children of the Sun, comprised of rulers and athletes, possessed qualities derived from Apollo. They were generally pious, sporting, and in possession of good beards, long foreheads, and fair bodies. The merry and sensual offspring of Venus, goddess of beauty, love, and pleasure, included courtiers, lovers, and musicians. As the god of eloquence and trade, Mercury presided over painters, sculptors, clock-makers, organ-makers, scribes, and goldsmiths. They were smart, probing, industrious, and generous. Finally, the Moon, the deity linked to the element of water and the phlegmatic temperament, reigned over the inconstant, lazy, jealous, mad, and greedy, as well as those associated with the sea, particularly fishermen and sailors.

Although specific versions vary in some particulars, the types associated with each of the planets remained remarkably consistent from the origins of the convention at the beginning of the fifteenth century through its eventual decline two centuries later. Importantly, the traits inspired by each of the planets did not infringe upon free will; rather than determining the course of one's life, the celestial bodies merely produced natural tendencies that required cultivation or suppression depending on their beneficent or harmful qualities.

Overview of Depictions of the 'Children of the Planets'

Images showing the 'Children of the Planets' first appeared at the turn of the fifteenth century in several seemingly independent contexts. The earliest surviving example of the pictorial convention occurs in an astrological manuscript—Bibliothèque Nationale Suppl. Turc. 242, fols. 32v. and 33r.—completed in Baghdad in August 1399 (Baer 1968). A double-page opening from the Arabic *Kitab al-Burhán*, now at the Bibliothèque Nationale in Paris, displays figures in a grid. In the column to the far right, the planets follow the order established by Ptolemy, which was based on the distance of the planets from the earth. In this instance, the most distant planet, Saturn, appears at the top, while the nearest, the Moon, occupies the bottom of the page. Although most of the planets are shown in personified form, the Sun and Moon appear as faces inscribed on solar and lunar discs. Arranged in rows to the left, the planetary progeny represent various crafts and professions associated with the governing deities. Saturn, for example—depicted as a dark figure in the upper right-hand corner of the grid—appears alongside a blacksmith, a stonemason, and a pitch-maker, all trades related to the god's traits in Islamic culture derived from classical sources like the *Picatrix* (Baer 1968: 528).

The tabular format reappeared in two sixteenth-century Ottoman manuscripts now in Paris and New York: Pierpont Morgan Library, MS 788, fols. 31v. and 32r. and Bodleian Library, MS Or. 133, fols. 25v. and 26r. These two works, both dated 1582, followed the earlier Arabic example in most details, including the selection of the planets' children. Despite such examples, however, pictures of the 'Children of the Planets' were not widespread in either Arabic or Ottoman culture, and there does not seem to have been much of a connection between this tradition and the one that gained popularity in Europe during roughly the same period.

The pictorial composition that would eventually dominate European versions of the 'Children of the Planets' initially appeared during the first decade of the fifteenth century in French manuscripts of Christine de Pizan's *Epistre Othéa*, an allegorical work in which Othéa, a fictional goddess, offers advice to the Trojan hero, Hector (Hindman 1986: 78-94; Desmond and Sheingorn 2006: 41-45). Born in Venice, Christine (1364–c. 1430) was raised in France at the royal court of Charles V, where her father served as a court physician and astrologer. In the years following 1400, she produced several autograph versions of the *Epistre Othéa* for royal patrons, including Jean, Duke of Berry and Isabeau of Bavaria. The miniatures illustrating portions of Christine's text portray the planetary deities on clouds with corresponding terrestrial figures below. As the god of eloquence, for example, Mercury is pictured above a group of gesticulating rhetoricians, while bellicose Mars presides over a battle scene (Figs. 1 and 2). The other planets appear in similar compositions with their own human cohorts.

Figure 1. Christine de Pizan, *Mercury and his Children, Epistre Othéa* (1407), London, BL Harley MS 4431, f. 102v (detail). Image: British Library.

Figure 2. Christine de Pizan, *Mars and his Children, Epistre Othéa* (1407), London, BL Harley MS 4431, f. 101v (detail). Image: British Library.

It is thought that Christine may have combined her knowledge of Arabic astrology with a compositional scheme borrowed from Christian imagery to create the standard portrayal of the 'Children of the Planets', with the planetary deities juxtaposed with their progeny in vertical registers separated by clouds (Saxl and Panofsky 1933: 246). However, this hypothesis of the origins of Christine's imagery has been contested in recent decades (Hindman 1986: 78-94, 90-91; Desmond and Sheingorn 2006: 41-45). Although this format reappeared consistently over the next two centuries, especially after the middle of the fifteenth century, Christine's French manuscripts likely had a limited role in the establishment and dissemination of the convention.

It is more likely that the intellectual framework and standard composition for the 'Children of the Planets' developed primarily in German poetry and graphic art during the late fourteenth and early fifteenth centuries (Blume 2000: 158-76; 2004). The Germanic engagement with the theme began with poems and songs describing the seven planets and their children in rhyming verses. In subsequent decades, this poetic popularization of astrological concepts expanded into the pictorial realm with the production of numerous manuscripts and block-books—books printed from woodblocks—depicting the 'Children of the Planets' (Mertens, Purpus, and Schneider 1991).

Primacy, according to an extensive analysis by Blume (2000: 160, 553-54, 559), belongs to a block-book published in Basel around 1430, Schweinfurt, Bibliothek Otto Schäfer, OS 1033. The Basel work paired explanatory texts with images of the planets and their children, who appear on facing pages. The circular frames surrounding the planets likely represent the planetary orbits, and the nudity of the deities, except for the stars that cover their genitalia, serves as an indication of their divine status, further distinguishing them from their children. In the text the planets speak directly to the viewer, specifying their zodiacal houses—shown flanking the planets—and describing the physical and behavioural traits commonly found in their progeny. This work, which was copied several times in subsequent years, helped to spread the convention through the use of reproducible media, making the imagery accessible to a wider audience. Blume (2004: 559) notes that copies made in 1437, 1444, and 1445 helped him to establish the early date of the Schweinfurt block-book.

The Basel block-book or a similar work certainly provided the impetus for the series included in a lavishly illustrated Milanese manuscript, Modena, Biblioteca Estense, Ms. lat. 209, which was likely produced between 1450 and 1460 and originally owned by Francesco Sforza

(1401–1466), who succeeded Filippo Visconti as Duke of Milan (Milano 1996). Known as the Este *De sphaera*, the work contains only sixteen folios, with most given over to depictions of the 'Children of the Planets' and their accompanying verses. The manuscript, which has been in the Estense Library in Modena since at least the end of the seventeenth century, presents each of the seven planets and their children in double-page openings with miniatures. Despite the likely absence of a signature, the images can almost certainly be attributed to Cristoforo de Predis (1440–1486), a Lombard illuminator (Milano 1966: 55). Personified planetary deities appear on the left, or verso, side, while their children pursue various activities in the space below and to the right. A short verse inscription in Italian accompanies each of the openings. With the exception of Mars, the planets appear nude within disks of multi-colored concentric circles, with depictions of the winds above and medallions containing signs of the zodiac below.

Figure 3. Cristoforo de Predis, *Mars and his Children*, Milan (c. 1450–60), Modena, Biblioteca Estense, MS lat. 209 (fol. 7v). Image: Biblioteca Estense Universitaria.

Unlike the crude images of the early German block-books, the illuminations in the Este *De sphaera* achieve a high level of refinement and detail in their depiction of the planets and their children. Mars, for example, rules over well-articulated landscapes filled with soldiers engaged in a variety of martial activities (Fig. 3). To the left, knights with lances ride toward an encampment that sits before a fortified city under siege, while on the right, nobles on horseback look on as armoured soldiers confront one another in bloody combat. Such imagery would have appealed to the courtly patron of the manuscript, especially since Francesco Sforza was known for his prowess in battle.

A series of drawings in the so-called 'Medieval Housebook', a Middle Rhenish manuscript, was likewise intended for an aristocratic patron (Kok 1985; Wolfegg 1998). Several scholars have suggested that the manuscript may have originally belonged to a member of the circle of Frederick III, who reigned as Holy Roman Emperor from 1452 until his death in 1493 (Kok 1985: 218; Blume 2000: 177-78). Such an attribution is supported by the accurate drawing of the imperial encampment used during the siege of Neuss in 1475, as well as by depictions of the imperial standard in various illustrations. Produced between 1475 and 1485 in what is now western Germany, the Housebook presents a unique assemblage of information, including directions for purifying wine, removing stains, making candles, soap, and dyes for textiles, a recipe for hazelnut torte, and one of the earliest depictions of a pedal-operated spinning wheel. The manuscript also contains sections on military tactics, metallurgy and minting, medical treatments for humans and horses, mnemonic techniques, recipes for various aphrodisiacs, lascivious drawings of a pleasure garden and a bathhouse, and of course, the 'Children of the Planets', which appears in the first gathering of the manuscript.

Rather than painted miniatures, the 'Medieval Housebook' includes monochrome drawings executed primarily by an unknown artist referred to in modern scholarship as the 'Housebook Master' or the 'Master of the Amsterdam Cabinet'. This shadowy figure, who played an important role in the development of engraved prints during the last quarter of the fifteenth century, portrayed the planetary deities as jousting knights astride richly caparisoned horses hovering above landscapes peopled by figures engaged in a variety of related pursuits. The manuscript's portrayal of the 'Children of Mercury', for example, depicts a wide range of vocations, including a blacksmith at his forge, a sculptor receiving a cup from a woman behind a well-laid table, a schoolmaster disciplining one of his wards, a clockmaker, an astronomer, an organ maker, and a painter at work on an altarpiece. Text on the facing page (Blazekovic 2003: 269-70) offers Mercury's description of his offspring:

> My children faithfully instill, with lust for beauty, greed for skill. No long journey for them too hard, strange new knowledge is their reward. Their faces are full and pale and round, their bodies white, their limbs unsound. Their clocks and organs are the best, excellent scribes, they take no rest. Dexterous goldsmiths, painters good, people praise them, and they should. They are a smart, hardworking lot, but ask for help, they give it not.

In listing the attributes of his progeny, Mercury praises their manual and mental dexterity, while noting their lack of generosity. While the sumptuous versions of the 'Children of the Planets' contained in the Este *De sphaera* and the German 'Housebook' certainly represent a high level of artistic achievement, neither attained a wide audience outside their immediate sphere of ownership.

Figure 4. Bacci Baldini, *Mercury and his Children*, engraving, Florence (1464). Image © Trustees of the British Museum.

This was not true, however, of Baccio Baldini's inmuential engravings produced in Florence in 1464 (Fig. 4). Baldini (1436–c. 1487) depicted the planetary deities riding in triumphal chariots with zodiacal signs of the planetary houses on their wheels. Pulled by symbolic animals, these chariots hover in the air above the planetary progeny, who engage in various activities and trades in naturalistic settings, several of which include recognisable Florentine landmarks, such as the Piazza della Signoria in the depiction of the 'Children of Mercury' and the Ponte della Carraia in the 'Children of the Moon' (Blume 2004: 562). The inclusion of familiar places and pursuits in Baldini's series would have appealed to the local, upper-class audience for whom they were likely produced.

Figure 5. George Pencz, *Mars and his Children*, woodcut, Nuremberg (1531). Image © Trustees of the British Museum.

Baldini's engravings stand at the beginning of a chain of influence, with the use of graphic media allowing for fertile exchanges between artists working in Italy, Germany, and the Lowlands. Friedrich Lippman (1895) was the first to trace the influence of this particular version of the 'Children of the Planets'. In addition to inspiring several close copies in

Italy, Baldini's works served as the models for Georg Pencz's (c. 1500–1550) German woodcuts. Published by Albrecht Glockendon (c. 1500–1545) in Nuremberg and dated 1 August 1531, Pencz's images present updated versions of the Italian prototypes (Fig. 5). As in Baldini's engravings, the German woodcuts portray the planets in chariots bearing zodiacal signs on their wheels and pulled by the same symbolic animals. To the Italian models, however, Pencz added the planetary glyphs as well as bands of cloud beneath the planetary chariots, further separating the planets from their children below.

Figure 6. Harmen Jansz Muller after Maerten van Heemskerck, *Luna and her Children*, engraving, Haarlem (1568). Image © Trustees of the British Museum.

These works, in turn, influenced Maerten van Heemskerck (1498–1574), who designed the first Netherlandish series of the 'Children of the Planets' in 1568 (Veldman 1980: 163-66). Engraved by Harmen Jansz Muller (c. 1538/9–1617) and published by Hieronymous Cock (1518–1570) in Antwerp, the series follows Pencz in showing the personified planets atop cloudbanks in chariots drawn by figures or symbolic animals. The signs of the zodiacal houses appear behind each of the deities along with elliptical striations indicating the planetary orbits. In the depiction of Luna, the planet nearest to the earth, the planetary goddess appears in the upper register holding a crescent and a horn as she rides in a chariot pulled by two maidens, a feature explained by the deity's dual guise as Luna and Diana; the latter serves as the protectress of girls until they reach the age of marriage (Fig. 6). The sign for Cancer appears nearby as an indication of Luna's zodiacal house. Below, fishermen cast their nets as others bathe in the water. The representation of aquatic activities accords with Luna's role as the planet associated with the element of water.

In comparison to his predecessors, Heemskerck amplified the classicism of his deities, portraying each of the planetary figures semi-nude and well-muscled, except for the figure of Sol, who wears the vestments of a king, and Mars, who dons classical armor. Unlike Baldini or Pencz, Heemskerck used horizontal rather than vertical sheets for his engravings, extending the spaces available for the depiction of the planets and their children. Although the planetary progeny engage in their typical activities, they appear in antiquated costumes and occupy classical settings, a departure from the contemporized and localized portrayals included in the Italian and German versions. At the bottom of each image, inscriptions in Latin by an unknown author provide descriptions of the children's character traits and typical occupations. The inscription beneath the 'Children of Luna', for example, indicates that 'those whose mistress is the Moon pass their lives as in the water, due to their innate wateriness, working either in ships or in fishing. Many are prone to paralysis' (Veldman 1980: 164).

Figure 7. Crispijn de Passe I after Marten de Vos, *Mars and his Children*, engraving, Antwerp (c. 1590). Image © Trustees of the British Museum.

Heemskerck's series of the 'Children of the Planets' inspired two versions of the theme by Marten de Vos (1532–1603), Antwerp's pre-eminent painter and designer of prints during the final decades of the sixteenth century. The first was engraved in 1585 by Johannes Sadeler I (1550–1600) (Hollstein 1996: 1380-87) and the second around 1590 by Crispijn de Passe (c. 1564–1637) (Hollstein 1996: 1373-79; Kaulbach and Schleier 1997: 83-88, cat. nrs. 17.1-17.8). The two series were published in Antwerp by Crispijn de Passe and Hieronymous Cock, respectively. In these two series, de Vos used distant, elevated views that greatly altered the scale of the earthly figures in relation to their surroundings. The images portrayed diminutive figures dominated by expansive landscape settings that stretched toward the horizon. Despite the small size of the figures, many of the conventional activities of the 'children' can still be observed, with groups of planetary progeny arrayed along the most proximate foreground spaces at the bottom edge of each image. In the depiction of Mars from the de Passe series, for example, the foreground shows a group of soldiers carousing with a pair of female camp followers on a hilltop as other soldiers kick in a door to the right (Fig. 7). In the background, a phalanx marches near a port, where smoke pours from a burning building. The rendering of these scenes from a greater height and distance increases the terrestrial area included in each image and amplifies the geographical aspects of the planets' dominions.

One of the final iterations of the series came in Haarlem in 1596, when Hendrick Goltzius (1577–1660) portrayed the planets as earthbound statues in public squares almost unnoticed by the contemporary figures that surround them (Kaulbach and Schleier 1997: 88-91, 18.1-18.7). Engraved by Jan Saenredam (1565–1607) and published in Haarlem, Goltzius reduced the otherworldly status of the planetary deities by literally bringing them down to earth. Ilja Veldman cites the series as a prime example of the progression 'from allegory to genre', in which symbolic representations of cosmological concepts were replaced by scenes of everyday life at the end of the sixteenth century (Veldman 2006). Although they no longer occupy the celestial sphere, the planets still seem to exert control over their children, who assemble around the bases of the statues as they participate in their typical activities. The zodiacal signs that appear in the sky above remind the viewer of the astrological significance of the scenes despite their otherwise terrestrial content, and the literal and metaphorical elevation of the statues them-selves implies a dominance consistent with the influential role of the planets. Pedestals beneath the statues raise the planets above their chil-dren, and the classical character of the sculptures confers an eminence and timelessness that distinguishes them from the localised settings and contemporary figures. In the depiction of the 'Children of Mercury', for example, the nude statue of the god stands in a city square with his caduceus in his outstretched left hand. The sculpted deity is surrounded by sixteenth-century figures engaged in painting, sculpting, and rhetorical oratory (Fig. 8). These figures take little notice of the statue; only the zodiacal signs in the sky indicate the cosmological implications of the scene. Produced at the end of the sixteenth century, Goltzius's series of the 'Children of the Planets' represents one of the last versions of the convention before it practically disappeared during the following century.

Figure 8. Jan Saenredam after Hendrick Goltzius, *Mercury and his Children*, engraving, Antwerp (c. 1596). Image © Trustees of the British Museum.

The 'Children of the Planets' as a Reflection of Society

Depictions of the 'Children of the Planets' flourished across Europe during the fifteenth and sixteenth centuries, appearing in a variety of media and appealing to a broad audience. This accessible convention classified diverse figures according to common traits, parsing the larger population based on shared inclinations, appearances, or preferred activities. In doing so, the 'Children of the Planets' employed astrological concepts to reflect and affirm prevailing social structures. Most versions of the series, for example, make distinctions according to class and rank. The fortunate children of Jupiter, Venus, and Sol typically belong to nobility; engaging in courtly activities like hunting and dancing, they serve as rulers and dispensers of justice. The representatives of Mercury and Luna—practitioners of various trades and professions—occupy a middle ground. The rapacious 'Children of Mars' were often portrayed in a negative light, while the lowest classes—cripples, criminals, and the destitute—appear under the banner of Saturn. The relative consistency of the convention from its inception in the early fifteenth century to its decline two centuries later demonstrates the persistence of the social classifications reflected in and strengthened by its imagery. The frequent depiction of these groupings in the series of the 'Children of the Planets' codified contemporary social relations and schematized current notions of corporate identity.

Despite the stability of the tradition, differences among audiences of the series could sometimes influence the portrayal of a particular group. The depiction of the 'Children of Mars' in the Este *De sphaera* (Fig. 3), for example, deviates from renderings elsewhere. Intended for an aristocratic patron proud of his exploits on the battlefield, the pictures in the manuscript offer a relatively positive portrayal of the conduct of war. The illuminations show organized troops besieging a city and combat- ants engaged in honourable combat under the gaze of their noble leaders. The opposite is true, however, in other versions of the series, where the violence of conflict is viewed through eyes of frightened peasants.

In his version of the 'Children of Mars' (Fig. 5), Georg Pencz presents a more negative portrayal of the god's bellicose offspring. His German woodcut of 1531 shows farmers defending themselves and their children from murderous soldiers, an image that likely evoked similar events that occurred during the so-called Peasants' Revolt of 1524–25, when mercenaries employed by the Holy Roman Emperor killed thousands of rebels engaged in a popular uprising. The similarly disparaging depiction of Mars' earthly progeny by Marten de Vos c. 1590 (Fig. 7), which depicts soldiers carousing and pillaging, emerged from the context of the ongoing conflict between Spain and the Low Countries that began during the final decades of the sixteenth century. The recurrence of similar motifs suggests that such imagery reflected and reaffirmed contemporary attitudes about soldiers and war.

In depictions of the 'Children of the Planets', professions could also be defined and categorized through comparison to related activities and through associations with the qualities of a particular planet. The planets played an important role, for example, in defining the value and position of artistic and artisanal activity during the fifteenth and sixteenth centuries. The status of painters and sculptors changed greatly in this period as artists attempted to distance themselves from manual labourers by asserting the liberal status of their professions. During the Renaissance, numerous writers and artists promoted the intellectual underpinnings of their vocations by establishing a link between artistic endeavor and the melancholic temperament governed by Saturn (Klibansky, Panofsky, and Saxl 1964: 241-76). Disseminated through depictions of the 'Children of the Planets' and other related imagery and literature, negative opinions of those aligned with the god Saturn were commonplace from the late Middle Ages into the early modern period and beyond.

The Florentine Neoplatonists, however, attempted to redeem Saturn and the melancholic temperament he induced. Marsilio Ficino (1433–1499), the influential humanist philosopher, and his sixteenth-century disciples argued that melancholy inspired brilliance, portraying the Saturnine artist as a solitary genius working alone in his studio, constantly moving between complete apathy and divine frenzy (Wittkower and Wittkower 1963: 98-113). According to Ficino, such figures were paralyzed by thought rather than laziness, and their isolation resulted not from misanthropy but from a willingness to forego the company of their fellow men or the fairer sex in pursuit of artistic or intellectual perfection. Also, by emphasizing artists' knowledge of geometry, such theories attempted to raise the status of artistic enterprise from manual and mechanical craft to the cerebral realm of the liberal arts. The Saturnine artist—an isolated, irascible, and inspired figure not unlike our modern stereotype—differs from the classification of painters and sculptors as children of Mercury in series of the 'Children of the Planets'. Although both characterizations derive from the same astrological theories of planetary influence, the two models promote different aspects of artistic activity.

In depictions of the 'Children of Mercury', painters and sculptors appear alongside the practitioners of other trades and professions linked through their Mercurial character. According to J. Sylvius in his *Almanach of Prognosticatie voor 1551* (fragment), published by Albert Pafraet in 1550, Mercury's authority extended to 'philosophers, doctors, astronomers, orators, rhetoricians, merchants, lawyers, writers, printers, and all the clever artists concerned with the free arts' (Honig 1998: 1). Despite the apparent variety of such professions, the diverse figures represented under the banner of Mercury share a mutual engagement in like-minded tasks. Described as industrious, probing, and smart, the children of Mercury comprised expert craftsmen, artisans, and others whose professions required a combination of *arte* and *ingegno,* or 'technical skill' and 'innate talent' (Geronimus and Waldman 2003: 118). By emphasizing the combination of manual prowess and intellectual virtue, depictions of the 'Children of Mercury' served as visual arguments for the improved status of painters and sculptors.

More than merely theoretical, the promotion of artistic professions also had financial ramifications, as the social recognition of artists was closely bound to their commercial success. Karel van Mander (1548–1606), a Dutch poet, painter, and biographer, linked artistic value with monetary value, arguing that artistic skill merits remuneration akin to other liberal professions (Melion 1991: 26-27). The commercial aspect of artistic and artisanal production was acknowledged in many versions of the 'Children of the Planets', in which artists are shown not only making works of art but also selling them in stalls, as in Baldini's Florentine engravings (Fig. 4). Perhaps the most obvious example of this is the Este *De sphaera,* where the various trades associated with Mercury are shown within small enclosures that double as workshops and salesrooms (Fig. 9). Such imagery demonstrates that commerce, like artistic skill, fitted within Mercury's purview, helping to define the industrious artist whose unique manual and intellectual expertise deserved financial recompense at the market.

·MERCVRIVS·

crcurio di ragion lucios ftella
Predice edoquonsa gran fontana
Subnli ingicgni er ciafebunorre bella
Et climoto rogni cofa usns :

Figure 9. Cristoforo de Predis, *Mercury and his Children*, Milan (c. 1450–60), Modena, Biblioteca Estense, MS lat. 209 (fols. 10v-11r). Image: Biblioteca Estense Universitari.

This combination of features, I would argue, not only aligned artists with Mercury, but also defined the ideal Netherlandish artist of the sixteenth century, particularly in Antwerp. Mercury's dual role as God of artistic skill and of trade was also central to civic identity in Antwerp during the city's Golden Age in the mid-sixteenth century. Between roughly 1525 and 1575, the city served as the centre of European mercantile exchange and functioned as a hub for the nascent global trade (van der Wee and Materné 1993). The preeminence of Antwerp's market attracted merchants from throughout Europe, and their presence, in turn, enticed numerous artists to settle in the city as well (Honig 1998). In his *Het Leven* (219r.), Van Mander described Antwerp in its heyday as the 'mother of artists', noting, 'The famed, wondrous city of Antwerp, which rose through trade, lured to herself from everywhere the most excellent in our art, who also moved there in great numbers because art is happy where wealth reigns' (Honig 1998: 13). During the city's commercial and artistic ascendancy in the middle decades of the sixteenth century, the painters' Guild of St Luke included around 300 masters, a number that represents a significant percentage of the city's population (Vermeylen 2003: 129). For more than half a century, Antwerp identified and promoted itself as the capital of commerce and of art, both areas over which Mercury presided.

Figure 10. Joost Amman, *Allegory of Trade with a View of Antwerp*, woodcut, 1585. Image © Trustees of the British Museum.

Mercury's endorsement of Antwerp served as a recurring trope in the city's self-representations during the sixteenth and seventeenth centuries. A morality play performed in Antwerp in 1561 as part of a competition between chambers of rhetoric from various towns and cities, Antwerp's *Lischbloeme* chamber included a dialogue between Mercury and the Maid of Antwerp, a personification of the city, in which the two figures acknowledge the great success resulting from their common aims and cooperation (Honig 1998: 234 n. 2). Similar portrayals existed in the visual realm. In 1585, the Augsburg artist Jost Amman (1539–1591) produced a large woodcut depicting an 'Allegory of Trade with a View of Antwerp', possibly as a commission for an Augsburg commercial enterprise operating in the city (Fig. 10) (Van der Stock 1993: 281, cat. no. 136). Measuring almost a meter in height and requiring six wood-blocks for printing, the immense print is packed with numerous figures and explanatory texts. At the top of the image, Mercury appears above the Antwerp skyline holding a gigantic scale that balances credit and debt. The fountain that dominates the centre of the image bears an inscription identifying it as an allegory of 'capital'. To the right of the fountain, figures exchange goods freely and amicably, while to the left, depictions of war and robbery show potential perils to profitable trade. The various vignettes at the bottom of the image portray typical commercial activities representing the qualities of the ideal merchant, including 'Obligation', 'Freedom', 'Good Fortune', 'Integrity', and 'Command of Languages' (Van der Stock 1993: 281). With Mercury presiding in his role as God of Trade, Antwerp dominated European and global exchange for much of the sixteenth century.

Figure 11. Crispijn de Passe I after Marten de Vos, *Mercury and his Children*, engraving, Antwerp (c. 1590). Image © Trustees of the British Museum.

Figure 12. Johannes I Sadeler after Marten de Vos, *Mercury and his Children*, engraving, Antwerp (1585). Image © Trustees of the British Museum.

Mercury's dual role as the patron of merchants and artists is highlighted in representations of the 'Children of the Planets' produced and printed in Antwerp. Both versions of the series designed by Marten de Vos depict Mercury in his chariot above harbour scenes filled with figures loading and unloading barrels and bushels from ships as others perform on stage, play music, and sell artisanal wares from stalls (Figs. 11, 12). The inclusion of the seascape in both works separates De Vos's portrayals of the 'Children of Mercury' in previous versions, including that by Marten van Heemskerck, his immediate predecessor in Haarlem, whose series of the 'Children of the Planets' served as the direct influence for De Vos's designs, in most instances. Seafaring occupations, typically included under the purview of Luna, were essential to international trade in Antwerp. Beneath Mercury's chariot, the portrayal of artists in their stalls and industrious merchants engaged in maritime trade would have appealed to the members of Antwerp's cultural elite who comprised the works' primary audience.

Figure 13. Johannes I Sadeler after Marten de Vos, *Title-Print*, engraving,
Antwerp (1585). Image © Trustees of the British Museum.

De Vos's 1585 series, which was engraved by Johannes Sadeler, makes
the connection between Mercury and Antwerp even more explicit. The
title-print for the series portrays a warship carrying a large plaque with
the title of the series, as well as an encomiastic inscription in praise of
Alexander Farnese (1545–1592), the Habsburg regent of the Netherlands
(Fig. 13). Farnese served as the leader of the Spanish army that forced
the capitulation of Antwerp on 17 August 1585, the same year the
engravings were published. Sitting on an eagle, the monumental figure of
Jupiter appears above the inscription with the arms of Philip II in one
hand and a cosmic diagram in the other. The pairing of Philip's blazon
with a representation of the cosmos serves as a flattering depiction of the
monarch's vast authority.

According to the description of the series included on the title-print,
the engravings portray planetary rule over various 'provinces, regions,
and cities'. The lists of towns and districts in the spaces below each of
the planetary images include numerous places within the Habsburg
Empire, implying an association between the territorial dominion of the
planets and that of the Spanish king. Antwerp, newly reacquired for the
crown by Farnese, heads the list of cities presided over by Mercury, who
appears in his chariot above (Fig. 12). The panoramic depiction of

Mercury's territory shows a winding river flanked by numerous settlements. In the immediate foreground, figures load and unload wares from docked ships, while merchants, many dressed in foreign costumes, conduct transactions. Despite the absence of any recognizable landmarks, it is tempting to view this riverside commercial centre as a depiction of Antwerp on the Scheldt. In addition to serving as the location of the series' publication and the site of Farnese's triumph, the city was also an important hub for international trade and a valuable part of the Spanish domain.

Despite the projection of prosperity depicted in such images, Antwerp's fortunes progressively deteriorated during the final decades of the sixteenth century as a result of religious and political conflicts in the Netherlands. A majority of the city's Protestant population, including numerous artists and merchants, departed after Antwerp's capitulation to Spanish forces in 1585 (Arnade 2008). The Dutch blockade of the River Scheldt, initiated the same year, prevented access to international trade and precluded a full recovery of the city's once thriving economy.

The decline of Antwerp's position as a vital commercial and artistic centre received a symbolic treatment in the 1635 triumphal entry of the new Spanish governor of the Southern Netherlands, Cardinal-Infante Ferdinand of Austria (c. 1609/10–1641) (Martin 1972: 180-87; McGrath 1974: 212). Designed by Peter Paul Rubens (1577–1660), the decorations for the entry included the so-called 'Stage of Mercury' as the penultimate display, with a painting of *Mercury Departing Antwerp* (Fig. 14) occupying a central space. Preserved in a contemporary etching by Theodoor van Thulden (1606–1669), the picture shows Mercury alighting from a pedestal with Antwerp's harbour in the background. To his right, a personification of the River Scheldt appears in bondage, while to his left, the Maid of Antwerp kneels in distress as she reaches out to the fleeing god. The inscription in Latin that accompanied the original painting appears at the bottom of the etching. It offers a plea from the Maid of Antwerp to the city's new ruler: 'Do not, I beseech you, O Prince, let Mercury take swift might and desert the city dedicated to him, and may fugitive commerce return once more to my Scheldt' (Martin 1972: 186). Although imminent, Mercury's departure is not a *fait accompli*; the picture served as an appeal to the new ruler to forestall such a fate by reinvigorating Antwerp's commercial and artistic prospects. That Mercury plays such a prominent role in the petition demonstrates the close association that existed between the city and its planetary ruler.

Figure 14. Theodoor van Thulden after Peter Paul Rubens, *Mercury Departing from Antwerp*, etching (1635). Image © Trustees of the British Museum.

For over two centuries, series of the 'Children of the Planets' offered a means of comprehending the invisible influence of the celestial realm. In reducing the complex correspondences between macrocosm and microcosm to simple, genealogical relationships conveyed through accessible imagery, the convention helped to popularize astrological concepts during the fifteenth and sixteenth centuries. The wide audience for the series, its broad geographical reach, and its frequent repetition in manuscripts, prints, and paintings, demonstrates its effectiveness at illustrating the place of individuals in the universe. In portraying planetary authority over the terrestrial realm, the series helped to define and schematize the place of individuals in relation to society.

Many scholars across time have viewed astrology as a primitive form of astronomy, arguing that modern rationality replaced the irrational perspectives of earlier eras. Others have suggested that astrology provided a means for psychological investigation, as celestial movements were thought to determine individual temperament. Few, however, have explored the possibility that astrological beliefs could serve as the basis for a nascent sociology. The 'Children of the Planets' provided a justification for a rigid and persistent cultural hierarchy, with privilege or its absence preordained by one's planetary heritage. The convention also offered a framework for corporate classification by helping to define certain social groups. Many portrayals of the 'Children of Mars' reinforced negative perceptions of soldiers and their atrocities amongst conflict-weary audiences. In contrast to the disparagement of martial qualities, artistic pursuits were elevated through their association with rhetoric and commerce in depictions of the 'Children of Mercury'. Such correspondences served as the basis for civic identity in Antwerp, where citizens took pride in the city's commercial and artistic preeminence. The 'Children of the Planets' expanded the potential applications of astrological concepts by operating as a mirror for society, demonstrating the role of such imagery in reflecting and endorsing contemporary attitudes toward certain classes and professions.

References

Arnade, Peter. 2008. *Beggars, Iconoclasts, and Civic Patriots: The Political Culture of the Dutch Revolution* (Ithaca, NY: Cornell University Press).

Baer, Eva. 1968. 'Representations of the "Planet-Children" in Turkish Manuscripts', *Bulletin of the School of Oriental and African Studies, University of London* 31.3: 526-33.

Barkan, Leonard. 1975. *Nature's Work of Art: The Human Body as Image of the World* (New Haven: Yale University Press).

Blazekovic, Zdravko. 2003. 'Variations on the Theme of the Planets' Children, or Medieval Musical Life according to the Housebook's Astrological Imagery', in *Art and Music in the Early Modern Period*, ed. Katherine A. McIver (Aldershot: Ashgate): 241-86.

Blume, Dieter. 2000. *Regenten des Himmels: Astrologische Bilder in Mittelalter und Renaissance* (Berlin: Akademie).

———. 2004. 'Children of the Planets: The Popularization of Astrology in the 15th Century', *Micrologus* 12: 549-63.

Burnett, Charles, Keiji Yamamoto, and Michio Yano, eds. 1994. *Abu Ma'shar—the Abbreviation of the Introduction to Astrology: Together with the Medieval Latin Translation of Adelard of Bath* (Leiden: E.J. Brill).

Desmond, Marilynn Robin, and Pamela Sheingorn. 2006. *Myth, Montage, and Visuality in Late Medieval Manuscript Culture: Christine de Pizan's Opistre Othéa* (Ann Arbor: University of Michigan Press).

Filipczak, Zirka Zaremba. 1987. *Picturing Art in Antwerp, 1550–1700* (Princeton: Princeton University Press).

Geronimus, Dennis V., and Louis A. Waldman. 2003. 'Children of Mercury: New Light on the Members of the Florentine Company of St. Luke (c. 1475–c. 1525)', *Mitteilungeb des Kunsthistorisches Institutes in Florenz* 47.1: 118-58.

Hauber, Anton. 1916. *Planetenkinderbilder und Sternbilder: zur Geschichte des menschlichen Glaubens und Irrens* (Strassburg: Heitz).

Heninger, S.K. Jr. 1974. *Touches of Sweet Harmony: Pythagorean Cosmology and Renaissance Poetics* (San Marino, CA: Huntington Library).

Hindman, Sandra L. 1986. *Christine de Pizan's 'Epistre d'Othea': Painting and Politics in the Court of Charles VI* (Toronto: Pontilcal Institute of the Mediæval Studies).

Hollstein. 1996. *Hollstein Dutch and Flemish Etchings, Engravings and Woodcuts ca. 1450–1700.* Vol. 44, *Marten de Vos*, comp. Christian Schuckman, ed. D. De Hoop Scheffer (Ouderkerk an den Ijssel: Sound & Vision).

Honig, Elizabeth A. 1998. *Painting and the Market in Early Modern Antwerp* (New Haven: Yale University Press).

Jacquart, Danielle. 1990. 'Theory, Everyday Practice, and Three Fifteenth-Century Physicians', *Osiris* 6 (2nd series): 140-60.

Kaulbach, Hans-Martin, and Reinhart Schleier, eds. 1997. *Der 'Welt Lauf': Allegorische Graphikserier des Manierismus* (Stuttgart: Gerd Hatje).

Klibansky, Raymond, Erwin Panofsky, and Fritz Saxl. 1964. *Saturn and Melancholy: Studies in the History of Natural Philosophy, Religion, and Art* (New York: Basic Books).

Kok, J.P. Filedt, ed. 1985. *Livelier Than Life: The Master of the Amsterdam Cabinet, or, the Housebook Master, 1470–1500*, 2 vols. (Princeton: Princeton University Press).

Lippmann, Friedrich. 1895. *Die Sieben Planeten* (Berlin: Internationale Chalkographische Gesellschaft).

Martin, John Rupert. 1972. *The Decorations for the Pompa introitus Ferdinandi* (London: Phaidon).

McGrath, Elizabeth. 1974. 'Rubens's Arch of the Mint', *Journal of the Warburg Institute* 37: 191-217.

Melion, Walter S. 1991. *Shaping the Netherlandish Canon: Karel van Mander's Schilder-Boeck* (Chicago: University of Chicago Press).

Mertens, S., E. Purpus, and C. Schneider, eds. 1991. *Blockbücher des Mittelalters: Bildfolgen als Lektüre* (Mainz am Rhein: Gutenberg Museum).

Milano, Ernesto. 1996. 'De Sphaera', in *Astrologia: Arte e Cultura in età Rinascimentale*, ed. Daniel Bini (Modena: Bulino): 45-76.

Savonarola, Michele. 1485. *De Balneis et Thermis Naturalibus omnibus Italiae gewidmet Borso d'Este* (Ferrara: Andreas Belfortis).

Saxl, Fritz. 1918–19. 'Probleme der Planetenkinderbilder', *Kunstchronik und Kunstmarkt* 54: 1013-21.

———. 1938. 'The Literary Sources of the "Finiguerra Planets"', *Journal of the Warburg Institute* 2.1: 72-74.

Saxl, Fritz, and Erwin Panofsky. 1933. 'Classical Mythology in Mediaeval Art', *Metropolitan Museum Studies* 4.2: 228-80.

Van der Stock, Jan, ed. 1993. *Antwerp: Story of a Metropolis* (Antwerp: Martial & Snoeck).

Van der Wee, Herman, and Jan Materné. 1993. 'Antwerp as a World Market in the Sixteenth and Seventeenth Centuries', in Van der Stock 1993: 19-31.

Veldman, Ilja M. 1980. 'Seasons, Planets and Temperaments in the Work of Martin van Heemskerck: Cosmo-Astrological Allegory in Sixteenth-Century Netherlandish Prints', *Simiolus* 11: 149-76.

———. 2006. 'From Allegory to Genre', in *Images for the Eye and Soul: Function and Meaning in Netherlandish Prints (1450–1650)* (Leiden: Primavera): 193-222.

Vermeylen, Filip. 2003. *Painting for the Market: Commercialization of Art in Antwerp's Golden Age*, Studies in European Urban History [1100–1800], 2 (Turnhout: Brepols).

Wittkower, Rudolf, and Margot Wittkower. 1963. *Born Under Saturn: The Character and Conduct of Artists: A Documented History from Antiquity to the French Revolution* (London: Weidenfeld & Nicolson).

Wolfegg, Christoph, Graf zu Waldburg. 1998. *Venus and Mars: The World of the Medieval Housebook* (Munich: Prestel).

MAPPING THE HEAVENS: THE CEILING OF THE SALA BOLOGNA IN THE VATICAN PALACE

Emily Urban

1520 S Broad St #3, Philadelphia, PA, 19146, USA
emily.a.urban@gmail.com

Abstract

Commissioned in 1575 by Pope Gregory XIII, the Sala Bologna, a small dining room located in the Vatican Palace, represents a monumental expression of Renaissance artistic and scientific achievement. Frescoed on the ceiling is an extraordinary vision of the heavens that is complemented by three maps of Bologna painted on the walls. In contrast to similarly themed decoration, this ceiling does not depict the horoscope of its patron, but instead presents a cartographically accurate rendition of the entire universe. Through an interpretation of the painted iconography, as well as an examination of the tradition of celestial frescoes, I demonstrate that this ceiling is remarkable not only for its cartographic accuracy, but for its representation of Renaissance astronomy. Moreover, by looking at contemporary artistic theory and scientific advancement, I argue that this fresco gives visual expression to the goals and aspirations of the Boncompagni pope who sought to use empirical inquiry as an ideological tool of the Counter Reformation.

Keywords

Pope Gregory XIII, Vatican Palace, Counter Reformation, art history, celestial cartography, ceiling frescoes, Giovanni Antonio Vanosino da Varese, Renaissance.

Introduction

Decorated for the Jubilee of 1575, the Sala Bologna, a small room located on the Terza Loggia of the Cortile di San Damaso in the Vatican Palace, is among the most important ensembles commissioned by

Pope Gregory XIII (7 January 1502–10 April 1585, head of the Catholic Church 13 May 1572 until his death in 1585), whose name is synonymous with the reformed calendar. The room is a monumental expression of Italian Renaissance artistic and scientific achievement, with a vision of the heavens frescoed on the ceiling and detailed maps of the pope's hometown of Bologna painted on the walls (Fig. 1).[1] Its imagery concretizes the goals and aspirations of Gregory's entire pontificate, that is, the use of empirical investigation in service of the Counter Reformation.

Figure 1. Sala Bologna, Vatican Palace. View of the south wall with the frescoed *City of Bologna*, and the west wall with the frescoed *Country-side of Bologna*. Photo: Archivio Fotografico, Musei Vaticani.

Strategically positioned to capitalize on the views of the Roman countryside available to the north and the cityscape to the east, the room was originally punctuated with five windows. During the construction of the adjacent Palazzo Sisto V in 1585, however, the three windows on the eastern wall were filled in. Several clues provide evidence to the *sala*'s original use as a dining room, including a description by the pope's principal biographer Marc'Antonio Ciappi (1577–1601) who wrote of Gregory XIII's fondness for dining in the Terza Loggia in the summer, enjoying the fresh air and the views its rooms provided (Ciappi 1591: 100-101). Additionally, an *avviso* dated to 30 July 1580 (and first

1. The most recent literature to date on the Sala Bologna is Urban 2013 and Ceccarelli and Aksamija 2011.

published by Courtright 1990: 87, 266 n. 87), noted the pope's custom for dining in the 'loggia detta la Bologna' (Vatican Library, Urb. lat. 1048, f. 226). Moreover, the two small rooms to the west of the *sala*, as recorded in Martino Longhi il Vecchio's (1534–1591) design plans for the Terza Loggia, were likely used as a pantry and small kitchen in service of the salon (Sambin de Norcen 2011a: 26). Finally, the display of celestial iconography on dining room ceilings is a celebrated practice dating back to antiquity, and such an artistic heritage may suggest a relationship of function and decoration in Gregory XIII's room to those from the ancient Roman past.

Known to contemporaries simply as 'la Bologna', as noted in the 'Memorie sulle pitture et fabriche di Gregorio XIII' (Vatican Library, Bonc. D.5, ff. 240r-241v) and 'Descrizione del Palazzo Pontificio di San Pietro in Vaticano fatta nel pontificato di s.m. di Benedetto XIII' (Archivio di Stato di Roma, MS. 496, f. 811), as well as by Agostino Taja (1750: 497) and Giovanni Pietro Chattard (1766: 370), the room takes its name from the majestic representations of that city frescoed on its walls. To the south is a grand cityscape of Bologna, painted to mimic the irregular shape of the city's medieval walls and measuring 456×607 cm at its largest span (Ceccarelli 2011a: 104).[2] Two historical scenes border the map, with Gregory IX Promulgating the Decretals to the left and Boniface VIII Delivering the Sixth Book of the Decretals to the Doctors of Bologna on the right.

To the west is the fresco of the Bolognese countryside, measuring 466×850 cm (Ceccarelli 2011c: 124),[3] and flanked by the allegories *Pax* (Peace) and *Annona* (the Grain Harvest). Between the two windows on the north side is a small perspectival view of Bologna measuring about 175×225 cm (Ceccarelli 2011c) and now in ruinous condition. Completing the Bolognese iconography on the lower walls is an allegory of *Bononia* (Bologna) seated below the perspectival view. Little of the imagery remains on the room's eastern wall, but the allegories of *Iustizia* (Justice) and *Securitas* (Security) are still identifiable (Sambin de Norcen 2011b; Urban 2013: 142-43).

Located above the walls and in the curvature of the vault is a fictive loggia designed by Ottaviano Mascherino (1536–1566), in which sit ten figures painted by Lorenzo Sabatini (1530–1577) (Fig. 2). Placed

2.   This measurement is the most current and corrects the erroneous reports by Roberto Almagià (1955: 34) who recorded 525×695 cm, and Manuela Ghizzoni (2003: 143) who recorded 466×638 cm.

3.   Ceccarelli (2011b: 124) offers current measurements, once again correcting those listed by Almagià (1555: 35) of 850×675 cm.

between paired columns of polychrome marble, each figure is identified by name in the centre of the arch above. On the north side, above the perspective of Bologna, the Old Testament figure Seth sits next to the Egyptian god Thoth. Above the eastern wall, the Egyptian goddess Isis is centred between the mythical Titan Atlas and the Greek philosopher Thales (c. 624–c. 546 BCE). On the south side, above the city map, Anaximenes (585–528 BCE), another Greek philosopher, is painted next to the Greek poet Aratus (c. 310–c. 240 BCE). On the east side, above the Bolognese countryside, sits the astronomer and geographer Ptolemy (90–168 CE), the Roman poet Marcus Manilius (flourished early first century CE), and Alfonso X (1221–1284), a medieval Castilian king and astrologer.

Figure 2. Sala Bologna, Vatican Palace. Detail of the frescoed ceiling (from the top and moving clockwise are the directions of east (with the figures Thales, Isis, and Atlas); north (with the figures Thoth and Seth); west (with the figures Alfonso, Manilius, and Ptolemy); and south (with the figures Aratus and Anaximenes). Photo: Archivio Fotografico, Musei Vaticani.

Crowning the entire room on the ceiling is a painted map of the heavens that is, as I have argued elsewhere, unlike any other in fresco (Urban 2011, 2013). Visually supported by Mascherino's *quadratura*, the map is displayed on a canopy with a border of decorative circles, lion heads, and female masks, and is held in place by a single putto in each of the four corners of the vault. In the centre and represented in their traditional allegorical form denoted since Aratus are the forty-nine constellations known in the Renaissance, including those that Ptolemy observed with the naked eye in the Mediterranean and subsequently listed in his *Almagest* (c. 150 CE). This star catalogue described 1026 individual stars located in forty-eight unique constellations: the twelve constellations of the zodiac, twenty-one constellations in the northern hemisphere, and fifteen to the south. The forty-ninth constellation in the Sala Bologna is Antinous, added to the sky by Emperor Hadrian in 132 CE. First appearing in Early Modern cartography with the 1536 globe of German cartographer Caspar Vopel (1511–1561), this constellation is now obsolete and combined with Aquila in modern astronomy.

Painted in brilliant gold leaf, the individual stars in the Sala Bologna shine against the dark blue background and are thus highly visible from below. Such a rich and deep shade of blue contrasts with the softer earth tones—mostly greens, browns, and reds—of the terrestrial frescoes, and, therefore, through a difference of colour, provides a visual culmination to the decoration of the room. This ceiling is not only remarkable for its cartographic accuracy, but it is, as my ongoing research has shown, unique among all other celestial frescoes as it gives visual expression to the goals and aspirations of Gregory XIII, that is, the use of natural philosophy as an ideological tool of the Counter Reformation (Urban 2011, 2013).

Designed by Giovanni Antonio Vanosino da Varese (active in Rome 1562–1590) and executed by Sabatini and his workshop, the ceiling contains a representation of the entire cosmic sphere, with the northern celestial hemisphere painted in the centre and the southern hemisphere broken into two crescents and painted on either side. Comparing this orientation to any modern terrestrial map shaped as an oval, one finds that the outer (southern) crescents of the ceiling wrap around the back of the central (northern) hemisphere and connect. This is demonstrated by the constellation Gemini, wherein the feet of the Twins appear on the right edge of the map and their bodies on the left.

The sky is painted from an outer-celestial point of view, meaning the constellations are oriented as if viewed from the heavens above, rather than from the Earth below. This perspective is observed in the depiction of the constellations themselves, all of which face the opposite direction from how one would observe them from Earth, and also in their reverse ordering. Virgo, for example, is painted to the right of Leo, instead of appearing to the lion's left side. Outer-celestial positioning originated in antique celestial globes, and this point of view was common in Renaissance globe making (Herlihy 2007: 115).

Completing the figural iconography of the Sala Bologna ceiling is a representation of *The Fall of Phaethon*, which, although not a constellation, is an allegorical warning against hubris commonly painted on ceilings (Urban 2013: 51-66). Golden stars fill the background of the ceiling, and the Milky Way, represented as a grayish-white line, cuts through the celestial landscape and splits into two paths between Cygnus and Ophiuchus. The fresco is also divided by the principle meridian lines inscribed in gold, including the North and South Poles, the Arctic and Antarctic Circles, the Tropics of Cancer and Capricorn, the Autumnal and Vernal Equinoctial Colures, the Summer Solstitial Colure, the celestial equator, and the ecliptic. The ecliptic, the apparent path of the Sun and the planets through the sky and divided into twelve signs, each of which extends 30° of longitude, is marked with the zodiacal glyphs, also painted in gold.

The zodiacal symbol for Virgo is inexplicably missing, but this is perhaps due to the restoration of the ceiling. The reparation reports of 1936 (Biagetti 1936) discuss the structure of the vault and indicate that large cracks were first found in the ceiling upon inspection in 1934. Crossbeams were added to stabilize the structure, and iron plates were inserted throughout to reinforce the vault. These plates were placed in empty sections of the sky, of which Biagetti (1936: 184) has published a diagram. The figure of Boötes, however, had to be completely removed to install two large plates, after which he was reattached to the ceiling. Inspections also indicated that the humidity and lack of circulation in the room damaged the fresco, and thus fifteen small ventilation pipes were added to the perimeter of the ceiling. The accounts of 1940 (Biagetti 1940) describe the restoration of the fresco itself, beginning with the repainting of sections that had been sacrificed for the application of the metal plates. Older restorations that had altered the colour of the ceiling were removed, resulting in the reappearance of the original blue of the background. This restoration additionally demonstrated that many details were originally painted in gold leaf (such as the stars themselves and the glyphs of the zodiac), and therefore this colour was restored.

The figurative and allegorical representation of Gregory XIII's constellations derive from classical mythology, and more specifically from the ancient poetry of Aratus and Marcus Manilius, both of whom are represented in the fictive loggia below the ceiling. Aratus's astrological poem *Phaenomena*, complete with descriptions of the constellations and their mythological origins, remained the paradigmatic astrological source since its debut, and its popularity was bolstered in the Renaissance by the German printer Erhard Ratdolt's (1442–1528) numerous printed copies. Although Manilius's *Astronomicon libri V* was less ubiquitous, the depiction of this ancient astrologer within the Sala Bologna demonstrates the Boncompagni pope's familiarity with his work, and it follows that this poem also provided inspiration for the ceiling fresco.

Dating back to antiquity, most famously with Emperor Nero's *Domus Aurea* (c. 64 CE), celestial ceilings have an extensive heritage, and although there is a lack of extant monuments, examples of such decoration survive in the descriptions of ancient authors. For example, in his *Roman History* (LXXVII.11), Cassius Dio (c. 155–235) relays Septimius Severus's campaign against the British:

> Severus, seeing that his sons were changing their mode of life and that the legions were becoming enervated by idleness, made a campaign against Britain, though he knew he should not return. He knew this chiefly from the stars under which he had been born, for he had caused them to be painted on the ceilings of the rooms in the palace where he was wont to hold court, so that they were visible to all… (trans. Earnest Cary).

Philostratus gives a similar description in his account of the palaces of Babylon in *The Life of Apollonius of Tyana* (I.25, trans. F.C. Conybeare): 'They say that they also visited men's quarters with a domed roof imitating a kind of sky, roofed with sapphire…' In *The Twelve Caesars* (VI.31, trans. J.C. Rolfe), Suetonius describes the famous dining room in Nero's *Domus Aurea*: 'The main dining room was circular, and its roof revolved slowly, day and night, in time with the sky'. Similar descriptions are also found in Martial's *Epigrams* (VII.56) and Varro's *On Agriculture* (III.5.17). In addition to iconographic descriptions, these historical accounts are useful for their indication of room type for which these frescoes were commissioned: a Babylonian audience chamber (from Philostratus), a reception room (Cassius Dio), and an Imperial dining room (Suetonius). It is significant that each of these rooms was a space in which the patron would receive or entertain illustrious guests, thereby indicating, I argue, that ancient rulers and other powerful patrons wished for such decoration to reach visitors and members of the court.

The Early Middle Ages (up to the eleventh century) saw a shift in the use of celestial iconography, and the walls and ceilings of palaces were no longer decorated with astrological imagery. Instead, the constellations were featured abundantly in mathematical, mythological, and literary manuscripts, leading to a wide diffusion of this imagery in the medieval world (Saxl 1915; Panofsky and Saxl 1933; Kamborian 1987; Page 2002). Additionally, although medieval horoscopes are certainly known, it was the depiction of the constellations celebrating the cycles of the months and found within Books of Hours that became ubiquitous throughout the Middle Ages. Here the signs of the zodiac were associated with the twelve months, while the planets were often connected to the days of the week.

Concurrent with Renaissance humanism, illustrations of the cosmos were once again commissioned for the walls and ceilings of both public and private buildings and became celebrated images of illustrious patrons. The rediscovery and translation of ancient astrological and astronomical texts from the East, including Ptolemy and others, led to a rise during the Renaissance in the popularity of this subject matter and also inspired patrons to commission works of art based on Aratus' *Phaenomena*, Eratosthenes's *Catasterism*, Hyginus's *Fabulae*, and Manilius's *Astronomicon*. This ancient poetry provided the names, descriptions, and myths for all of the constellations and planetary gods, and as such they became the source books for artists charged with representing celestial themes (Cox-Rearick 1984: 169; Bornoroni 2006: 36).

Given such ancient precedents, it is unsurprising that Early Modern patrons avidly commissioned such works of art. Moreover, the profusion of examples found in Italy between the fourteenth and seventeenth centuries, as well as their location in reception and dining rooms inside important palaces and civic halls, demonstrates that celestial imagery was not reserved for private chambers, but was instead, as I have explored previously, commissioned for public spaces and used by the patron to glorify their illustrious birth, power, or rule (Urban 2013: 194-235).

Renaissance and Baroque astrological frescoes are usefully divided into four categories.[4] The first can be described as encyclopaedic, as they contain all the signs of the zodiac or planets in groupings that do not form a cartographically accurate representation of the sky. Commissioned by Duke Borso d'Este (1413–1471) and painted by Francesco del Cossa (1430–1477), Cosmè Tura (1430–1495), and Ercole de' Roberti (1451–1496), the decoration on the walls of the Sala dei Mesi in the Palazzo Schifanoia in Ferrara is a striking and comprehensive example of

---

4. In his discussion of Andrea Sacchi's ceiling in the Palazzo Barberini, John Beldon Scott (1991: 69-70) distinguishes between three common types of astrological murals: encyclopedic, accurate, and horoscopic. My encyclopedic and horoscopic categories are based upon his model.

this type (Warburg 1922, 1988; Lippincott 1990, 1992, 1994; Federici Vescovini 2006; Incerti 2008). The walls of this room are divided into nineteen vertical sections, twelve of which represent the months of the year and include depictions of d'Este's dukedom, the zodiac, celestial decans, and monthly labours. Derived from and modelled upon medieval Books of Hours (Saxl 1985: 80-81; Warburg 1988: 236, 240; Bini 1996: 24), the placement of this terrestrial imagery within the rooms of powerful Renaissance rulers added the additional meaning of a patron's unspoken claim of having control over nature, just as he presided over the territories of his actual domain (Alberti 1988; Urban 2013: 236-48). The celestial iconography meanwhile indicated, as I have argued elsewhere, his desire to be in concord with the heavens (Urban 2013: 199-214), reflecting the manner of astrological authors of the time who dedicated their works to God in order to be in harmony with the divine.

The second category consists of horoscopic ceilings, or those that contain the planets and/or zodiacal constellations relevant to the patron, but which again are not arranged cartographically. Painted by Baldassare Peruzzi in c. 1511, the careful assemblage of constellations on the vault of the Sala di Galatea in the Villa Chigi (now Farnesina) in Rome references the natal horoscope of its patron, Agostino Chigi (Saxl 1934, 1957, 1985; Quinlan-McGrath 1984, 1986, 1995, 2013; Rowland 1984; Lippincott 1990, 1991; Taylor 2004; Urban 2010). Examples of this type need not display an entire horoscope, but may include only a select few constellations or planets that are meaningful to the patron. This is demonstrated by the 1574 ceiling of the Sala del Mappamondo in the Palazzo Farnese at Caprarola designed by Vanosino and painted by Giovanni de'Vecchi (Fig. 3). The presence of the planet Jupiter, the skewed direction of the constellation Argo, the inclusion of the star Capella and a fleur-de-lis, each of which references an element of the Farnese *imprese*, indicates that this ceiling alludes to Alessandro Farnese's horoscope (Partridge 1995: esp. 421).

Frescoes that commemorate an event through the precise depiction of the sky at a specific date and time, as exemplified by the frescoed cupola above the altar in the Old Sacristy of San Lorenzo in Florence attributed to Giuliano d'Arrigo (c. 1367–1446) after 1422, makes up the third type of celestial iconography (Warburg 1912; Brown 1981; Parronchi 1984; Lapi Ballerini 1986, 1988, 1989a, 1989b; Beck 1989; Campione 1995; Vuilleumier 2000; Blume 2006). Here, the location of the painted Sun and Moon in the constellations of Cancer and Taurus indicates the date of 6 July 1439, thus marking for posterity the Council of Florence (Brown 1981; Cox-Rearick 1984).

Figure 3. Sala del Mappamondo, Palazzo Farnese, Caprarola. Detail of
the frescoed ceiling. Photo: Alfredo Dagli Orti/ The Art Archive at Art
Resource, NY.

Similar in precision to commemorative cycles is the ceiling in the
Sala Bologna, the only example of the fourth category, the complete
cartographic representation of the heavens. Therefore I am defining the
difference between horoscopic, commemorative, and cartographic cycles
as the absence of planets in the latter, thus precluding any indication of
date or time. Moreover, the Sala Bologna is different from encyclopaedic
examples, as the arrangement of the constellations is cartographically
accurate. From this categorical listing the uniqueness of Gregory XIII's
ceiling becomes apparent.

The decoration of the Sala Bologna was born out of the new atmosphere of natural inquiry that marked the sixteenth century in Italy, and
that found outstanding expression in both the painted loggia and the
celestial map in the *sala*. Representing this renewed interest in the history
of astrology and astronomy are the figures painted in Mascherino's
loggia. The answer as to why these personalities were selected is gleaned
only when the group is considered as a whole and examined within the
context of the decoration of the entire room. If, as has been suggested by
others (Lippincott 1990: 206; Fiorani 2005: 149), the intention was to
illustrate the various sciences needed for map-making or for Gregory
XIII's later calendar reform, then a few notable individuals such as

Euclid and Aristotle are missing, and further, the inclusion of the mythical gods is inappropriate. Instead, I contend that these ten figures represent a compilation of each of the founders or inventors of Western astrology, astronomy, and geography, as well as a few of these subjects' most famous practitioners. With this mix of mythical, biblical, and historical figures, Sabatini has painted a unique and complete visual history of these disciplines without precedent or comparison, with a narrative that begins in antiquity and continues into the Middle Ages.

The visual history begins with Isis and Thoth, as the Egyptian queen of heaven and inventor of astronomy respectively. Atlas carries this tradition into the classical world, and Seth into the Judeo-Christian. The remaining personalities constitute a representation of key figures from the Greco-Roman world to medieval Spain. In addition, this combination of astrological and astronomical imagery demonstrates how these two branches of learning were seen as one and the same in antiquity and into Gregory XIII's own day. Thoth, Atlas, Seth, and Ptolemy also represent, in this worldview, the lineage of knowledge of cartography and geography, from ancient Egypt into the Latin West. Altogether, these figures, and more importantly, the history they represent, connect thematically the terrestrial maps on the walls with the celestial map on the ceiling, and unify the overall decorative program of the room.

Similar to the maps on the walls, the ceiling fresco of the Sala Bologna acts as a celebration of the Renaissance interest in cartography. Although the background stars appear to be placed randomly, those within the constellations are accurately plotted when compared to Ptolemy's *Almagest* (Ptolemy 1998: 2). For example, the bright star Arcturus is painted between the legs of Boötes, described by Ptolemy (1998: 347) as 'The star between the thighs, called "Arcturus"'; Sirius is painted within the face of Canis Major, described by Ptolemy (1998: 387) as 'The star in the mouth, the brightest, which is called "the Dog" and is reddish'; and Spica is painted within the wheat held by Virgo, described by Ptolemy (1998: 368) as 'The star on the left hand, called "Spica"'. The plotting of the constellations and meridian lines are also remarkably accurate when compared to the *Almagest*. As discussed, images of the constellations date back to antiquity and flourished during the Middle Ages, but they were portrayed as independent illustrations in the medieval world, not in accurate maps. Such mapping of the heavens was left to the globe-maker who could, in three dimensions, accurately render the celestial realm. The few flat maps that existed in the Middle Ages were praised for their decoration, not for their accuracy (Warner 2005: 17). What radically changed the production of cartography was the development of the printing press in the mid-fifteenth century, which allowed for the first time the wide-scale manufacturing of flat—and thus portable—maps (Warner 1979: x).

The rediscovery of Ptolemy's second-century *Geography* in the early fifteenth century also played a critical role in the renewed interest of both celestial and terrestrial cartography (Warner 1979: x). Contained within its pages were fundamental keys and instructions for the construction of accurate maps, as well as for the plotting of coordinates. Based on the information gained from the *Geography*, the most influential celestial map of the time was that by Albrecht Dürer (1471–1528), printed in 1515 in Nuremberg (Weiss 1888; and Warner 2005) (Fig. 4). Not merely a star catalogue or decorative image of the heavens, Dürer's print is the first accurately rendered map of the sky in two dimensions, with each of the constellations in the northern and southern hemisphere carved on separate woodblocks. Resulting from this paradigm was a surge in the methodical production of celestial map-making, as well as the invention of stylistic differences in the depiction of the constellations (Warner 1971: 337).

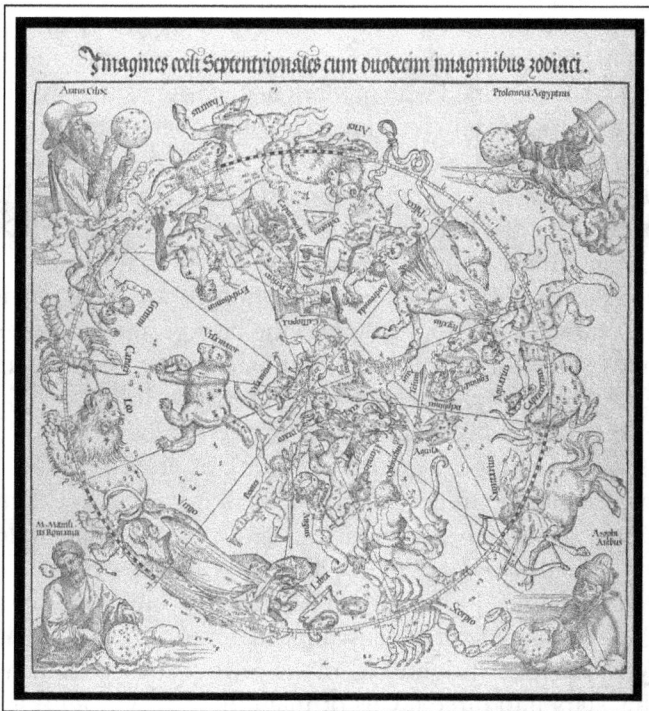

Figure 4. Albrecht Dürer, *Imagines Coeli Septentrionales cum duodecim imaginibus zodiaci*, 1515, woodcut, 24 1/8 inches × 17 15/16 inches. Photo: The Metropolitan Museum of Art.

Since any projection of a three-dimensional sky onto a two-dimensional plane will include some unavoidable distortion, a celestial map has to be rendered in three dimensions to be completely measurable. Commenting on Jacopo Barozzi da Vignola's 1583 perspectival treatise *Le due regole della prospettiva practica*, Egnazio Danti (1583: 90) observed of the Sala Bologna ceiling that, '…it is impossible to reduce the eighth celestial sphere with its images onto a flat oval'. Indeed, to eliminate any distortion, two-dimensional maps must be plotted with a stereographic projection in which the globe is divided into two hemispheres, as seen with Dürer's print, or divided into cartographic gores, as used by François Demongenet (flourished mid-sixteenth century) in c. 1560. The projection methods used by Dürer and Demongenet, however, may create an image that is useful for navigation but is difficult to read as an entire unit. Such a projection was therefore inappropriate for the Sala Bologna, where decoration was the first priority, as Danti (1583: 90) himself noted.

In spite of the slight distortions caused by its pseudocylindrical projection, when compared to Ptolemy, Vanosino designed a precise representation of the heavens in which each of the constellations is correctly proportioned and positioned in relation to one another. This accuracy can be confirmed with modern planetarium software that allows the user to enter a date and location to create a chart of the sky as seen at the time, in this case, Rome 1575.[5]

In addition to this cartographic precision, other iconographic details more closely align the Sala Bologna fresco with the maps of Dürer and Ptolemy than with the similar ceiling at Caprarola to which it is often compared. For example, with the exception of the constellation Ursa Major, the stars at Caprarola fade into the background and are scarcely visible between the mythological figures that are here given greater emphasis. Additionally, the inclusion in the Sala Bologna of the Arctic and Antarctic meridian lines, as well as the depiction of the zodiacal glyphs along the ecliptic, suggests a priority of precision.

Further distancing Gregory XIII's ceiling from that at Caprarola are the differing sizes and shapes of the painted stars that reflect their varying magnitudes (degrees of brightness) as also described by Ptolemy and carved by Dürer. In the *Almagest*, Ptolemy indicated six different levels of magnitude; Dürer, meanwhile, cut three differently shaped stars to signify variances in brightness. In the ceiling at Caprarola, Vanosino divided his stars into three levels of magnitude. The brightest stars are large with six points, followed by smaller stars of the same shape, and

5. My thanks to Darrelyn Gunzburg for her help with this.

his faintest stars have five points. Given the similarity between each shape, two of which are separated only by a slight alteration in size, the depicted magnitudes at Caprarola are difficult to read. In contrast to this is the artist's later design in the Sala Bologna, in which four different stars were presented. Magnitude 1 stars are the largest in size, and have eleven points. Next in line are eight-point stars that are slightly smaller, followed by medium-sized stars with six points, and lastly by the faintest stars with only five points. Given that each magnitude is distinct in shape, the degrees of brightness on the Vatican ceiling are clearly seen and easily understood. Such a development in Vanosino's work suggests that the Boncompagni pope desired a greater emphasis on accuracy than what had been accomplished previously at Caprarola.

The most striking contrast between the two frescoes is found in the Sala Bologna's lack of personal emblems compared to those found throughout the Caprarola ceiling (Partridge 1995: 421), and which emphasize the Vatican's adherence to Ptolemaic cartography. The inclusion of various horoscopic elements at Caprarola as noted above, as well as the modification of the constellations to incorporate them, particularly the depiction of the planet Jupiter and the adjustment of Ursa Major's location, precludes, I argue, this fresco from the category of accurate cartography.

One final comparison between the two frescoes solidifies their dissimilarity. In contrast to the painted clouds on the outer edges of the Caprarola ceiling that suggest a realistic vision of the sky as if seen through an opening in the vault, the constellations of the Sala Bologna appear as if painted on a canopy. Karl Lehman (1945: esp. 2-14) remains the authoritative source on painted ceiling canopies, tracing the iconography's origins to the early fifth-century BCE Etruscan Tomb of the Monkey, and although there are few extant examples, he notes that the descriptions of Greco-Roman authors provide evidence of this decoration's ubiquity (Lehman 1945: 2, 4, 5, 8; figs 5, 8). Given the origin of painted canopies, it follows that Gregory XIII's ceiling was intended as a reference to antiquity, specifically to the age of the astronomers, astrologers, and poets painted in the *quadratura*. Moreover, the rich blue and red colours of the canvas recall the colouring of the ceiling in the Sala della Volta Dorata in Nero's *Domus Aurea*, as reconstructed by the painter Francisco de Hollanda (1517–1585) in 1538.

Additionally, the compositional use of a canopy in the Sala Bologna emphasizes the apparent flatness and map-like quality of the scene, especially when viewed in conjunction with the fictive loggia just below. This flatness must be considered a conscious choice, as the *quadratura* demonstrates that illusionistic perspective was not only possible, but was

successfully employed in the room. Inside the fictive architecture
daylight illuminates each niche and pergola, as well as the four corners
of the ceiling between the putti and convex edges of the canopy. The
manifestation of night, evidenced by a darker shading of blue, as well as
by the appearance of the stars themselves, establishes that the celestial
scene was made to look as if it were painted on a two-dimensional
surface, and it is therefore more closely related to a printed map than a
miraculous vision. This conceptual break between daylight in the
quadratura and the representation of night on the canopy demonstrates
that the viewer was meant to read the two ideas separately. The loggia
exists as a fictive continuation of the room's architecture, while the
constellations are depicted on a flat surface that is disconnected from this
illusion and is instead held above it.

Although the late sixteenth-century dating of Gregory XIII's commission, as well as its reliance upon the revival of Ptolemaic map-
making, suggests that its decoration was intended as a celebration of
cartography, monumental map cycles were a well-established tradition of
political and religious aggrandizement used by patrons to demonstrate
their control—intellectual, actual, or otherwise—over the terrestrial world
(Alberti 1988: 287; Fiorani 2005: 12; 2007: 805). The profusion of maps
in Gregory XIII's other artistic commissions—including the frescoes in
the Vatican Terza Loggia and Galleria delle Carte Geografiche—demonstrates his immense interest in cartography, as well as its propagandistic
possibilities. What makes the Sala Bologna unique, I argue, is the fact
that this was the first instance in which mapmaking was employed in an
effort to understand heavenly space. Similar to golden backgrounds in
late medieval paintings, the use of a blue wash and golden stars in church
and chapel ceilings was a common iconographic method of displaying
heaven, exemplified perhaps most famously with the original 1480s
decoration of the Sistine ceiling before Michelangelo's ground-breaking
commission in 1508. This iconography, however, represents heaven, but
does not explore it. In contrast, the celestial decoration of the Sala
Bologna, I suggest, calculates and maps the heavens in an attempt to
obtain an understanding of the divine realm and gain access to God.

The theories and opinions of Gabriele Paleotti (1522–1597), then
Bishop of Bologna and Gregory XIII's close friend, may have played an
important role in the cartographic decoration of the Sala Bologna
(Fiorani 2005: 152-57). In his post-Tridentine treatise on art, *Discorso
intorno alle imagini sacre e profane* (1582), Paleotti devoted a chapter to
the usefulness of secular images for spiritual contemplation, and
included maps of both the terrestrial and celestial realms as examples
(Paleotti 1961 [1582]; Jones 1995: 135). Referencing the writings of both

Augustine (354–430) and Thomas Aquinas (1225–1274) as the basis of his arguments, the bishop described how representations of God's creation, if understood correctly and meditated upon properly, could help one reach an understanding of the divine. Paleotti argued that a learned viewer who looked at such a painting would not merely see a map or landscape, but would be able to contemplate metaphysically each aspect of the image and comprehend God's presence in everything depicted (Paleotti 1961 [1582]: 384-85; Jones 1995: 135-36; Fiorani 2005: 154; 2011: 18). Critical to this notion was Paleotti's statement regarding the required accuracy of such imagery. Similar to his descriptions concerning the correct use of iconography and decorum in sacred paintings, he argued that a secular or scientific image must be accurate in order to represent God most truthfully. Cartography by definition seeks to illustrate fact, and Paleotti's theories on the usefulness of maps help explain why the ceiling of the Sala Bologna upholds a strictly Ptolemaic representation of the heavens devoid of any horoscopic iconography.

Although Paleotti's treatise was not published until 1582, given his personal involvement in the Council of Trent it can be assumed that he formulated his arguments regarding the proper use of art prior to publication. Moreover, his close relationship with Gregory XIII should not be overlooked. For example, the bishop and pope were both educated at the University of Bologna, they each participated in the Council of Trent, and they shared similar opinions about Catholic reform (Fiorani 2005: 150). It is likely that the two exchanged ideas with one another, and that Gregory XIII agreed with Paleotti's views concerning the usefulness of secular imagery. The cartographical and emblematic decoration of the Sala Bologna, I argue, must therefore be seen as Gregory's testament to the validity of Paleotti's *Discorso*, as well as the pope's own endorsement of the Counter-Reformatory efficacy and value of cartographic imagery. Not merely an illustration of the stars, the Sala Bologna fresco therefore represents the contemporary advancements and interests in map-making and also acts as a demonstration of God's creation that could be used as a visual aid for spiritual meditation. No other celestial fresco, I contend, can claim such complex implications.

To conclude, when examined in the rapidly changing context of late sixteenth-century astronomy, the remaining iconography and meaning of the Sala Bologna's vault is revealed. Paired with the inclusion of the mythic founders and various historical authorities of the astronomical sciences, the ceiling represents a critical juncture in the evolution of natural philosophy: mathematics was becoming increasingly sophisticated and ancient theories of the universe were eagerly read, but there were still many truths and mysteries yet to be discovered. While the precision and placement of the constellations in the Sala Bologna testify to the advancement in celestial calculation and cartographic methodo- logy, the absolute absence of stars in the frescoed Milky Way provides a snapshot of astronomical knowledge in the mid- to late sixteenth century before Galileo's telescopic observations in 1610.

There is a tendency for modern historians to focus on the relationship between astronomy and Catholicism in the post-Galilean era and argue that the two were always at odds. This notion, however, is overtly simple and emphatically false. Indeed, at the time of the Sala Bologna's decora- tion, Copernicanism had yet to be condemned and Galileo's observations would not be made for another thirty-five years. Gregory's ceiling there- fore represents the Church's official attitudes towards sixteenth-century astronomy, meaning the fresco does not incorporate contemporary philosophical debate regarding the nature of the heavens brought about by the publication of Copernicus's *De Revolutionibus* in 1543 and the appearance of a supernova in 1572, but instead, according to the writings of Cardinal Paleotti, it shows the sky as part of God's miraculous creation. It is telling, then, that it is the only ceiling of its kind, given its chronological position on the cusp of the tumultuous scientific revolution of the next century, a time when the spiritual implications of such inquiries could no longer be ignored by the papacy.

References

Alberti, Leon Battista. 1988. *On the Art of Building in Ten Books*, trans. Joseph Rykwert, Neil Leach, and Robert Tavernor (London and Cambridge: MIT Press).

Almagià, Roberto. 1955. *Monumenta cartographica vaticana*. Vol. IV. *Le pitture geografiche murali della terza loggia e di altre sale Vaticane* (Vatican City: Biblioteca Apostolica Vaticana).

Beck, James. 1989. 'Leon Battista Alberti and the "Night Sky" at San Lorenzo', *Artibus et Historiae* 10: 9-35.

Biagetti, B. 1936. 'Pitture Murali Restauri: Sala Bolognese', in *Rendiconti della pontificia academia romana di archeologia*, serie III (Vatican City: Tipografia Poliglotta Vaticana): 182-87.

———. 1940. 'Pitture Murali Restauri: Sala Bolognese', in *Rendiconti della pontificia academia romana di archeologia*, serie III (Vatican City: Tipografia Poliglotta Vaticana): 240-43.

Bini, Daniele. 1996. *Astrologia: arte e cultura in età rinascimentale = art and culture in the Renaissance* (Modena: Bulino).

Blume, Dieter. 2006. 'Astrologia come scienza politica. Il cielo notturno della Sagrestia Vecchia di San Lorenzo', in Morel 2006: 149-64.

Bornoroni, Marina. 2006. 'Linguaggi astrologici tra scienza e mito dal Medioevo al Rinascimento', in Morel 2006: 35-53.

Brown, Patricia Fortini. 1981. '*Laetentur Caeli*: The Council of Florence and the Astronomical Fresco in the Old Sacristy', *Journal of the Warburg and Courtauld Institutes* 44: 176-80.

Campione, Monica, and Lorena Gianlorenzi. 1995. 'Firenze: il planetario della Sagrestia Vecchia di San Lorenzo', *Anagkē* 9: 84-91.

Cassius Dio. 1982. *Roman History*, trans. Earnest Cary (Cambridge, MA and London: Harvard University Press).

Cato, Marcus Porcius, and Marcus Terentius Varro. *On Agriculture*, trans. William David Hooper and Harrison Boyd Ash, ed. G.P. Goold, The Loeb Classical Library, 283 (Cambridge, MA: Harvard University Press, 1934).

Ceccarelli, Francesco. 2011a. 'Parete Sud: Lorenzo Sabatini (probabilmente su disegno di Domenico Tibaldi): *Pianta prospettica di Bologna, 1575*', in Ceccarelli and Aksamija 2011: 104-109.

———. 2011b. 'Parete Ovest: Lorenzo Sabatini (su disegni di Domenico Tibaldi e Scipione Dattari): *Corografia del Bolognese, 1575*', in Ceccarelli and Aksamija 2011: 124-25.

———. 2011c. 'Parete Nord: Lorenzo Sabatini (su disegno di Domenico Tibaldi?): *Veduta di Bologna dalla chiesa di San Giovanni in Bosco, 1575*', in Ceccarelli and Aksamija 2011: 135.

Ceccarelli, Francesco, and Nadja Aksamija, eds. 2011. *La Sala Bologna nei Palazzi Vaticani: Architettura, cartografia e potere nell'età di Gregorio XIII* (Venice: Marsilio Editori).

Chattard, Giovanni Pietro. 1766. *Nuova descrizione del Vaticano o sia della sacrosanta Basilica di S. Pietro*, vol. II (Rome: Barbiellini).

Ciappi, Marc'Antonio. 1591. *Compendio delle heroiche et gloriose attioni et santa vita di Papa Greg. XIII* (Rome: Stamperia de gli Accolti).

Courtright, Nicola. 1990. 'Gregory XIII's Tower of the Winds in the Vatican' (PhD diss., New York University).

Cox-Rearick, Janet. 1984. *Dynasty and Destiny in Medici Art: Pontormo, Leo X, and the Two Cosimos* (Princeton: Princeton University Press).

Danti, Egnazio. 1583. *Le due regole della prospettiva pratica di M. Jacopo Barozzi da Vignola con il commentario del R.P.M. Egnatio Danti* (Rome: Francesco Zannetti).

Federici Vescovini, Graziella. 2006. 'Gli affreschi astrologici del Palazzo Schifanoia e l'astrologia alla Corte dei Duchi d'Este tra Medioevo e Rinascimento', in Morel 2006: 55-82.

Fiorani, Francesca. 2005. *The Marvel of Maps: Art, Cartography and Politics in Renaissance Italy* (New Haven and London: Yale University Press).

———. 2007. 'Cycles of Painted Maps in the Renaissance', in Woodward 2007: 804-30.

———. 2011. 'Da Bologna al mondo: Astronomia, cartografia, giurisprudenza e la Chiesa universale di Gregorio XIII', in Ceccarelli and Aksamija 2011: 13-23.

Ghizzoni, Manuela. 2003. 'L'immagine di Bologna nella veduta vaticana del 1575', in *Imago Urbis: L'immagine della città nella storia d'Italia*, ed. Francesca Bocchi and Rosa Smurra (Rome: Viella): 139-65.

Herlihy, Anna Friedman. 2007. 'Renaissance Star Charts', in Woodward 2007: 99-122.

Incerti, Manuela. 2008. 'Geometrie, astrologiche, e astronomiche nel Salone dei Mesi di Schifanoia', *F.D.: bollettino della Ferrariae Decus* 24: 46-57.

Jones, Pamela. 1995. 'Art Theory as Ideology: Gabriele Paleotti's Hierarchical Notion of Painting's Universality and Reception', in *Reframing the Renaissance: Visual Culture in Europe and Latin America, 1450–1650*, ed. Claire J. Farago (New Haven and London: Yale University Press): 127-39.

Kamborian, Kelly. 1987. 'Children of the Planets: Medieval Astronomical Imagery', in *Survival of the Gods: Classical Mythology in Medieval Art* (Providence: Brown University Press): 125-32.

Lapi Ballerini, Isabella. 1986. 'L'emisfero celeste della Sagrestia Vecchia: rendiconti da un giornale di restauro', in *Donatello e la Sagrestia Vecchia di San Lorenzo* (Florence: Centro di): 75-85.

———. 1988. 'Gli emisferi celesti della sagrestia vecchia e della cappella Pazzi', *Rinascimento* 28: 321-55.

———. 1989a. 'Il planetario della Sagrestia Vecchia', in *Brunelleschi e Donatello nella Sagrestia Vecchia di S. Lorenzo*, ed. Umberto Baldini and Donatella Valente (Florence: Il Fiorino-Alinari): 113-66.

———. 1989b. 'Considerazioni a margine del restauro della "cupolina" dipinta nella Sagrestia Vecchia', in *Donatello-Studien* (Munich: Bruckmann): 102-12.

Lehman, Karl. 1945. 'The Dome of Heaven', *The Art Bulletin* 27: 1-27.

Lippincott, Kristen. 1990. 'Two Astrological Ceilings Reconsidered: The Sala di Galatea in the Villa Farnesina and the Sala del Mappamondo at Caprarola', *Journal of the Warburg and Courtauld Institutes* 53: 185-207.

———. 1991. 'Aby Warburg, Fritz Saxl and the Astrological Ceiling of the Sala di Galatea', in *Aby Warburg: Akten des internationalen Symposions, Hamburg 1990*, ed. Horst Bredekamp, Michael Diers, and Andreas Beyer (Weinheim: VCH, Acta Humaniora): 213-32.

———. 1992. 'I decani di Schifanoia e la ricostruzione artistica di Maurizio Bonora', in *Lo Zodiaco del Principe*, ed. Elena Bonatti (Ferrara: Tosi): 15-21.

———. 1994. 'Gli dei-decani del Salone dei Mesi di Palazzo Schifanoia', in *Alla Corte degli Estense*, ed. Marco Bertozzi (Ferrara: Università degli Studi): 181-97.

Martial. 1919. *Epigrams*, trans. Walter C.A. Ker (Cambridge, MA and London: Harvard University Press).

Morel, Philippe, ed. 2006. *L'Arte de la Renaissance entre science et magie* (Paris: Somogy, Academie de France à Rome).

Page, Sophie. 2002. *Astrology in Medieval Manuscripts* (London: The British Library).

Paleotti, Gabriele. 1961 [1582]. 'Discorso Intorno alle Imagini Sacre e Profane', in *Trattati d'Arte del Cinquecento: fra Manierismo e Controriforma*, vol. II, ed. Paola Barocchi (Bari: Laterza e Figli): 117-509.

Panofsky, Erwin, and Fritz Saxl. 1933. 'Classical Mythology in Mediaeval Art', *Metropolitan Museum Studies* 4: 228-80.

Parronchi, Alessandro. 1984. 'L'emisfero settentrionale della Sagrestia Vecchia', in *Il complesso monumentale di San Lorenzo: la basilica, le sagrestie, le cappelle, la biblioteca*, ed. Umberto Baldini and Bruno Nardini (Florence: Nardini Editore): 72-79.

Partridge, Loren. 1995. 'The Room of Maps at Caprarola, 1573–1575', *The Art Bulletin* 77: 413-44.

Philostratus. 1912. *The Life of Apollonius of Tyana*, trans. F.C. Conybeare (Cambridge, MA and London: Harvard University Press).

Ptolemy, Claudius. 1998. *Ptolemy's Almagest*, trans. G.J. Toomer (Princeton: Princeton University Press).

Quinlan-McGrath, Mary. 1984. 'The Astrological Vault of the Villa Farnesina: Agostino Chigi's Rising Sign', *Journal of the Warburg and Courtauld Institutes* 47: 91-105.

———. 1986. 'A Proposal for the Foundation Date of the Villa Farnesina', *Journal of the Warburg and Courtauld Institutes* 49: 245-50.

———. 1995. 'The Villa Farnesina, Time-Telling Conventions and Renaissance Astrological Practice', *Journal of the Warburg and Courtauld Institutes* 58: 52-71.

———. 2013. *Influences: Art, Optics, and Astrology in the Italian Renaissance* (Chicago and London: The University of Chicago Press, 2013).

Rowland, Ingrid. 1984. 'The Birth Date of Agostino Chigi: Documentary Proof', *Journal of the Warburg and Courtauld Institutes* 47: 192-93.

Sambin de Norcen, Maria Teresa. 2011a. 'Il progetto della Sala Bologna: architettura e iconografia', in Ceccarelli and Aksamija 2011: 25-33.

———. 2011b. 'Parete est e personificazioni nella Sala Bologna: Parete est e serie delle figure allegoriche: *Securitas* (parete est), *Pax* (parete ovest), *Annona* (parete ovest), *Bononia* (parete nord)', in Ceccarelli and Aksamija 2011: 140-45.

Saxl, Fritz. 1915. *Verzeichnis astrologischer und mythologischer illustrierter Handschriften des lateinischen Mittelalters* (Heidelberg: C. Winter).

———. 1934. *La Fede Astrologica di Agostino Chigi: Interpretazione dei dipinta di Baldassare Peruzzi nella Sala di Galatea della Farnesina* (Rome: Reale Accademia d'Italia).

———. 1957. 'The Villa Farnesina', in *Lectures* (London: The Warburg Institute): 189-99.

———. 1985. *La fede negli astri dall'antichita al Rinascimento*, ed. Salvatore Settis (Turin: Boringhieri).

Scott, John Beldon. 1991. *Images of Nepotism: The Painted Ceilings of Palazzo Barberini* (Princeton: Princeton University Press).

Suetonius. 1914. *The Lives of the Twelve Caesars*, trans. J.C. Rolfe (Cambridge, MA and London: Harvard University Press).

Taja, Agostino. 1750. *Descrizione del Palazzo Apostolico Vaticano* (Rome: Pagliarini).

Taylor, Paul. 2004. 'Boötes on the Farnesina Ceiling', *Journal of the Warburg and Courtauld Institutes* 67: 295-300.

Urban, Emily. 2010. 'Depicting the Heavens: The Use of Astrology in the Frescoes of Rome', paper presented at the seventh annual INSAP (Inspiration of Astronomical Phenomena conference, Bath, England.

———. 2011. 'Quadratura con figure nell'intradosso della volta della Sala Bologna, 1575', in Ceccarelli and Aksamija 2011: 154-61.

———. 2013. 'The Sala Bologna in the Vatican Palace: Art and Astronomy in Counter-Reformation Rome' (PhD diss., Rutgers University).

Vuilleumier, Florence. 2000. 'Oriona et istiusmodi signa micantia: l'hémisphère céleste de la Sagrestia Vecchia da San Lorenzo', in *Leon Battista Alberti*, vol. 2, ed. Francesco Furlan (Paris: Vrin): 599-621.

Warburg, Aby. 1912. 'Eine astronomische Himmelsdarstellung in der alten Sakristei von S. Lorenzo in Florenz', *Mitteilungen des Kunsthistorischen Instituts in Florenz* 2: 34-36.

———. 1922. 'Italienische Kunst und internationale Astrologie im Palazzo Schifanoja zu Ferrara', in *L'Italia e l'arte straniera* (Rome: Maglione & Strini): 179-93.

———. 1988. 'Italian Art and International Astrology in the Palazzo Schifanoia in Ferrara', in *German Essays on Art History*, ed. Gert Schiff (New York: Continuum): 234-54.

Warner, Deborah Jean. 1971. 'The Celestial Cartography of Giovanni Antonio Vanosino da Varese', *Journal of the Warburg and Courtauld Institutes* 34: 336-37.

———. 1979. *The Sky Explored: Celestial Cartography 1500–1800* (New York: Alan R. Liss).

———. 2005. 'Star Charts: Their Lore and Meaning', in *Celestial Images: Antiquarian Astronomical Charts and Maps from the Mendillo Collection* (Boston: Boston University Art Gallery): 17-20.

Weiss, Edmund. 1888. 'Albrecht Dürer's geographische, astronomische und astrologische Tafeln', *Jahrbuch der Kunsthistorischen Sammlungen des Allerhoechsten Kaiserhauses* 7: 207-20.

Woodward, David. 2007. *Cartography in the Renaissance*, vol. III of *The History of Cartography* (Chicago and London: The University of Chicago Press).

COSMOS, CULTURE AND LANDSCAPE: DOCUMENTING, LEARNING AND SHARING AUSTRALIAN ABORIGINAL ASTRONOMICAL KNOWLEDGE IN CONTEMPORARY SOCIETY*

John Goldsmith

International Centre for Radio Astronomy Research/Curtin Institute of Radio Astronomy, GPO Box U1987, Perth 6845, Western Australia
John.Goldsmith.MSc@gmail.com

Abstract

The Cosmos Culture and Landscape project investigated two contemporary examples of Western Australian Aboriginal astronomical knowledge and cultural beliefs. Radio astronomers from the Murchison Radio-astronomy Observatory and Square Kilometre Array radio telescope project in the Murchison Region, and local Aboriginal communities were brought together in a collaborative endeavour, so that both groups could share their respective knowledge of the night sky. Aboriginal perspectives were examined of the 300,000+ year old Wolfe Creek Crater in the East Kimberley region. In-depth video interviews documented Aboriginal knowledge and extensive digital imaging (360° and timelapse) of key locations were used to record landscapes. New resources were developed (a video exhibit and virtual tour) and successfully applied to encourage learning and appreciation of Australian Aboriginal sky knowledge.

Keywords

Australian Aboriginal sky mythology, astronomy, digital imaging, *Ilgarijiri—Things Belonging to the Sky*, Wolfe Creek Crater, Emu constellation, Australian Aboriginal Dreamtime.

* Readers are respectfully advised that this chapter contains the image and names of Aboriginal people who have passed away.

Introduction

The cosmos, in its complexity, elegance and mystery, inspires humanity to wonder, imagine, and to expand its understanding of its place in the cosmos. These motives have been expressed by many cultures throughout the world, from ancient times up to the scientific endeavours of the present day. Examples from ancient cultures include Egyptian civilisations that were inspired by and worshipped the Sun, as evidenced by astronomical alignments of temples (Belmonte 2011), observations of the Sun, Moon, and bright planets by the Maya and Aztecs, as indicated in codices and monumental hieroglyphics (Šprajc 2011), ancient Chinese cultures that observed and documented the night sky (Krupp 1997), and ancient Vedic texts from India that dealt with the movements of the Sun and Moon (Kochhar 2011). Cultures with oral traditions have also passed on astronomical knowledge gained by direct personal experience and observation to successive generations.

In Australia, cultural knowledge of the night sky held by distinctive Aboriginal communities has a long tradition. This chapter explores two contemporary examples from Western Australia, examined by the Cosmos, Culture and Landscape project (Goldsmith 2014). The first is a collaboration between Aboriginal Elders, artists, and radio-astronomy scientists associated with the Murchison Radio-astronomy Observatory and Square Kilometre Array (SKA) radio telescope project in the Murchison Region. The second example examines Aboriginal knowledge relating to Kandimalal, Wolfe Creek Crater in the East Kimberly, a 300,000+ year old meteorite crater and site of scientific and cultural importance.

Aboriginal Australia in Context

Research by Richard Gillespie revealed evidence of Australian Aboriginal culture that is at least 42,000–48,000 years old (Gillespie 2002: 469), suggesting that Australian Aboriginal culture may represent one of the longest continuous cultures in the world. The National Indigenous Languages Survey Report (Commonwealth of Australia 2005) noted that at the time of European colonisation, there were approximately 250 different Indigenous languages, which provides an indication of the cultural diversity of Aboriginal Australia. The first contact between early European explorers, and the subsequent colonisation of Australia by the British, in 1788, has resulted in profound and far-reaching changes to virtually all aspects of Aboriginal life to the present day. These impacts have included dispossession of land, impact of disease, and overt conflict. One indicator of such impacts is the twenty-year discrepancy in life expectancy between Aboriginal and non-Aboriginal Australians (Australian Bureau of Statistics 2002).

Various initiatives ranging from the symbolic to the highly practical have taken place in Australia to help redress these issues. Some key highlights include the historic transfer of Uluru and Kata Tjuta (Ayres Rock and the Olgas) back to traditional owners (Uluru–Kata Tjuta Aboriginal Land Trust), in 1985, by the Australian Government (Australian Government Director of National Parks 2010). In 1992, the then Australian Prime Minister Paul Keating delivered the 'Redfern Speech' (Keating 1992), a powerful public acknowledgment of the challenges faced by Aboriginal people. This speech, and subsequent developments, helped pave the way for the major modern day social process of Reconciliation, which was formally adopted by the Common-wealth of Australia, via the *Council for Aboriginal Reconciliation Act 1991*. The Council for Aboriginal Reconciliation (2000) articulated key issues essential to the process of Reconciliation: the importance of greater understanding about the significance of land and sea, better rela-tionships between Aboriginal people and the wider community, recogni-tion and valuing of Aboriginal cultures and heritage as part of Australia's heritage, and a shared sense of ownership of Australia's history. Since that time, many Aboriginal and non-Aboriginal people, communities, and organisations have been working towards finding practical steps to help address Aboriginal disadvantage in Australia, and to encourage greater opportunities, self-determination, employment, leadership, cul-tural renewal, and more broadly, greater understanding and appreciation of Australian Aboriginal cultures.

An Introduction to Australian Aboriginal Sky Knowledge

Astronomical symbolism lies at the heart of the Australian national identity of both Aboriginal and non-Aboriginal people. The Australian National Flag features both the Southern Cross and the six pointed 'Commonwealth Star', also known as the 'Star of Federation', which symbolically represents the states and territories of Australia. The Aboriginal Flag contains three symbolic elements: black (representing Aboriginal people of Australia); red (representing the red earth, red ochre, and a spiritual relation to the land); and yellow (representing the sun, giver of life and protector) (Fig. 1) (AIATSIS 2012).

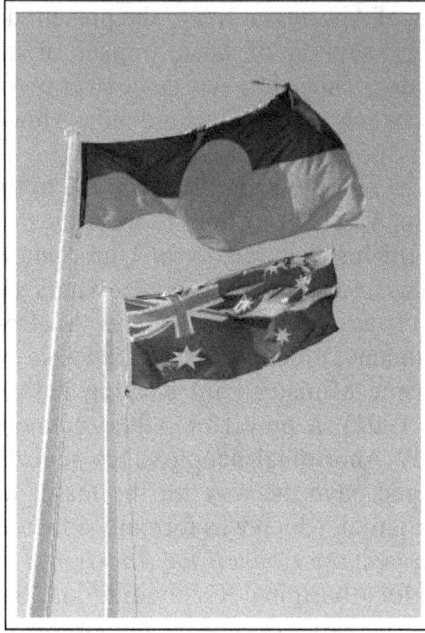

Figure 1. The Australian National Flag (below), and the Aboriginal Flag (above). Photo: © John Goldsmith.

Researchers such as Philip Clarke (1998) have noted the general lack of knowledge and research dedicated to Australian Aboriginal beliefs and knowledge regarding the night sky and cultural astronomy:

> In general, there has been little recording of Australian Aboriginal beliefs in astronomy. This is in spite of the predominance of astronomical themes in Aboriginal art... The investigation of beliefs concerning the Heavens, considered by many Aboriginal groups to exist as a distinct Skyworld, is important to the study of the cultural perceptions of all space... (Clarke (1998: 1).

Whilst investigation into Aboriginal astronomical and sky knowledge began early in the colonial settlement of Australia, the field is still comparatively small. Since the mid-1990s, a significant number of academic papers, books, book chapters, and articles have been published in this area, by researchers such as Clarke (1998), and Hugh Cairns and Bill Harney (2003) and in previous work that I have published (Goldsmith 1999) and together with Duane Hamacher (Hamacher and Goldsmith 2013). The primary repository of such knowledge is the Australian Institute of Aboriginal and Torres Strait Islander Studies (AIATSIS) located in Canberra. The field of Australian cultural astronomy crystallised in

2009 when the first national forum dedicated to this subject was held. Research has rapidly expanded since the 2009 national forum. Some examples of such research include Ray Norris and Cilla Norris (2009), Steven Tingay (2011), and, as noted above, my collaborative work (Hamacher and Goldsmith 2013), to name just a few. Such research efforts are helping to address the issues to which Clarke referred.

Researchers have adopted several approaches to Aboriginal astronomy. The first contact between European culture and Aboriginal people in Australia, along with colonisation, led to early efforts at trying to understand Aboriginal languages, some of which included vocabularies based on word list translations, of the names of astronomical bodies such as Sun, Moon, and stars. Captain Phillip King compiled a Noongar vocabulary in 1821 that included the word 'Sun' which was recorded as 'Djaät' (King 1827: 144) during a survey along the South Western coastline of Western Australia. William Edward Stanbridge (1858) provided another example of documenting Aboriginal astronomical knowledge and beliefs of the Boorong people in Victoria, stating that the Boorong people 'pride themselves upon knowing more of Astronomy than any other (Australian) tribe' (Stanbridge 1858: 137).

Other approaches attempted to reconstruct Aboriginal knowledge relating to the stars prior to the first European contact in Australia. Such approaches can be fraught with difficulties, including language barriers, researcher interpretation, and the influence and modification of cultural knowledge over time. For example, Bednarik (2011) discussed the complexities and challenges of interpreting Aboriginal rock art. Whilst the issue of interpretation remains a complex one, some astronomical/cultural research lends itself to analytical and scientific methods. For example, the Wurdi Youang Aboriginal stone arrangement in Victoria, Australia, has been analysed by Norris et al. (2013) for possible solar alignments and it is concluded that the evidence strongly suggests 'that the stone arrangement was deliberately intended by its builders to point to the setting Sun at the solstices and equinox'. The authors, however, take care not to claim Wurdi Youang as an 'Aboriginal observatory' (Norris et al. 2013: 63).

Aboriginal art often deals with subjects relating to 'Country' (the landscape) and some artworks present astronomical subjects, such as the Seven Sisters (The Pleiades) and the 'Emu in the sky', which represents the Emu (Goldsmith 1999). The Emu is Australia's largest flightless bird and stands approximately 1.7 metres tall. The Emu sky pattern is highly significant because it is recognised not by the patterns formed by a group of stars, but by the 'negative space' created by the absence of stars (formed by the dark dust lanes of the Milky Way, between the constellations Crux [Southern Cross] and Scorpius). Aboriginal artist Bonnie Deegan, from Halls Creek, expressed her story of the 'Emu in the sky' via artwork (Fig. 2), which she regards as a 'dreamtime' story. The 'Dreamtime', likewise referred to as 'the Dreaming', are generic terms that refer to a period of creation in which ancestral beings travelled across the landscape, giving form to the land itself. The Dreamtime can also be understood as a state of being (Willis 1996: 279). Other stories of the 'Emu in the sky' also relate the visibility of the Emu pattern and the actual behaviour of Emus on the ground. From the vantage of Australia's 'outback' (desert regions), the best views of the Emu in the sky typically occur when the moon is absent and when rains cleanse the atmosphere of dust. With such conditions, the 'Emu in the sky' stands out in striking contrast and is easily recognisable. As my previous research has shown, this timing also corresponds with when Emus lay their eggs, which are a sought-after food source (Goldsmith 1999).

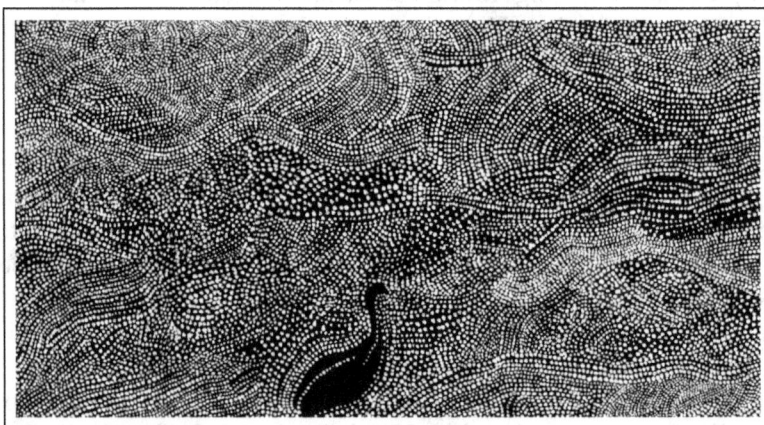

Figure 2. 'The Emu in the Sky' painting by Aboriginal elder Bonnie Deegan, Halls Creek. From the Cosmos, Culture and Landscape/ Goldsmith collection. Photo: © John Goldsmith.

Factors Contributing towards Aboriginal Astronomy Research

The first national symposium on Aboriginal Astronomy in Australia took place in 2009, at AIATSIS, Canberra, where several factors contributed towards renewed efforts to investigate the documentation, sharing, and communication of Australian Aboriginal sky knowledge. First, the role of Reconciliation in Australia set the basis for renewed efforts for improved cultural understanding and collaborations. Second, 2009 was declared the International Year of Astronomy, marking 400 years since Galileo turned his telescope skyward for astronomical observation. Many countries throughout the world showcased and celebrated astronomy, and diverse cultural interests and perspectives relating to astronomy were highlighted, including many historical and contemporary examples (International Astronomical Union 2010).

Coinciding with IYA 2009 was the continued development of the SKA radio telescope project, a major international astronomy initiative. The SKA project aims to investigate fundamental questions in cosmology and is described as 'an ultrasensitive radio telescope, built to further the understanding of the most important phenomena in the Universe, including some pertaining to the birth and eventual death of the Universe itself' (Dewdney et al. 2009: 1482). The SKA represents a major scientific initiative for the twenty-first century. Australia and Southern Africa were identified as the final two shortlisted candidate sites for the project. Ultimately, both candidate sites were selected for a shared project (SKAtelescope 2012). The extreme sensitivity of the radio antennas necessitated locations with very low artificial radio noise, which is why the SKA facilities are located in remote areas. A special characteristic of radio astronomy is its ability literally to see through interstellar dust clouds (which block visible light) to reveal distant astronomical sources, which would otherwise be obscured from view. Ironically, it is these same dust clouds in the Milky Way that are of particular significance to many Aboriginal communities in Australia.

The focus of SKA initiatives in Australia is the Murchison region of Western Australia, where the Murchison Radio-astronomy Observatory is located. Development of the SKA project is supported by the Australian SKA Pathfinder (ASKAP), which functions as a technology demonstrator for SKA development (Tingay et al. 2012). ASKAP comprises an array of 36 antennas, 12 metres in diameter. This facility is complimented by the Murchison Widefield Array, which consists of thousands of low frequency fixed radio antennas, spread across the outback landscape of the Murchison Radio-astronomy Observatory (Fig. 3). In Australia, Aboriginal support for the SKA project is evident in the historic Indigenous Land Use Agreement (ILUA), formally agreed to in 2009 (ANZSKA 2009). An example of the recognition of Wajarri Yamatji Aboriginal culture in the project is shown by the naming of the ASKAP antennas, in which each of the 36 antennas were formally given a Wajarri name. For example, Antenna 3 is known as Bundara (pronounced bun-da-ra), which means 'stars' and Antenna 8 is called Jirdilungu (jir-di-lu-ngu), which means Milky Way (CSIRO 2011).

Aboriginal astronomy research has also been supported by the advancement of digital imaging, exemplified by The World at Night (TWAN), an international network of astronomical landscape photographers. TWAN applied advanced digital imaging to document nocturnal landscapes throughout the world (Seip, Meiser, and Tafreshi 2010), and the greatly expanded capabilities of digital imaging cameras provided impetus to apply these methods to Aboriginal astronomy research.

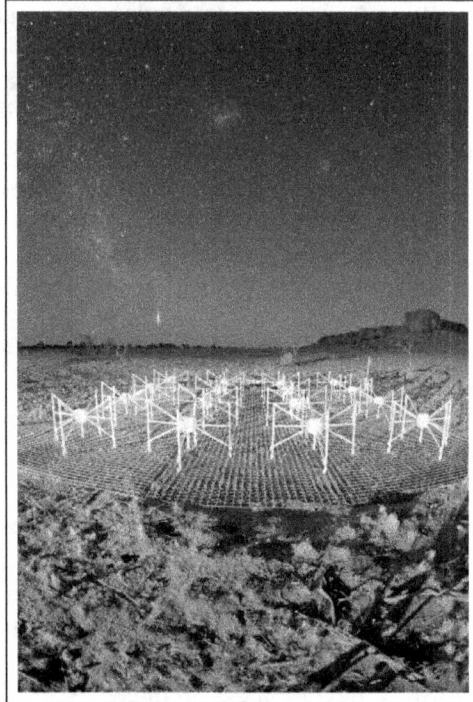

Figure 3. Radio astronomy dipole antennas (illuminated) at the Murchison Radio-astronomy Observatory. A scene from a timelapse sequence, showing the southern sky, Milky Way, Southern Cross, Magellanic Clouds, and a fireball meteor. Photo: © John Goldsmith.

Research Objectives

The Cosmos, Culture and Landscape project focussed on three main objectives: to investigate the variety of ways in which people engage with Australian Aboriginal astronomical knowledge in contemporary society; to gain an understanding of the issues and sensitivities regarding such cultural knowledge and reflect on the ways in which these issues can be addressed; and to collaborate with Aboriginal people to document and communicate in a culturally appropriate manner contemporary astronomical knowledge. Given the substantial diversity of Aboriginal cultures in Australia, the research focussed on three main geographical areas of Western Australia: the South West; the Mid West (Geraldton / Murchison) region; and the East Kimberley (Wolfe Creek Meteorite Crater) (Fig. 4). The first two geographical areas were selected as the locations coincided with the focus of the Australian radio astronomy initiatives (Square Kilometre Array radio telescope). The third location provided a special opportunity to investigate Aboriginal cultural knowledge of the night sky in relation to a major meteorite crater.

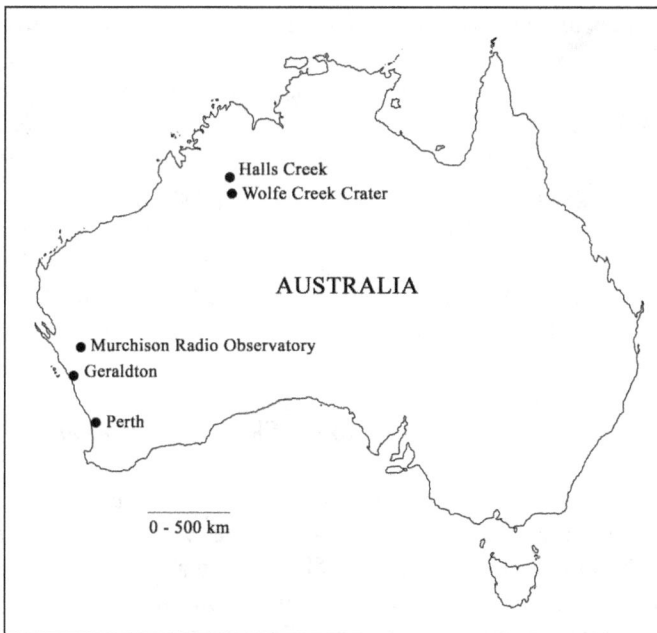

Figure 4. Location diagram showing Perth, Geraldton, the Murchison Radio-astronomy Observatory, Halls Creek, and Wolfe Creek Crater. Image: © John Goldsmith.

Research Methodologies

After gaining research ethics approval, the principal research methodology was to conduct video-based interviews with Aboriginal Elders and artists during site visits, resulting in detailed transcripts of discussions. I conducted interviews for the Cosmos, Culture and Landscape project between 2010 and 2011 and also transcribed and analysed interviews that I conducted during previous site visits to Wolfe Creek Crater, which commenced in 1998. The interview results were comprehensively presented for the first time in Goldsmith (2014). The flexibility provided by the use of interviews was important, as this enabled complex subjects to be explored over time, and progressive layers of meaning to emerge from discussions. Site visits enabled extensive digital photography to be conducted on site, including the use of techniques such as astronomical timelapse photography and spherical (360° by 180°) imaging. These techniques have developed a substantial digital photographic record of the sites. Another important source of information was Aboriginal artwork and drawings made by Aboriginal elders and artists, which helped to express different aspects of Aboriginal astronomical knowledge.

The project gained appropriate permissions, respected sensitive cultural information, and addressed intellectual property in accordance with the wishes of participants. The research also took into account the issue of Aboriginal people who had recently passed away, as in parts of Australia the name (and image) of a deceased person is avoided for a period of time after death. Finally, there were practical issues of conducting fieldwork in remote areas, which included travel and logistics, to ensure well-planned and safe operations.

The Ilgarijiri—Things Belonging to the Sky *Collaboration*

Ilgarijiri means 'things belonging to the sky' in the local Wajarri Yamatji language (Tingay 2011: 203). The very name of *Ilgarijiri* indicates the importance of a sense of belonging and relationships, rather than a sense of individual ownership of astronomical knowledge. The *Ilgarijiri* project developed out of a collaboration between Yamaji Arts (Geraldton, Western Australia) and the International Centre for Radio Astronomy Research (ICRAR), under the leadership of Professor Steven Tingay. Radio astronomers and research scientists involved in the SKA project met with Aboriginal Elders and artists during site visits at Boolardy Station, the site of the Murchison Radio-astronomy Observatory and the Australian SKA Pathfinder project. The site visits involved an exchange and sharing of knowledge, and the gathering of ideas and material. This later formed the basis of the *Ilgarijiri* art exhibition (Tingay 2011; Drok 2009/10; Brophy 2009). After the site visits, artists and Elders continued to explore and learn about the night sky and developed artworks along several broad themes: traditional Aboriginal stories about the night sky; representations of the night sky, as experienced during site visits; paintings that record journeys and site visits to Boolardy Station; and other themes.

During the *Ilgarijiri* project, the participants considered how to deal with sensitive cultural knowledge and the general question about the right of Aboriginal people to share stories via art. The then manager of Yamaji Art, Charmaine Green, explained:

> Well, anything with the sky is sort of culturally problematic and it took the committee at least eight months to even say yeh, we will go there. It took them a long time sitting in with the board, throwing it back and forth, shall we do this? Are we doing the right thing? Are we going to get in trouble? What sort of stories? But then the positive side of it out-weighed that because there is not a lot of opportunities to tell stories to the wider public and not enough opportunities to tell stories to our kids or our community, so that side of it, sort of... People knew their boundaries. They knew that there is stories connected to the sky that they can't tell, and they won't tell.

Margaret Whitehurst, a Yamatji artist, first reacted with scepticism and doubt regarding the *Ilgarijiri* exhibition concept. Her views were trans-formed, however, when she experienced the views of the night sky, the use of a telescope, and the interaction with radio astronomy scientists:

> Well, when I first started I thought, oh, well nah...it was going to be boring. I thought it was going to be boring. Nah...I haven't got much stories of the sky. When they first approached us and said that we are going to do these stories about the sky, look I don't know much about stories in the sky. All I knew was about this Emu in the sky and Charmaine and Kathryn said: You go out and you look at the sky and you will see, so we did, and we went out and I just couldn't believe all the things that we saw in the sky, you know. I didn't even know even half of the things that was in the sky, because we didn't look for them things. All we did was look for the seven sisters, and the pot in the sky, what they used to tell us, the seven sisters, the emu in the sky, that was it. I didn't know any more, till I saw the ones in the sky. Now I think I could do more stories of it, you know tell more stories about it. Just looking... through the telescope, into the sky, yeh. It's really given me a lot of things that I can go back, and well, I went back and told my kids and my grandkids all about it, but they didn't believe me. They didn't believe there were that many things in the sky. Yeh...

During one of the Boolardy Station site visits, collaborations between scientists, artists, and Elders allowed participants to share their knowledge amongst the group. Several of the artists commented about their experience of the Boolardy Station visit, and the experience of interacting with radio astronomy scientists. As Kevin Merritt describes:

> I thought that was very positive, because we were able to relate our stories, in the… They were able to show close-up views of the constellations that we looked at over our life, we could see that even though we thought it was just a star, it was another constellation, you know. It just blows your mind away…
>
> To be able to have their [the astronomers] expertise tell us about all these things, and I think some of the older people learnt a great deal more than what they knew before, about the stars and the constellations, about where we fit in, our own little world, where we fit in this great cosmos we live in.

The excitement of a practical viewing night, in a group setting, and the sharing of knowledge out in the country was clearly expressed by Margaret Whitehurst:

> …and that night when we went home back to the station, sat around a big campfire and we told stories, and we even pointed out the sky, they saw the emu in the sky that night we pointed out up in the sky and the non-Indigenous people couldn't… They got so excited when they saw the emu in the sky. Yeh, they really…they couldn't believe it… We'll show you the emu in the sky when it gets dark and we showed it to them…they just couldn't believe it because we saw it plain as anything out there at Boolardy. And all the stars, it was so…and Mr Tingay showed us a lot of other things that he saw, that we can see up in the sky and what we never seen before, that's where I saw a lot in the sky that night. I can't remember all the names but, because they were, some of them weren't Australian, so, but really enjoyed Boolardy. A good trip. It was wonderful out there, yeh.

However, the anticipation of interacting with astronomers and scientists did cause some anxiousness on the part of some Aboriginal participants, as expressed by Charmaine Green:

> But um, everyone was quite anxious on how we were going to interact and how we were going to connect with the astronomers but the good thing was people like talking about the sky and just like looking at the stars. So the connection there was when the sun came down, people had lots to talk about.

Many of the artists and Elders commented about the way in which the exhibition and collaboration affected them, primarily as a learning process. Charmaine Green reported examples of self-motivated informal learning:

> ...Doing checks on the internet, thinking what's this about, reading more stories. People were finding videos about astronomy. We had about twelve people sitting in my lounge room one night, just looking at this video on the universe, the sky and the planets, so it just opened a whole wide world of different discussions, and looking at the night sky.

Learnings from the Ilgarijiri *Collaboration*

The *Ilgarijiri—Things Belonging to the Sky* project provided a cross-cultural experience in which scientific knowledge and Aboriginal cultural knowledge was shared, interaction between people encouraged, and creative works of art developed and exhibited. The collaboration proved to be very successful. The use of video interviews as a research method proved to be highly effective as a method to document the experiences of participants. Aboriginal Elders and artists felt that the project was of value to them, suggesting that the project encouraged significant informal learning amongst participants, and provided a way of 'taking back' or reclaiming the right of Aboriginal people to tell and share their stories. It is clear that participants experienced the project in a very positive way, in part because it encouraged the recognition and celebration of Aboriginal knowledge, under their own management and direction, and provided a way of sharing such knowledge in an engaging way via the artworks with the broader Australian and international community.

The *Ilgarijiri* exhibition resulted from this interaction and represented Western Australia's largest Aboriginal art exhibition primarily based on astronomical themes. The first phase of the *Ilgarijiri* exhibition presented more than eighty artworks from thirty Aboriginal artists from the Murchison region, centred on Geraldton. Many of the artworks showed the diversity of styles used to represent astronomical subjects. The story of the Seven Sisters (Pleiades) was a strong theme, in addition to the 'Emu in the sky' pattern. Artworks included both traditional and modern styles (Fig. 5).

Figure 5. The Ilgarijiri Exhibition at Curtin University, Western Australia, 2009. Photo: © John Goldsmith.

The *Ilgarijiri—Things Belonging to the Sky* exhibition has been adapted and developed over time into several exhibitions since its first public exhibition in June 2009. Eight exhibitions have occurred to date, including exhibitions in Australia (Geraldton, Perth, and Canberra) (Fig. 6), South Africa (Cape Town), United States (Washington, DC), Netherlands (The Hague), Belgium (Brussels), and Germany (Berlin). The exhibition's showing in Canberra in 2009 coincided with the opening of the first national Indigenous Astronomy Symposium, hosted at the Australian Institute for Aboriginal and Torres Strait Islander Studies (AIATSIS), Canberra (AIATSIS 2011).

Figure 6. Wajarri Elder Teddo Ryan (left), and Kevin Merritt (right), at the opening of the *Ilgarijiri—Things Belonging to the Sky* exhibition at Curtin University, Western Australia, 2009. Photo: © John Goldsmith.

Finally, the *Ilgarijiri—Things Belonging to the Sky* project enabled radio astronomers alongside Aboriginal communities and artists to experience the night sky together and to share their respective knowledge in the context of the development of major radio astronomy initiatives in the Murchison region of Western Australia. The development of the exhibition enabled Aboriginal artists to express their understanding creatively to a local, national, and international audience. Having examined collaborations between Aboriginal communities and radio astronomers, we now examine Aboriginal knowledge associated with a meteorite crater.

Meteorite Craters

The Earth Impact Database provides a worldwide listing of known meteorite impact sites. Fewer than 200 meteorite craters and impact sites are listed on the database (PASSC 2011), with twenty-six impact sites listed in Australia. However, recent discoveries, such as the Hickman Crater (Glickson, Hickman, and Vickers 2008) in Western Australia have not yet been listed. Alex Bevan and Ken McNamara indicate thirty impact sites in Australia, with seven additional structures (lacking conclusive proof of meteoritic origin), and a further twelve 'enigmatic structures under investigation' (Bevan and McNamara 2009: 45). This context indicates that there are relatively few meteorite impact structures known globally. The presence of Wolfe Creek Crater in Western Australia provides an opportunity to investigate Aboriginal perspectives relating to a meteorite crater, in the broader context of Aboriginal astronomical and sky knowledge. The crater has been incorporated into Aboriginal knowledge and creative endeavours, which are examined below.

Kandimalal, Wolfe Creek Crater

'Kandimalal' is the Jaru Aboriginal name of Wolfe Creek Crater, one of the best-preserved and most spectacular meteorite craters in the world and a highly significant site for scientific research (Fig. 7). The site is one of the few locations in the world where local Aboriginal knowledge and culture relate directly to a meteorite crater (Hamacher and Goldsmith 2013). The crater is often incorrectly described as the second largest meteorite crater in the world, whereas Bevan and McNamara (2009) described the crater more precisely as the second largest impact crater from which meteorite fragments have been recovered. The crater is now protected as a National Park and is managed by the Department of Parks and Wildlife (Western Australia). Furthermore, the site has become an important tourist attraction. Although studied by numerous scientists, the cultural significance of the crater is only now beginning to be more fully appreciated. The crater is situated at latitude 19° 10' 18.2" S and 127° 47' 43.56" E, in the East Kimberley region of Western Australia, approximately 130 km south of Halls Creek, on the edge of the Great Sandy Desert. It is located on a vast flat plain north east of the junction of two river systems, Wolfe Creek and Sturt Creek, which join to drain into an extensive lake system called Lake Paraku (Lake Gregory) (Bevan 1996; Goldsmith 2000).

Figure 7. Aerial view of Kandimalal, Wolfe Creek Crater. 1999. Photo: © John Goldsmith.

Formation of Wolfe Creek Crater

Planetary scientists note that 'projectiles usually less than a few tens of metres in diameter produce "simple", bowl shaped craters with raised rims, like Wolfe Creek (Crater)...' (Bevan and De Laeter 2002: 173).

Such projectiles weigh in the order of thousands of tonnes. The tremendous speed of the meteor on impact caused a massive blast, comparable in force to a nuclear explosion, creating the near-circular Wolfe Creek Crater, almost 900 metres in diameter and 150 metres deep. The impact probably occurred more than 300,000 years ago (Bevan and McNamara 2009: 41). Since then, the process of erosion has slowly worn down the crater walls. Wind-blown sand and dust has partially filled the crater floor. The crater walls remain quite steep, and in places there are sheer cliffs, particularly on the inner side of the northeastern crater wall. The crater walls presently stand up to about thirty-five metres above the surrounding flat plain, and the almost flat crater floor is fifty-five metres deep, about twenty metres below the surrounding plain. The outer portion of the crater floor is sandy, while the central portion consists of encrusted salt deposits. Soakwaters, also referred to as sink-holes, are located near the middle of the crater, and some water is present virtually all the year. Vegetation in the base of the crater has also formed in a distinctive partial arc, and the central salty region is ringed by low trees. Although some small iron meteorite fragments have been discovered in the vicinity of the crater, very few particles of the original meteorite have survived. During the millennia that have passed since the impact, the meteorite fragments have largely rusted away, and, in more recent times, people have removed much of this material.

Aboriginal People and the Crater

Aboriginal people have known about the crater for a long time. The first confirmed non-Aboriginal recognition of the crater occurred in 1947. F. Reeves, N.B. Suave, and D. Hart observed the crater from the air during an aerial survey of the Canning basin in 1947 (Bevan and McNamara 2009: 20). A field visit took place two months later. After the first reports of the crater, speculation developed about its origin, whether it was of volcanic or meteoric origin (e.g. Leonard 1949a, b). There is at least one claim of an earlier 'discovery' of the crater by a non-Aboriginal person. Ronele and Eric Gard noted: 'Constable A.J. Jones of Halls Creek, the trooper...claims he was shown the crater by a black tracker as early as 1935, but he could not prove his claim' (Gard and Gard 1995: 434). US Anthropologist Peggy Reeves Sanday (daughter of Frank Reeves, 'co-discoverer' of the crater) visited the crater in the late 1990s and developed an exhibition of Aboriginal art that featured the crater.

Her book, *Aboriginal Paintings of the Wolfe Creek Crater, Track of the Rainbow Serpent* (Sanday 2007) presents the story of her personal connection to the crater, her interactions with contemporary Aboriginal people, and the exhibition of Aboriginal art relating to the crater.

The main Aboriginal language groups in the vicinity of the crater are the Jaru, the Ngarti (to the south east), the Kukatja (south west including Sturt Creek and Lake Paraku), Walmatjarri (west), and the Warlpiri (east of the crater) (Horton 1996). The crater itself lies at the approximate boundary of three language groups, the Jaru, Kukatja, and the Ngarti. Whilst English is widely spoken, many Aboriginal people are also multilingual. Since many language groups in the Kimberley are based on small populations, local languages are at risk of decline and loss. As a result, there have been significant efforts to document and maintain local languages, such as the work by the Halls Creek based Kimberley Language Resource Centre (Wrigley 1992). Population density is extremely low and the nearest permanently occupied settlement to the crater is the Billiluna community, some 70 km south west of the crater, with a population of approximately 200 people. Halls Creek is the nearest major town (about 130 kilometres to the north of the crater); in 2014, it had a population of some 3000 residents.

Oral Accounts of Kandimalal, Wolfe Creek Crater and Representation in Aboriginal Art

The crater features prominently in the art of several Aboriginal artists (Fig. 8), including such notable artists as Stan Brumby (deceased 2012) and Barbara Sturt. Knowledge about the crater comprises stories and accounts of its origin (despite the actual age of the crater far exceeding that of known human occupation in Australia). Other stories refer to the role of meteors, which reveal an unexpected practice of 'listening to the shaking country' after a large meteor has been seen. Large meteors are also interpreted as indicating the death of a person. Additionally there is a range of stories that relate to the physical form of the crater, and in particular to the soakwaters in the central salt-encrusted crater floor. The strikingly circular form of the crater is reinforced by the appearance of the roughly circular salty area in the centre. The concentric partial arc of vegetation on the crater floor, and the circular pattern of the crater are shown in several Aboriginal artworks of the crater.

Figure 8. Aboriginal paintings featuring Kandimalal, Wolfe Creek Crater. Top row: (*left*) Crate landscape (*right*) crater, paintings by Stan Brumby. Central row: Three representations of 'the star falling to the earth', paintings by Stan Brumby. Lower row: Representations of the crater and nearby Wolfe and Sturt Creek (paintings by Barbara Sturt). *Photo*: From the Cosmos, Culture and Landscape / Goldsmith collection. Reproduced by permission / Yarliyil Art Centre.

Our video interviews with Elders Jack Jugarie (Fig. 9) and Stan Brumby (both of whom are now deceased), provided particular insight into Aboriginal knowledge about the crater. Jack Jugarie's account of the origin of the crater takes the form of an eye-witness narrative:

Well, this thing been fall, well, the Blackfellas reckon in the early days, the first mob, you know, they never saw any white people, or anyone, they only know their own colour, you know, like us. They reckon, star, second star from the big one, you know, been fall. Well we call him wada, that star. Wada it been fall in this ground and it makes big noise and shakes this country and...made a round, what's a name, rim right round, and he made a hole...there, and in the centre, down there, it's a hole there, no water stay in there. Doesn't matter how much rain can be here, the water don't stay here in the middle, it goes in the hole, and come out through down there, where we came, inside... Yeh, sink holes, right in the middle.

Well, when this thing been fall, in those days, and it made a great big
hole, and right in the centre it made another big hole. And I think that
powerful that thing been fall inside, when it hit the ground, that half a
piece would go inside, see, and made a big hole inside there and the water
don't stay there; it go down the creek, from a little hole, you know, make
'im bigger and bigger, every rain come bigger and bigger inside,... hole.
Water don't stay there,...that big rain...water don't stay, it go inside, go
down to the river. Inside now...

From my old grandfather told me, yeh, Father Mike, yeh, from those
one, and they got the word from their father (Grandfather Mike, and
grandmother), from their father, and that father with them, he told by his
father again, all the way like that, that word from the beginning, come
little by little it come right up big, right up to us fella... I don't know
from how many years, how long Blackfella been living here? From that
time, that story.

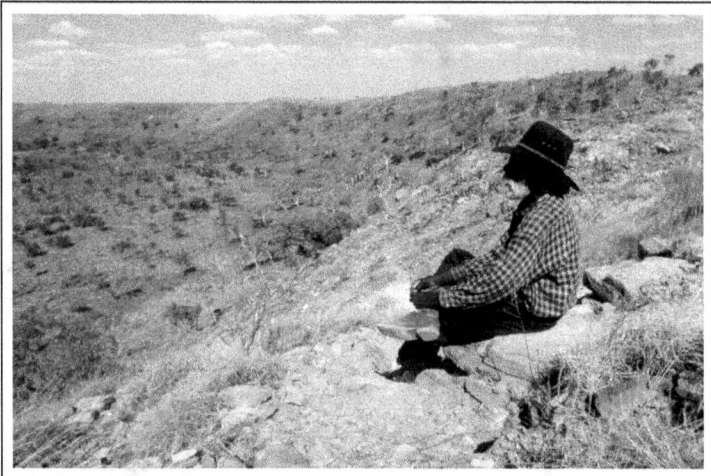

Figure 9. Jaru Aboriginal elder Jack Jugarie, at Kandimalal, Wolfe Creek
Crater, 1999, approximately one month before he passed away. Photo: ©
John Goldsmith.

The Star Falling Down Song

Stan Brumby's song of the crater and the 'falling star' is a rhythmic,
repetitive and brief song, made up of only three words: 'warda' (star)
'wandinga' (fall down), and 'morungai' (the ground). His song was
recorded and features in the Cosmology Gallery video exhibit, which is
discussed later. A transcription of Stan Brumby's song follows:

Warda wandinga
Warda wandinga morungai
Warda wandinga
Warda wandinga morungai
Warda wandinga
Warda wandinga
Warda wandinga morungai
Warda wandinga
Warda wandinga morungai
Warda wandinga
Warda wandinga
Warda wandinga morungai
Warda wandinga
Warda wandinga morungai
Warda wandinga
Warda wandinga morungai
Warda wandinga
Warda wandinga

How and from where such a song develops was unknown, until Elder Stan Brumby explained that much of his knowledge of culture came to him via dreams (not to be confused with the concept of the 'Dreamtime'):

> Yeh I can hear him, I can dream him. When I sleep, I dream, they give me…culture. Song, everything. Song… Yeh, I can dream. Like you got to come and dream and talk to me, 'Hello, Stan Brumby', 'Hullo', like that, I'm talking to you 'Hullo', dreaming, I dreaming you,… I'm dreaming like that, you talking to me, dreaming, they talk to me, they give that…culture, I sing that in the next morning, I sing him. In the night, in the morning. I sing him, this one, this one, this one, finish, you see. Same as that morning star. Morrungo been giving me that song, with the language, right there, I've been camped right there, in the crater. Take a photo…camp there, I've been dreaming at the same time. I've been looking at the place, from top, high, crater…

Stan Brumby's description of the role of subconscious states via sleep provides an important insight into the source of his knowledge.

Digital Imaging as a Means of Site Documentation

Recent advances in digital imaging and photographic image processing have substantially extended the capabilities and application of digital photographic cameras and there are now a wide range of digital photographic techniques available to support site documentation. Kandimalal,

Wolfe Creek Crater, provides a prime example of Aboriginal knowledge of the night sky being closely associated with knowledge about the land itself. The terrestrial context of a given site can therefore support a fuller understanding and appreciation of Aboriginal sky knowledge.

Timelapse and spherical imaging techniques were most extensively applied in the Cosmos, Culture and Landscape project, using methods described in my previous research (Goldsmith 2011a). Results from the digital imaging include timelapse sequences of the nocturnal landscape of Wolfe Creek Crater. These sequences have been produced as video clips (several of which are featured at The World at Night, htttp://www.twanight.org). Another product derived from these sequences is 'star trail' images (Fig. 10). For the Cosmos, Culture and Landscape project, twenty-one spherical (360° by 180°) images were recorded, including ten at Wolfe Creek Crater. One example is provided below (Fig. 11) from the vantage point of half way down the inside of the western crater wall. High definition video clips have been generated from the spherical (360° by 180°) imaging. This approach was used to create a smooth pan and tilt scene, featuring the crater and its rim. The extensive video interviews and digital imaging, including conventional photography, astronomical timelapse, and spherical (360° by 180°) imaging, provided the basis for creating new resources, which have been used to share and communicate Aboriginal sky knowledge.

Figure 10. Southern stars and the South Celestial Pole, above Kandimalal, Wolfe Creek Crater. Timelapse sequence photographed from the northern rim of the crater, looking south. Star trail image generated using www.startrails.de software. Photo: © John Goldsmith.

Figure 11. 360° by 180° image (spherical photo mosaic) of Kandimalal,
Wolfe Creek Crater, taken from approximately half-way down the inner
crater rim (western side). Photo: © John Goldsmith.

Communicating Aboriginal Sky Knowledge via New Resources:
The Cosmology Gallery Video Exhibit

The Cosmology Gallery, at Western Australia's Gravity Discovery
Centre, presents new visual interpretations of the cosmos, from cultural
and scientific perspectives including Indigenous, Christian, Buddhist,
Islamic, and Hindu traditions (Goldsmith 2011b; Gravity Discovery
Centre Foundation 2008). The late Emeritus Professor John De Laeter
played a critical role in the development of the Gravity Discovery Centre
and was chairperson of the Gravity Discovery Centre Foundation, since
its inception through to 2010. De Laeter conducted substantial research
in relation to meteorites, and one of his publications, *Meteorites: A
Journey through Space and Time*, prominently featured Wolfe Creek
Crater (Bevan and De Laeter 2002). In 2010, the Gravity Discovery
Centre Foundation established the De Laeter scholarship, in recognition
of De Laeter's contributions to science in Western Australia. In early
2011, the Cosmos, Culture and Landscape project was awarded the
inaugural De Laeter Tertiary Scholarship for Science Engagement. The
scholarship enabled the development of an eight-minute video exhibit for
the Cosmology Gallery. The exhibit presented both scientific and
Aboriginal perspectives about Kandimalal, Wolfe Creek Crater, and
featured Aboriginal Elders Jack Jugarie and Stan Brumby, who shared

views about Wolfe Creek Crater. The video used visually engaging methods and advanced imaging techniques for the production. The production applied appropriate cultural standards regarding the video content and featured a strong link to the research interests of the late Emeritus Professor De Laeter. The exhibit was also developed to relate to the practical scientific gravity experiments and demonstrations conducted at the Leaning Tower, Gravity Discovery Centre. The video production is part of the permanent collection of the Cosmology Gallery.

A Virtual Aboriginal Astronomy Tour

The Cosmos, Culture and Landscape project developed a DVD virtual tour, based on the digital imaging of Wolfe Creek Crater, the Murchison Radio-astronomy Observatory, and various sites of importance regarding Aboriginal astronomy, including the *Ilgarijiri* exhibition. Virtual tours provided a valuable educational tool by delivering a realistic, navigable visual environment of sites and locations, enabling audiences to experience remote sites and landscapes that would otherwise be difficult to access. Collaboration with Questacon resulted in the virtual tour being used as an educational tool in a live video link to schools and students across Australia.

Conclusions

The Cosmos, Culture and Landscape project identified numerous examples of publically available Australian Aboriginal astronomical and sky knowledge. Collaborative, cross-cultural projects such as *Ilgarijiri— Things Belonging to the Sky* shows that such projects can act as important catalysts to encourage the appreciation and respect of Aboriginal and scientific astronomical knowledge. In addition, it is clear that cultural astronomy and Aboriginal sky knowledge can be used as a contemporary tool to support Aboriginal and non-Aboriginal learning and education. Insights regarding issues and sensitivities about Aboriginal sky knowledge and the ways in which these issues can be addressed help to inform future research and collaborative initiatives. Conducting interviews with Elders associated with Wolfe Creek Crater was a high priority, due to the risk of loss of knowledge from the passing of Elders. The urgency to conduct this research was borne out during the project when key Elders associated with the crater passed away after irreplaceable documentary interviews had been recorded. Had this research not taken place, it is highly likely that the Aboriginal astronomical knowledge understood by these Elders would have never been documented, and therefore never have been recognised or appreciated. The participants and family members generously provided permission for the use of such knowledge in this research.

The collaboration with Aboriginal people to document and communicate contemporary astronomical knowledge led to the development of new resources, including a video exhibit and a virtual tour. Digital imaging was used as a site documentation method, with extensive use of 360° imaging. Ultimately the Cosmos, Culture and Landscape project contributed towards a new appreciation of the value, importance and significance of Aboriginal sky knowledge, the ways in which such knowledge can bring Aboriginal and non-Aboriginal people together, and how we can all respectfully honour the sharing of such knowledge.

Acknowledgments

This chapter is based on the PhD thesis entitled 'Cosmos, Culture and Landscape' by John Goldsmith (2014). The research was conducted at the Curtin Institute of Radio Astronomy and the International Centre for Radio Astronomy Research, Curtin University, Western Australia, under the supervision of Professor Steven Tingay (ICRAR), Kevin Cameron, Aboriginal Elder, and Professor Ray Norris, CSIRO. Research Ethics approval (RD 10-15) was provided by the Curtin University Research Ethics Committee. The support and participation of many individuals and organisations is gratefully acknowledged, including the Aboriginal Elders and artists featured (credited within the text), the Centre for Aboriginal Studies, Curtin University, the Western Australian Department of Aboriginal Affairs, Department of Environment and Conservation (now Department of Parks and Wildlife), Yamaji Art, Scitech/ Horizon Planetarium, Gingin Observatory, Scientists in Schools, CSIRO Education, Gravity Discovery Centre Foundation, Australian Institute of Aboriginal and Torres Strait Islander Studies (AIATSIS), Western Australian Museum, The World at Night, and Astronomers without Borders.

References

ANZSKA. 2009. 'Indigenous Land Use Agreement Complete', ANZSKA Newsletter no. 25, December 2009: 1. Online: http://www.ska.gov.au/multimedia/Documents/ Publications/anzSKANewsletterArchive/anzska_25_hr.pdf (accessed 10 March 2014).

Australian Bureau of Statistics. 2002. 'Mortality of Aboriginal and Torres Strait Islander Peoples, Mortality and Morbidity', in *Australian Bureau of Statistics* (Canberra, Australia: Bureau of Statistics): 86-90. Online: http://www.ausstats.abs.gov.au/ Ausstats/subscriber.nsf/0/C0A01711EAD911BFCA256BCD007D7F10/$File/ 41020_2002.pdf (accessed 9 February 2014).

Australian Government Director of National Parks. 2010. *Uluru-Kata Tjuta National Park, Management Plan 2010–2020. Tjukurpa Katutja Ngarantja* (Canberra: Director of National Parks). Online: http://www.environment.gov.au/system/ files/resources/f7d3c167-8bd1-470a-a502-ba222067e1ac/files/management-plan.pdf (accessed 31 March 2014).

Australian Institute of Aboriginal and Torres Strait Islander Studies. 2011. 'Ilgarijiri— Things Belonging to the Sky', Australian Institute of Aboriginal and Torres Strait Islander Studies. Online: http://www.aiatsis.gov.au/events/ilgarijir (accessed 22 November 2011).

Australian Institute of Aboriginal and Torres Strait Islander Studies. 2012. 'The Aboriginal Flag'. Online: http://www.aiatsis.gov.au/fastfacts/aboriginalflag.html (accessed 10 January 2012).

Bednarik, Robert G. 2011. 'Ethnographic Analogy in Rock Art Interpretation'. Online: http://home.vicnet.net.au/~auranet/interpret/web/index.html (accessed 1 March 2012).

Belmonte, Juan A. 2011. 'In Search of Cosmic Order: Astronomy and Culture in Ancient Egypt', in Valls-Gabaud and Boksenberg 2011: 74-86.

Bevan, Alex. 1996. 'A Blast from the Past', *Landscope Magazine* 12.1 (Western Australia: Department of Conservation and Land Management).

Bevan, Alex, and John De Laeter. 2002, *Meteorites: A Journey through Space and Time* (Sydney: University of New South Wales Press).

Bevan, Alex, and Ken McNamara. 2009. *Australia's Meteorite Craters* (Perth: Western Australian Museum).

Brophy, Lindy. 2009. 'Opening the Skies to the Past and the Future'. *UWA News* 28.14:1, 8-9 (Nedlands: University of Western Australia).

Cairns, Hugh, and Bill Harney. 2003. *Dark Sparklers, Yidumduma's Aboriginal Astronomy* (Sydney: Hugh Cairns).

Clarke, Philip. 1998. 'The Study of Ethnoastronomy in Australia', *Essays from Archaeoastronomy and Ethnoastronomy News, The Quarterly Bulletin of the Centre for Archaeoastronomy*, no. 29, September Equinox. Online: http://terpconnect. umd.edu/~tlaloc/archastro/ae29.html#PUBS (accessed 10 October 2009).

Commonwealth of Australia. 2005. *National Indigenous Languages Survey Report 2005* (Acton, ACT: Department of Communications, Information Technology and the Arts). Online: http://arts.gov.au/sites/default/files/pdfs/nils-report-2005.pdf (accessed 10 March 2014).

Council for Aboriginal Reconciliation Act. 1991. (Commonwealth). Online: http://www.austlii.edu.au/cgi-bin/download.cgi/cgibin/download.cgi/download/au/legis/cth/num_act/cfara1991338.txt (accessed 10 February 2014).

Council for Aboriginal Reconciliation (Australia). 2000. *Reconciliation, Australia's Challenge: Final Report of the Council for Aboriginal Reconciliation to the Prime Minister and the Commonwealth Parliament* (Kingston, ACT: Council for Aboriginal Reconciliation). Online: http://www.austlii.edu.au/au/other/IndigLRes/car/2000/16/ (accessed 10 October 2009).

CSIRO. 2011. 'Aboriginal Community Names CSIRO Telescope'. Online: http://www.csiro.au/Portals/Media/2011/Aboriginal-community-names-CSIRO-telescope.aspx (accessed 1 December 2013).

Dewdney, Peter E., Peter J. Hall, Richard. T. Schilizzi, and T. Joseph L.W. Lazio. 2009. 'The Square Kilometre Array', *Proceedings of the IEEE* 97.8: 1482-96.

Drok, Kelly. 2009/10. 'Paint the Sky with Stars', *CITE, The Magazine of Curtin University of Technology* 15 (Summer): 12-13.

Gard, Ronele, and Eric Gard. 1995. *Canning Stock Route, a Traveller's Guide*, 2nd ed. (Wembley Downs: Western Desert Guides).

Gillespie, Richard. 2002. 'Dating the First Australians', *Radiocarbon* 44.2: 455-72.

Glickson, A.Y., A.H. Hickman, and J. Vickers. 2008. 'Hickman Crater, Ophthalmia Range, Western Australia: Evidence Supporting a Meteorite Impact Origin', *Australian Journal of Earth Sciences* 55.8: 1107-17.

Goldsmith, John. 1999. 'The Emu in the Sky', *Australian Geographic, The Journal of the Australian Geographic Society* 55: 19.

———. 2000. 'Cosmic Impacts in the Kimberley', *Landscope Magazine* 15.3: 28-34.

———. 2011a. 'Documenting Natural and Cultural Places with 360° Spherical Images, Panoramic and Timelapse Digital Photography', *Rock Art Research* 28.1:123-27.

———. 2011b. 'The Cosmology Gallery, Unity through Diversity in a Vast and Awe Inspiring Universe', *Proceedings IAU Symposium no. 260*, 5.

———. 2014. 'Cosmos, Culture and Landscape: Documenting, Learning and Sharing Aboriginal Astronomical Knowledge in Contemporary Society' (PhD diss., Curtin University).

Gravity Discovery Centre Foundation. 2008. *The Cosmology Gallery: Unity through Diversity in a Vast and Awe Inspiring Universe* (Western Australia: Gravity Discovery Centre Foundation).

Hamacher, Duane, and John Goldsmith. 2013. 'Aboriginal Oral Traditions of Australian Impact Craters', *Journal of Astronomical History and Heritage* 16.3: 295-311.

Horton, D.R. 1996. *Aboriginal Australia Wall Map* (Aboriginal Studies Press).

International Astronomical Union. 2010. *International Year of Astronomy 2009 Final Report*, ed. Pedro Russo and Christensen L. Lindberg (UNESCO/IAU). Online: http://www.astronomy2009.org/resources/documents/detail/iya2009_final_report/ (accessed 15 January 2014).

Keating, Paul. 1992. *Redfern Speech (Year for the World's Indigenous People)— Delivered in Redfern Park by Prime Minister Paul Keating, 10 December 1992* (Transcript), https://antar.org.au/sites/default/files/paul_keating_speech_transcript.pdf (accessed 10 March 2014).

King, Phillip. 1827. *Narrative of a Survey of the Intertropical and Western Coasts of Australia, Performed between the Years 1818 and 1822*, vol. II (London: John Murray).

Kochhar, Rajesh. 2011. 'Scriptures, Science and Mythology: Astronomy in Indian Cultures', in Valls-Gabaud and Boksenberg 2011: 54-61.

Krupp, E.C. 1997. *Skywatchers, Shamans and Kings* (New York: John Wiley & Sons).

Leonard, Frederick. C. 1949a. 'Is the Crater of Wolf Creek, Western Australia (-1278,193) Meteoritic?' *Popular Astronomy* 57: 138-40.

———. 1949b. 'Further Evidence Concerning the Wolf Creek, Western Australia, Crater (-1278, 192)', *Popular Astronomy,* 57: 405-406.

Norris, Ray, and Cilla Norris. 2009. *Emu Dreaming: An Introduction to Aboriginal Astronomy* (Sydney: Emu Dreaming).

Norris, Ray, Cilla Norris, Duane Hamacher, and Reg Abrahams. 2013. 'Wurdi Youang: An Australian Aboriginal Stone Arrangement with Possible Solar Indications', *Rock Art Research* 30.1: 55-65.

Planetary and Space Science Centre. 2011. Earth Impact Database: Planetary and Space Science Centre. Online: http://www.passc.net/EarthImpactDatabase/index.html (accessed 20 July 2011).

Sanday, Peggy. 2007. *Aboriginal Paintings of Wolfe Creek Crater: Track of the Rainbow Serpent* (Pennsylvania: University of Pennsylvania Museum, Museum of Archaeology and Anthropology).

Seip, Stefan, Gernot Meiser, and Babak Tafreshi. 2010. *Zauber der Sterne* (*Magic of the Stars*) (Stuttgart: Kosmos).

SKAtelescope. 2012. 'Dual Site Agreed for Square Kilometre Array Telescope', 25 May. Online: http://www.skatelescope.org/news/dual-site-agreed-square-kilometre-array-telescope/ (accessed 28 May 2012).

Šprajc, Ivan. 2011. 'Astronomy and its Role in Ancient Mesoamerica', in Valls-Gabaud and Boksenberg 2011: 87-95.

Stanbridge, W.E. 1858, 'On the Astronomy and Mythology of the Aborigines of Victoria', *Transactions of the Philosophical Institute of Victoria* 2: 137-40 (Melbourne).

Tingay, Steven J. 2011. '*Ilgarijiri*—Things Belonging to the Sky: Connecting Australian Indigenous Artists and Astrophysicists', *The International Journal of the Arts in Society* 6.1: 203-11.

Tingay, S.J., R. Goeke, J.D. Bowman, D. Emrich, S.M. Ord, D.A. Mitchell, M.F. Morales et al. 2012. 'The Murchison Widefield Array: The Square Kilometre Array Precursor at Low Frequencies', *Publications of the Astronomical Society of Australia.* arXiv:1206.6945v1.

Valls-Gabaud, D., and A. Boksenberg, eds. 2011. *The Role of Astronomy in Society and Culture*, Proceedings of the International Astronomical Union (Cambridge: Cambridge University Press)

Willis, Roy, ed. 1996. *World Mythology: The Illustrated Guide* (London: Duncan Baird Publishers).

Wrigley, Matthew, and Kimberley Language Resource Centre. 1992. *Jaru Dictionary* (Western Australia: Kimberley Language Resource Centre).

AT NIGHT'S END

Tyler Nordgren

University of Redlands/International Dark-Sky Association,
1200 E Colton Avenue, Redlands, CA, 92373, USA
Tyler_Nordgren@redlands.edu

Abstract

The light of the Milky Way in a dark night sky has been a common sight for all of human history. In the last one hundred years, astronomical research has revealed the position, past and future, of the earth and sun within that band of stars. Unfortunately, during that same time, urban lighting has rendered the Milky Way invisible to a growing fraction of the world's population. In addition, many of the observatories that contributed to our understanding of our place in the Universe are threatened, if not rendered obsolete by these same city lights. This chapter considers how a number of local, city, and state governments in cooperation with organizations like the International Dark-Sky Association and the United States National Park Service are working to preserve the remaining dark, starry locations for the benefit of science, wildlife, natural resource conservation, economic considerations, and the health benefits and general esthetic enjoyment of humanity.

Keywords

Milky Way, night sky, International Dark-Sky Association (IDA), artificial light pollution, sky glow, national parks.

Introduction

For all of human history the Milky Way and a night full of stars were a common sight in the sky overhead. Knowledge of the heavens and their changing appearance were important for civilisation. The rising of the sun and moon and motions of the stars told you when to plant, when to harvest, and when to gather your people for celebrations. The three main monotheistic religions still time major holy days by the position of the sun and phases of the moon. Yet today we do not need to watch the sky to tell the time or date. In nearly every urban area, those stars that are visible are so sparse that few constellations can be seen in their entirety and their seasonal changes are not worth noticing. Current estimates are that fewer than 40% of US and 50% of European populations can still faintly glimpse the Milky Way from where they live (Cinzano, Falchi, and Elvidge 2001: 689). A World Health Organization (2010) report states that we have just crossed the point at which 50% of the world's population lives in cities. Given how little most people around the world travel from the places they were born, this leads to the sobering thought that roughly 50% of the children born this year will never see the Milky Way. This sight that was once familiar to everyone and that stimulated the production of art, myth, and science has now faded into obscurity (Moore, Richman, and Chamberlain 2011).

It has been said that 400 years ago everyone could see the stars but only Galileo had a telescope. Now everyone has access to telescopes, but almost no one can see the stars (Bogard 2013: 209). Thanks to his telescope, Galileo was the first human being to discover what the Milky Way actually is (Galileo 1610). In the twentieth century astronomers finally completed his work to understand our larger place within its band and the universe beyond. How sad then that in the twenty-first century we face the very real possibility that we will have reduced the visible universe to the glow of our own atmosphere punctuated by no more than the sun and moon beyond. So, while the view of the Milky Way yet remains in those few remote places, what does its luminous band tell us about our place in the universe? What is the Milky Way?

The Milky Way

The Milky Way is our Galaxy: a collection of roughly a hundred billion stars arrayed in an enormous flat pinwheel in space. We see it as a band across the sky because we live permanently within it. Hubble Space Telescope images of other galaxies show similar thin galactic disks. These photos also reveal that, in addition to stars, galaxies like our own contain vast clouds of dark material running along their spiral arms. These are enormous clouds of interstellar gas and dust that fill the 'empty' space between the stars, and are so dense that they blot out the light of the distant stars behind them. We see the same sorts of clouds in our own galaxy. These sometimes complex shapes are so obvious to the fully dark-adapted eye in pristine locations that pre-Columbian cultures joined them together in the sky to create special 'black' constellations (Krupp 1991: 263).

Figure 1. The Milky Way's band arches over Glacier National Park, Montana, USA. Distant stars and interstellar clouds of dust are visible in its glow. Image: Tyler Nordgren.

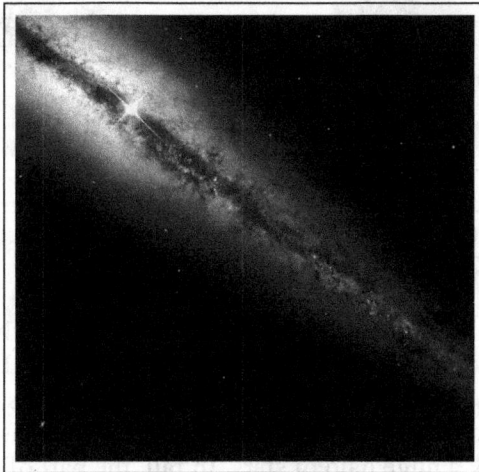

Figure 2. The glow of bright stars backlights interstellar dust in a distant edge-on spiral galaxy like the Milky Way. Image: NASA and The Hubble Heritage Team (STScI/AURA).

From a scientific perspective, these dark clouds are important because it is from within these regions that all the stars in the sky, including our sun, originated (Churchwell et al. 2009). Because they are so dense, no light reaches the hearts of these clouds and they become some of the coldest places in the universe. Without heat, there is little energy and thus little motion. Atoms of hydrogen gas, the most abundant element in the universe, are sluggish at these temperatures and gravity draws them together into clumps. When the gravitational pressure at the center of these clumps forces hydrogen atoms to fuse, the star turns on. Hydrogen fusion gives off energy and is the fuel that lights the stars. Our sun first turned on in a dark dust cloud like the ones we see at night and so the sight of these inky plumes is a window into where we all came from five billion years ago. They show us our origins.

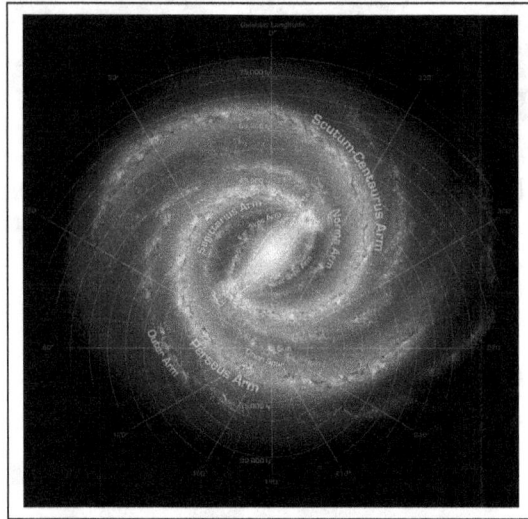

Figure 3. Artist's conception of our Galaxy as viewed from above. The Sun lies 25,000 light years away from the Galactic Center. Image: NASA/JPL-Caltech/R. Hurt(SSC-Caltech).

Over the course of a year, as the earth travels around the sun, different parts of the Milky Way's band become visible at night. The first thing to notice is the band is not uniformly bright in all directions. In summer, the part of the Milky Way visible at night is big and bright with bold dust lanes back-lit by a huge halo of stars. In fall, the part of the Milky Way overhead is split in two by a single dust cloud forming a rift through the constellation of Cygnus. In winter and spring the Milky Way fades away to a pale band with few noticeable features. This is not what you would expect if we lived at the center of the Milky Way. In such a privileged vantage point the Galaxy's disk would be universally bright all along its band. But we do not live at the heart of our galaxy. We live far out in the suburbs.

Our galaxy is measured to be about 100,000 light years in diameter (Churchwell et al. 2009). A light year is the distance light travels in a year. It is 6×10^{12} miles (9.5×10^{12} km) and our sun lies 25 thousand light years from our galaxy's core (Groenewegen, Udalski, and Bono 2008). Out here we see the centre of the galaxy in the direction of the summer constellation of Sagittarius. In that bearing lies the majority of the stars and thus it makes sense that we see it at its brightest in summer. In winter the earth is on the other side of the sun and the part of the Milky Way visible at night points directly away from the galactic centre. In fall we look up at the Northern Cross of Cygnus and see straight down the galactic arm in which our sun resides. It is in that direction that our solar system is heading in its 250-million-year trip around the galactic centre. The sight of the Milky Way in all its detail and changing glory therefore reveals where we are in the universe, where we have come from, and where we are going.

This, however, is nothing new. The sky has given us direction for probably as long as we have been humans. Our cardinal directions were defined by the sky before we had compasses and GPS units. All over the world there are archaeological sites that show some form of astronomical alignment. Keeping track of the calendar, and thus the seasons and attendant celebrations, is the most likely reason for aligning stones, rooms, buildings, or other structures with the sky.

Casa Rinconada is one such structure in Chaco Culture National Historical Park in northwestern New Mexico. It is a circular ceremonial enclosure, the largest kiva in Chaco Canyon and one of about a dozen 'Great Houses' found there, 60 ft (18 m) in diameter and 12 to 16 ft (4 to 5 m) deep. Two massive T-shaped doorways are cut into opposing walls of the kiva and allow entrance and descent down narrow stairs. The line connecting the two doors and the center of the kiva is aligned due north and south (Malville 1993: 37). You can easily see this alignment at night by standing within the southern door and observing Polaris, the North Star, shining directly above the door on the opposite side of the kiva. Today the kiva is open to the air, but a thousand years ago it was enclosed with a log roof supported by four massive posts. Astronomer Ray Williamson recounts a story told by the Acoma, one of the descendent peoples of the Chacoans (Williamson 1984: 138):

> When they built the kiva, they first put up beams of four different trees. These were the trees that were planted in the underworld for the people to climb up on... The walls represent the sky, the beams of the roof (made of wood of the first four trees) represent the Milky Way. The sky looks like a circle, hence the round shape of the kiva.

Park rangers used to tell visitors that little about the canyon is as its original inhabitants once saw it: the Great Houses have crumbled, the canyon walls have collapsed, the trees and grasses that covered the land have disappeared, and the climate has changed. One thing, however, was the same and that was the sky overhead. Yet the last two decades have shown that even that is not true. Today a visitor to an astronomical observatory beside the Chaco Visitor Center can look out on a star-filled sky and make out the lights of nearby towns backlighting the canyon walls in nearly every direction. Even the city of Albuquerque, 100 miles (160 km) away, casts its pale orange glow. We have changed the sky.

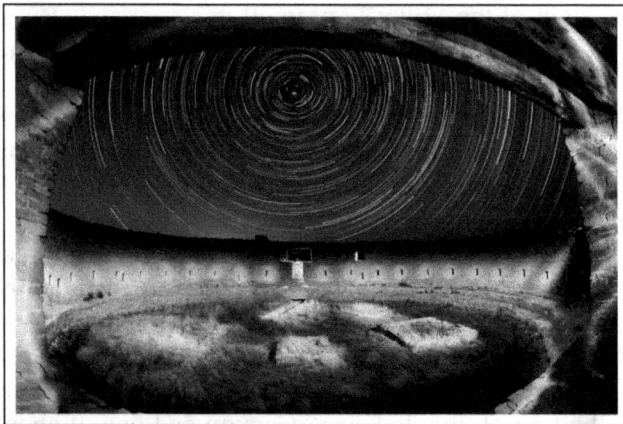

Figure 4. Stars circle over the great kiva of Casa Rinconada in Chaco Culture National Historical Park. The North Star is in line with the two doors into the kiva. Image: Tyler Nordgren.

Light Pollution

If aliens were to visit the earth, the easiest way for them to tell whether the planet was inhabited would be to view the planet at night. Our own spacecraft imagery reveals a planet laced with a luminous web and myriad knots of bright, orange light, the most recent of which was released by the NASA-NOAA Suomi National Polar-orbiting Partnership satellite, 2012.

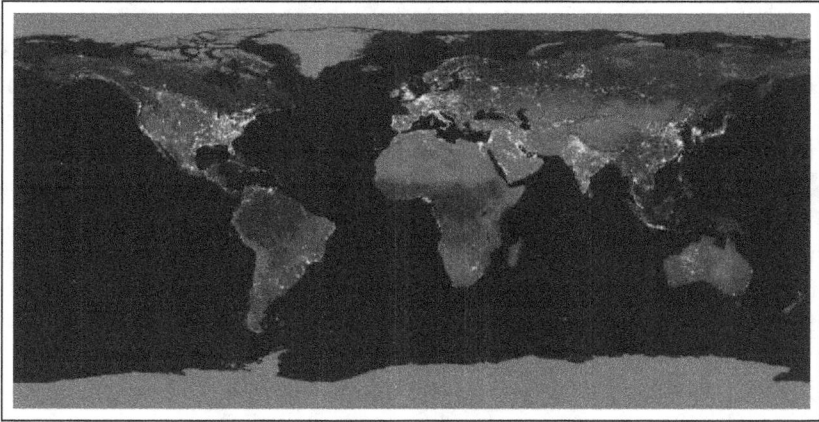

Figure 5. Composite map of the world at night showing the lights of civilisation. Image: NASA Earth Observatory/NOAA NGDC.

At first glance these lights are beautiful. But consider that every bright spot represents electricity wastefully illuminating a spacecraft. These photographs highlight a phenomenon known all too well to astronomers on the ground who recognise that our view of the stars (and the entire universe beyond our atmosphere) is steadily worsening with time. This is light pollution, defined by the International Dark-Sky Association (IDA) as, 'any adverse effect of artificial light, including sky glow, glare, light trespass, light clutter, decreased visibility at night, and energy waste'. In a recent history of light pollution and the loss of natural night, the writer Paul Bogard describes the components of this problem (Bogard 2013: 26):

> Sky glow—on display nightly over any city of any size—is that pink-orange glow alighting the clouds… It's that dome of light on the horizon ahead though the sign says you've still got 50 miles to go. Glare is that bright light shining in your eyes that you raise your hand to block. Trespass is light allowed to cross from one property to another. It's your neighbor's security light shining through your bedroom window… And clutter? A catchword for the confused lighting shining this way and that in any and every modern city.

Sky glow is created by light traveling up into the sky and scattering as it bounces off oxygen molecules, water vapor, dust particles, and smog. Some of the light shining directly upward makes it through to light up the undersides of spacecraft. Light shining horizontally, however, passes through significantly more air than light that shines directly upward (Luginbuhl et al. 2009). This light encounters far more particles with which it interacts and is scattered around the atmosphere and eventually back towards the ground. For observers on the ground it appears as if the sky is glowing and in fact it now is, like an artificial daylight. Since our ability to see stars depends on the contrast between the star and the sky, the brighter we make the background sky the fewer stars we can see.

Glare robs us of stars through its effect on our sight. Sight is the process where the light that enters the eye stimulates photopigments in the cones and rods of the retina. Light causes these chemicals to generate energy which travels from the optic nerve to the brain. Under daytime or bright-light conditions the cones in the retina are responsible for sight (photopic vision). There are three types of cones, each sensitive to a different wavelength range of light (short, medium, and long) and thus responsible for our color perception. Under low-light conditions, where the cones are not as sensitive, we see via the rods (scotopic vision). There is only one type of rod which means that under these conditions we have almost no sense of color.

When the eye is exposed to bright light, the photopigments in the rods and cones break down. The pigments in the low-light sensitive rods can take up to an hour to regenerate after exposure to bright light, while those photopigments in the less-sensitive cones can fully regenerate in as little as 15 minutes. Thus, after exposure to bright light (or glare), some measure of dark adaptation occurs after 15 minutes, but full dark sensitivity to the very faintest light requires nearly an hour or more without exposure to any bright sources. The fact that the low-light level rods are only sensitive to short-wavelengths of light means that observers at night can use dim long-wavelength red light without it affecting their dark sensitivity.

To add insult to injury, sky glow becomes glare when the glow of city lights becomes so bright that the sky itself prevents us from ever becoming truly dark adapted. It is estimated that about one tenth of the World population, more than 40% of the US population and one sixth of the European Union population no longer view the night sky with the eye adapted to night vision because of this (Cinzano, Falchi, and Elvidge 2001: 689).

Astronomers use a number of methods to quantify the darkness of a particular site. One method is to determine its 'limiting magnitude' (the faintest star one can see or photograph from a particular spot). The magnitude scale is a numerical scale devised by the ancient Greek astronomer Hipparchus (c. 190–120 BCE) who defined the brightest star he could see as a star of first magnitude. The next 'less-bright' star he could differentiate he defined as a star of second magnitude, and so on.

Today this has been converted to a mathematical scale, with the bright star Vega classified as a zero magnitude star and every increase of one magnitude is a factor of 2.51× dimmer in brightness. The faintest star that the human eye can pick out is usually 7 or 8 under the darkest conditions. For the naked-eye observer, having the patience and visual acuity to pick out the faintest star visible at night and determine its magnitude is particularly challenging and the results may only marginally reflect what another observer might be able to see.

In recent years, the Bortle Scale, developed by astronomer John E. Bortle at *Sky and Telescope Magazine*, has gained wide acceptance by those concerned about light pollution. It uses a range of factors in quantifying a location, some of which are: visible detail in the Milky Way, prominence of artificial light domes, and ability to discern color in the landscape and the sky. While some of the astronomical features used may be unknown to the layperson, each class contains enough identifying features for use by everyone from professional astronomers to novice stargazers. What follows is an abbreviated version of Bortle's original scale (Bortle 2001: 126):

The Bortle Scale

Class 1: Excellent dark-sky site. Even with direct vision, the galaxy M33 is an obvious naked-eye object. The Scorpius and Sagittarius region of the Milky Way casts obvious diffuse shadows on the ground. To the unaided eye the limiting magnitude is 7.6 to 8.0 (with effort); the presence of Jupiter or Venus in the sky seems to degrade dark adaptation. Airglow (a very faint, naturally occurring glow most evident within about 15° of the horizon) is readily apparent. If you are observing on a grass-covered field bordered by trees, your telescope, companions, and vehicle are almost totally invisible. This is an observer's Nirvana!

Class 2: Typical truly dark site. Airglow may be weakly apparent along the horizon. M33 is rather easily seen with direct vision. The summer Milky Way is highly structured to the unaided eye, and its brightest parts look like veined marble when viewed with ordinary binoculars. Any clouds in the sky are visible only as dark holes or voids in the starry background. You can see your telescope and surroundings only vaguely, except where they project against the sky. Many of the Messier globular clusters are distinct naked-eye objects. The limiting naked-eye magnitude is as faint as 7.1 to 7.5.

Class 3: Rural sky. Some indication of light pollution is evident along the horizon. Clouds may appear faintly illuminated in the brightest parts of the sky near the horizon but are dark overhead. The Milky Way still appears complex, and globular clusters such as M4, M5, M15, and M22 are all distinct naked-eye objects. M33 is easy to see with averted vision. Your telescope is vaguely apparent at a distance of 20 or 30 feet (10 m). The naked-eye limiting magnitude is 6.6 to 7.0.

Class 4: Rural/suburban transition. Fairly obvious light-pollution domes are apparent over population centers in several directions. The Milky Way well above the horizon is still impressive but lacks all but the most obvious structure. M33 is a difficult averted-vision object and is detectable only when at an altitude higher than 50°. Clouds in the direction of light-pollution sources are illuminated but only slightly so, and are still dark overhead. You can make out your telescope rather clearly at a distance. The maximum naked-eye limiting magnitude is 6.1 to 6.5.

Class 5: Suburban sky. The Milky Way is very weak or invisible near the horizon and looks rather washed out overhead. Light sources are evident in most if not all directions. Over most or all of the sky, clouds are quite noticeably brighter than the sky itself. The naked-eye limit is around 5.6 to 6.0.

Class 6: Bright suburban sky. Any indications of the Milky Way are apparent only toward the zenith. The sky within 35° of the horizon glows grayish white. Clouds anywhere in the sky appear fairly bright. You have no trouble seeing eyepieces and telescope accessories on an observing table. M33 is impossible to see without binoculars, and M31 is only modestly apparent to the unaided eye. The naked-eye limit is about 5.5.

Class 7: Suburban/urban transition. The entire sky background has a vague, grayish white hue. Strong light sources are evident in all directions. The Milky Way is totally invisible or nearly so. M44 or M31 may be glimpsed with the unaided eye but are very indistinct. Clouds are brilliantly lit. Even in moderate-size telescopes, the brightest Messier objects are pale ghosts of their true selves. The naked-eye limiting magnitude is 5.0 if you really try.

Class 8: City sky. The sky glows whitish gray or orangish, and you can read newspaper headlines without difficulty. M31 and M44 may be barely glimpsed by an experienced observer on good nights, and only the bright Messier objects are detectable with a modest-size telescope. Some of the stars making up the familiar constellation patterns are difficult to see or are absent entirely. The naked eye can pick out stars down to magnitude 4.5 at best, if you know just where to look.

Class 9: Inner-city sky. The entire sky is brightly lit, even at the zenith. Many stars making up familiar constellation figures are invisible, and dim constellations such as Cancer and Pisces are not seen at all. Aside from perhaps the Pleiades, no Messier objects are visible to the unaided eye. The only celestial objects that really provide pleasing telescopic views are the moon, the planets, and a few of the brightest star clusters (if you can find them). The naked-eye limiting magnitude is 4.0 or less.

In 2001, a team of Italian and American astronomers created the first World Atlas of light pollution (Cinzano, Falchi, and Elvidge 2001: 2001). They used spacecraft images of the earth taken by the US Air Force Defense Meteorological Satellite Program (DMSP) Operational Linescan System (OLS) to produce models of the sky brightness above any spot on earth. These models quantify how bright the zenith (the point directly overhead) appears for a given location. Comparing these models to population density databases, they determined that 'two-thirds of the World population and 99% of the population in the United States (excluding Alaska and Hawaii) and European Union live in areas where the night sky is above the threshold set for polluted status'. Their additional results that more than 60% of US and 50% European populations can no longer see the Milky Way implies that more than half of US and European populations live under Bortle Class 7 or greater skies.

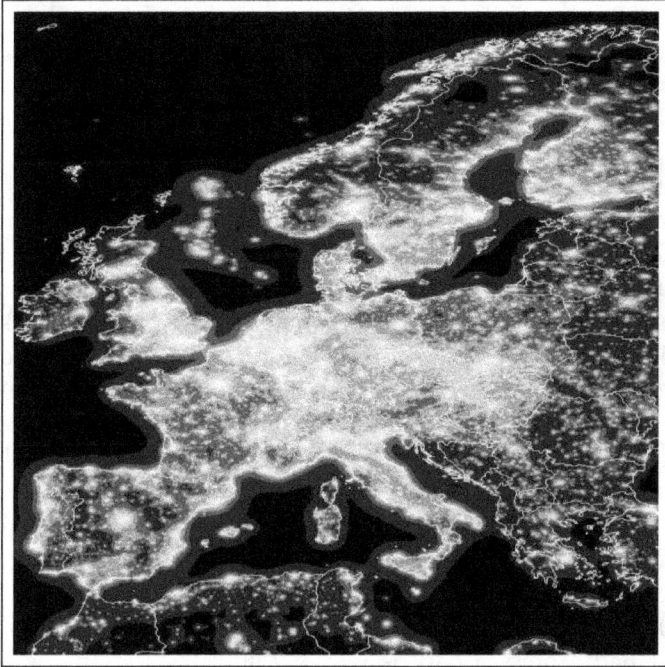

Figure 6. Model of European night sky brightness measured at the zenith. Image: Cinzano, Falchi and Elvidge 2001.

As startling as these results may seem, the loss of truly natural night may be even greater than this. Far from city lights the main visible aspect of artificial lighting is to produce light domes along the horizon. Many rural areas where the sky is relatively dark at the zenith can still have significant nocturnal degradation along the horizon. Efforts are underway to create a new world atlas that uses the same satellite data as Cinzano but that calculates an average brightness over the entire visible celestial hemisphere instead (Duriscoe et al. 2016). This new model better reflects an actual observer's experience under the sky where the lights of distant communities prevent the view from being described as truly pristine. Not surprisingly, the places we can go to see a truly natural, night sky are growing fewer in number and smaller in area.

The National Park Service Night Skies Team

The world's first national park came into being in 1872 when Yellow-stone National Park was created by an act of the US Congress to protect the unusual volcanic features of the newly explored Wyoming Territory. With the formation of subsequent national parks, the National Park Service (NPS) was formed in 1916 to preserve 'unimpaired the natural and cultural resources and values of the national park system for the enjoyment, education, and inspiration of this and future generations' (National Park Service Organic Act of 1916 [16 U.S.C. Sections 1, 2, 3 and 4]).

For much of the twentieth century, this meant protecting the physical manifestation of the landscape, the animals found there, and providing access for the public to both. Since the turn of the twenty-first century, there has been a movement within the park service to protect those qualities that are necessary for enjoyment of these traditional resources: air quality for viewing the landscape, natural quiet for hearing the sounds of the landscape, and pristine natural night for enjoying the half of the 'day' that happens at night. Surveys of park visitor experiences in two western US parks found that visitors considered seeing a sky full of stars as instrumental to their park experience as seeing wildflowers and water-falls (Mace and McDaniel 2013). Today, astronomy ranger 'campfire' talks are one of the most popular evening programs the park service provides (Moore 2013).

In 2000, two NPS rangers in California noticed a curious pheno-menon. Chad Moore, a park ranger at Pinnacles National Monument (now Pinnacles National Park) near San Jose, California, observed that over the previous three years the background sky brightness had become brighter in the direction of the nearby city. Meanwhile, Dan Duriscoe, a park ranger at Sequoia & Kings Canyon National Parks, had observed the same anomaly. Together they developed an automated camera system that can photograph the entire sky above a particular location using a series of between 45 and 104 individual frames (Duriscoe, Luginbuhl and Moore 2007). To be of maximum use for both astronomers and casual observers, each individual frame is photographed through what is called a Johnson V filter. This is a system of filters that has been in use by astronomers for over 60 years (Johnson and Morgan 1953). The V (for Visual) filter passes light at a mean wavelength of 540 nm. This is near the peak wavelength of light to which the human eye is most sensitive when dark-adapted (555 nm). This means that all-sky mosaics made from V filter photos are in a scientifically quantifiable scale while at the same time most closely capturing what the human eye would see in such a location.

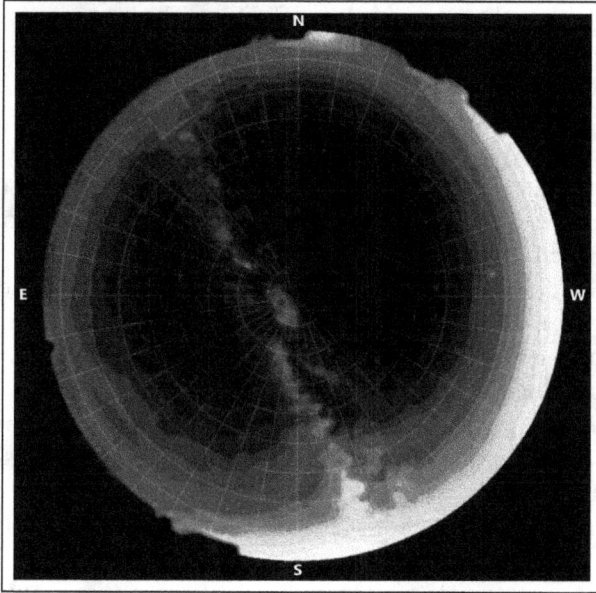

Figure 7. The Night sky above Yosemite National Park, California USA. The Milky Way is visible along with interstellar dust clouds along its band. Much nearer are the lights of Fresno CA to the south (bottom) and Sacramento and San Francisco CA to the west (right). Image: Duriscoe and Moore/NPS Night Sky Team.

Since 2001, Moore and Duriscoe, along with their team of ranger and astronomer assistants, have been travelling the US photographing and re-photographing the night sky above many parks looking to determine how dark the skies are, where sources of light pollution may be coming from, and how those light sources are changing in those communities visible from the parks. Their mosaics have revealed the sources of light pollution in and around parks, in some cases hundreds of miles away, as well as the efficacy of city ordinances to reduce those same sources of pollution (Duriscoe, Luginbuhl, and Moore 2007; Duriscoe, Luginbuhl, and Elvidge 2014).

Light Pollution's Effects

It is natural to imagine that light pollution is a phenomenon that solely affects astronomers. The growth of light pollution has required the construction of new observatories in ever more remote locations and has rendered existing observatories less effective. The best example of this in the United States is Mt Wilson Observatory in the San Gabriel Mountains above Los Angeles (total metropolitan population: 18 million). Mt Wilson hosted the largest telescope in the world, not once, but twice. Both telescopes were used to produce three of the most important results of the twentieth century: first, determining the location and distance to the center of the Milky Way (and thus completing the work of Copernicus and Galileo by revealing our sun is not at the center of the known universe [Shapley 1918]); second, revealing that the Andromeda Nebula (now, the Andromeda Galaxy) is outside our Milky Way and thus our Galaxy is just one of many galaxies in the universe (Hubble 1929a); and third, discovering the observational proof that the universe is expanding (Hubble 1929b). Today these telescopes sit awash in a million points of light emanating from the landscape beneath rather than the sky above.

New observatories are being built in the Atacama Desert of the Chilean Andes, the summit of Mauna Kea on Hawaii's Big Island, and in rural 'sky islands' of southeastern Arizona (Selingo 2001; Bunge 1990). But as astronomers move to more remote areas they naturally bring development in their wake. The remote ceases to be remote while sacred mountains sprout roads, domes, offices, and powerlines. The results are costly and create acrimonious fights between astronomers, environmentalists, and native populations.

The impact of light pollution on the environment, however, is not limited to the building of observatories. Many species around the world are nocturnal. These species have evolved to hunt, feed, breed, and give birth at night (Rich and Longcore 2006). Yet for many locations, particularly in Europe and North America, natural night no longer falls on what appear to be otherwise pristine habitats. On Florida's gulf coast, loggerhead sea turtles lay their eggs in the sand above the high water mark. When the baby turtles hatch, the young must crawl their way back to the relative safety of the sea. Too small to see the ocean above the surrounding dunes, studies show the hatchlings are predisposed to crawl away from dark places and towards those that are much lighter. At night, forests and dunes will appear dark under natural conditions, while open sea (possibly reflecting stars and moon) are brighter. Current levels of light pollution from nearby communities now result in hatchlings either setting out in random directions, or, under the worst conditions, crawling directly away from the sea where they are caught by predators, crushed by cars, or simply succumb to dehydration and exhaustion (Salmon et al. 1995).

Artificial lighting has been found to disorient migrating birds that find their routes over long distances by a still poorly understood method of visual cues and internal magnetic compasses. Light appears to play a role in both mechanisms, particularly for those birds that migrate at night. In laboratory settings, long-wavelength red-orange light has been found to disrupt or confuse birds' internal compass (Gauthreaux and Belser 2006). Birds that migrate at night across the North Sea can typically encounter up to ten oil drilling platforms in the course of their crossing. Massive bird kills have been observed where tall lighted structures (buildings, communications towers, lighthouses, drilling platforms, and so on) extend into the airspace where these birds are flying (Poot et al. 2008).

Even the lowly African ball-rolling dung beetle has been shown to depend upon the night sky. To reproduce, male dung beetles must present female beetles with a ball of excrement in which to lay her eggs. Competition amongst males for dung is therefore fierce around a dung heap (with faster males sometimes stealing the balls of slower males), so once a male produces a ball it is important to roll it directly away from the competition as quickly as possible. A study by Dacke et al. (2013) found that male dung beetles rolled their balls in straight lines under fully star lit skies but wandered randomly under skies with few to no stars. When tests were conducted in a planetarium, where the celestial cues could be varied, the researchers found that beetles appeared to use the Milky Way itself (a bright linear feature often high overhead in the African night). As the Milky Way and stars were eliminated, the ball-rolling tracks became more random. The only other species that appears to pay attention to and navigate by the Milky Way is us, but more may simply await discovery.

We humans are not immune to the health effects of our brightening skies. The International Agency for Cancer Research and American Medical Association now recognize nocturnal lighting as a probable carcinogen (IARC 2007; Blask et al. 2012). At night the human body produces melatonin (a hormone involved in the circadian rhythm and preventing tumor growth). Over the last decade, studies of women working night-shifts (thus exposed to increased levels of light at night) revealed increased risk of breast cancer (Davis, Mirick, and Stevens 2001) while blind night shift workers showed a decreased risk (Hahn 1991). Other research is finding similar results for those with increased levels of light in the sleeping environment, something which more of us will encounter as our cities get brighter (Reiter et al. 2007). As the American Medical Association put it in their recent Report of the Council on Science and Public Health (Blask et al. 2012: 1):

> Biological adaptation to the sun has evolved over billions of years. The power to artificially override the natural cycle of light and dark is a recent event and represents a man-made self-experiment on the effects of exposure to increasingly bright light during the night as human societies acquire technology and expand industry.

In banishing the night we are embarked on an experiment upon ourselves and our world, the effects of which we are only now just coming to learn at the very time we are starting to realize what we have already lost. But this loss is not just to science, the environment, aesthetics, and health. There is a direct economic loss as well.

A million years of human evolution have taught us to be wary of the dark. The increase in artificial lighting worldwide is a direct response to the perceived safety that light affords (Bogard 2013). In today's world, however, there are few-to-no natural predators, disasters, or criminals that regularly swoop out of the sky to prey upon us. All light that shines above the horizon (and really within 20 degrees of the horizon) is therefore wasted light, electricity, natural resources, and money. In a recent economic analysis, the annual costs of light pollution in the US alone are made clear (Gallaway, Olsen, and Mitchell 2010: 659):

> In the United States, roughly 6% of the 4,054 million megawatt hours (mwh) of electricity produced are used for outdoor lighting and an estimated 30% of this is wasted as light pollution (California Energy Commission 2005). This translates into 72.9 million mwh of electricity needlessly being generated at a cost of $6.9 billion a year. Furthermore, this unnecessary electricity usage generated an additional 66 million metric tons of CO_2 (Ristinen and Kraushaar 2006; DOE 2006). Eliminating light pollution would be the CO_2 equivalent of removing over 9.5 million cars from off the road (EPA 2006; DOT 2001).

In a particularly noxious feedback loop, the smog that blankets many cities (and which provides even more sources from which light can scatter to produce glow) may itself be increased by light pollution. Smog is composed of nitrogen oxides (NOx) and ozone that build up during the day as nitrogen dioxide from car exhausts reacts with sunlight and oxygen. But NOx is neutralized by the nitrate radical (NO_3) that builds up in the atmosphere each night (but is itself broken down each day by the light of the sun). New research by Stark et al. (2011) finds that increased levels of light pollution above cities breaks down NO_3 just like the sun, preventing it from neutralizing the smog causing NOx. As cities get bigger, they will produce more light and more smog in a positive feedback loop that will blanket our cities more effectively from the light of the universe beyond.

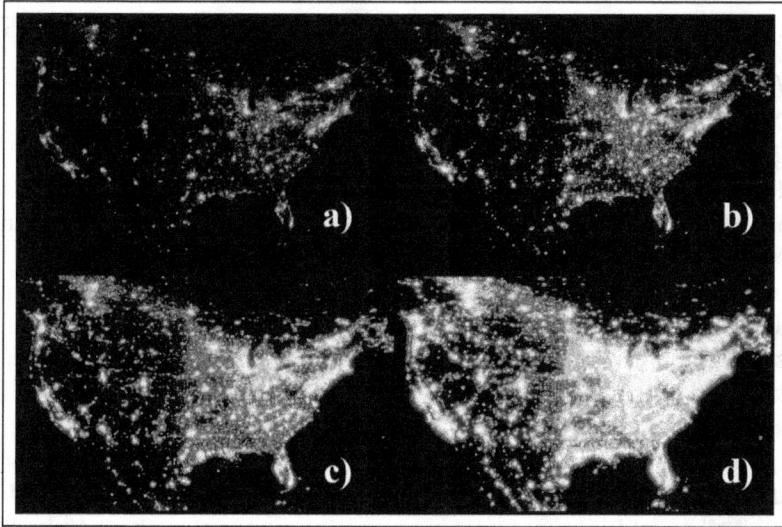

Figure 8. Observed and predicted growth of light pollution in the United States using the observations and models in Cinzano et al. 2001: a) 1950s, b) 1970s, c) 1997, d) 2025. Image: Cinzano, Falchi and Elvidge 2001.

Lastly, light pollution interferes with the important goal of detecting and cataloguing potential impact threats to the earth. Consider that 65 million years ago the impact of an asteroid or comet caused the extinction of the dinosaurs along with roughly 70% of all species on earth. Asteroids and comets still impact the planets (including earth) today. In 1994 virtually every astronomical observatory on Earth and in space watched as Comet Shoemaker-Levy 9 impacted Jupiter (Levy, Shoemaker, and Shoemaker 1995). In February 2013 the meteor that exploded over Chelyabinsk with the force of 300–500 kilotons of TNT was widely seen thanks to a plethora of car-mount video cameras (Durda 2013). Potentially Hazardous Asteroids (objects larger than 100m) are known to be on orbits that come close to the Earth's. To date, the vast majority of these objects have been discovered by ground-based observatories. Until the recent advent of automated telescopic surveys, most comets were still discovered by amateur astronomers. As urban illumination spreads and brightens the background sky, we limit our ability to find large objects on collision courses at far enough distances to have sufficiently long periods of time to divert. The Chelyabinsk Meteor was entirely unknown prior to entering our atmosphere and though no one was killed, the next time we may not be so fortunate.

Solutions

The natural nocturnal sky, unlike resources lost to other forms of pollution, is 100% recoverable (Duriscoe 2001). Shield the light and those errant photons leave the atmosphere at the speed of light. Since 1988 the International Dark-Sky Association (IDA) has been dedicated to reducing the amount of unwanted light flooding the world's skies. This non-profit, community driven organization, with fifty-eight chapters in sixteen countries, seeks to educate the public and encourage architects, engineers, and municipalities to design better-lighted and thus more energy-efficient communities. The IDA has done this in the past by helping individual communities to design effective lighting ordinances and today has partnered with the Illuminating Engineering Society (IES) to craft a Model Lighting Ordinance (MLO) to encourage broad adoption of comprehensive outdoor lighting ordinances to reduce glare, light trespass, and sky glow.

What all lighting ordinances have in common is the simple idea of using light efficiently, shining light towards the ground where it is needed. The simple solution is to place a shield on top of the light and ensure that the bottom of the shield is below the level of the lighting element. This is referred to as 'Full Cut-Off Shielding'. All light that used to shine upward is now reflected back to the ground increasing the amount of useful light that falls there. If you do not need more light on the ground, then fewer lights or lower wattage light bulbs can be installed. In addition, if nocturnal activity is the concern (aiding the good activity and detecting the bad) then the addition of motion sensors puts light exactly where it is needed, when it is needed.

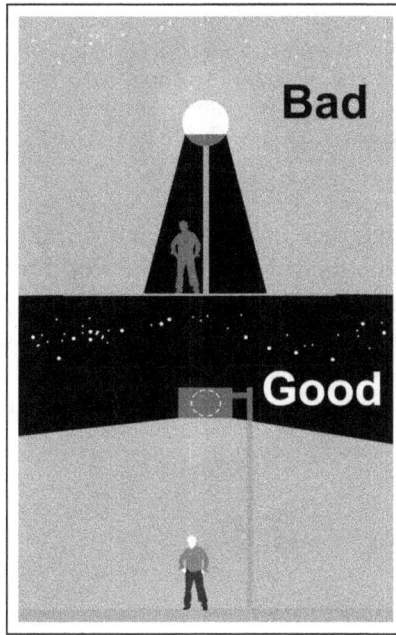

Figure 9. Examples of lighting: Bad lighting (light shines above the horizon and hides unsavory activity in shadows) and Good lighting (illumination goes only on the ground where it is needed. Image credit: Tyler Nordgren.

In addition to shielding, the IDA and other organizations seeking to reduce the amount of unwanted light in the environment also look at how the spectrum of light leads to more or less light pollution—blue light scatters in the sky better than red light—(IDA 2010), and what is the optimum amount of illumination that provides enough light for safety without adversely affecting the night (Luginbuhl et al. 2009). Flagstaff, Arizona (population 67,500 in 2012) has the longest history of regulating light levels to protect the sky, thanks to the presence of two major astronomical observatories (Lowell Observatory and the US Naval Observatory). In 1958, the city passed the first known law limiting what one could shine into the sky by banning the use of search lights within city limits (Portree 2002) and in 1989 the city passed one of the world's most comprehensive plans for reducing light pollution. Christian Luginbuhl at the US Naval Observatory has done extensive modeling of how city lights travel into the sky and creates sky glow. For the test case of Flagstaff (Luginbuhl et al. 2009: 202):

> [T]he adoption of the 1989 lighting code has reduced the growth of
> Flagstaff's sky glow from an expected 43% without the code to just 17%,
> while the population has increased by about 25%. If all ['grandfathered'
> pre-1989] lighting in Flagstaff could be brought within the standards of
> the 1989 code, Flagstaff sky glow could be reduced to 64% of the 2003
> value...

Flagstaff, Arizona, has demonstrated to the world that the night can be
saved. Since then, communities around the world have new put lighting
ordinances in place, including the state of New Mexico which has
declared the night sky to be a cultural resource, the Veneto region of
Italy, and most recently, France, where, starting in 2013, business lights
and store windows are turned off at 1:00am to save money, energy, and
the night sky.

International Dark Sky Parks

While local communities pass new ordinances, for the vast majority of
Americans (and international visitors to America) the most accessible
places to see a nearly pristine night sky remain the national parks.
A growing number of parks across the United States host annual night
sky festivals. Bryce Canyon National Park, in the midst of Utah's dark-
sky country, has been hosting four-day festivals with multiple parallel
nightly speakers, daytime activities, constellation tours, and over fifty
telescopes provided by volunteers from the nearby Salt Lake Astronomical Society since the year 2000. They have the longest tradition of continuous ranger astronomy programs, while parks like Yosemite National
Park in California have been inviting amateur astronomy clubs to set up
telescopes for the public on clear summer evenings for several decades.
Together with festivals at parks like Great Basin National Park in
Nevada, Grand Canyon National Park in Arizona, Chaco Culture National
Historical Park (which has its own observatory) in New Mexico, and
Acadia National Park in Maine, the public is introduced to the beauty,
scientific discoveries, and rich cultural legacy of the night sky and the
need to preserve it (Moore, Richman, and Chamberlain 2011).

To better promote night-sky tourism and preservation, the IDA and
NPS have partnered to create the International Dark-Sky Park program.
Beginning in 2007 Natural Bridges National Monument in southern Utah
was declared the world's first International Dark Sky Park (IDSP) based
upon NPS Night Sky Team imagery revealing that the center of the
Milky Way (and not the lights of a distant city) is the brightest feature in

a moonless summer sky. In 2013 Chaco Culture National Historical Park was added to this list. Because of the astronomical alignments of the Chacoan Great Houses, as well as what are thought to be astronomically themed pictographs and petroglyphs, it is clear that there have been night sky enthusiasts in Chaco for at least a thousand years. As of 2016, according to the IDA website, there are now thirty-four certified IDSPs around the world.

Figure 10. International Dark Sky Parks promote the enjoyment and conservation of exceptional dark-sky parks and preserves around the world. Image: Tyler Nordgren.

Conclusion

The Milky Way was once visible to everyone, everywhere, every clear moonless night. Fewer than half of Americans and Europeans can still see this sight from their homes. Consider the magnitude of this loss: for all of human history, ever since the first primates who would one day call themselves human climbed down out of the trees and set foot out into the African savanna, the stars overhead were a nightly occurrence. The patterns and motions of these stars gave us myths, morality tales, art, religion, and science. They measured the passage of time and allowed us to plant and to harvest, to predict the coming of the rains, the heat, and the cold. On land they guided our feet, and at sea they guided our ships. They were the catalyst for the scientific method that has subsequently prolonged life, harnessed the atom, and sent our spacecraft on their way to the stars. The stars we see at night link us to our past and hold the key to our survival in the future. Modern science has revealed that the atoms that compose everything we can see and touch, our entire world and our very bodies, were created in the hearts of stars. As the late astronomer Carl Sagan (1934–1996) once said, 'We are star stuff'. Without their presence overhead, our universe is rendered void, and together we are diminished.

References

Blask, D., G. Brainard, R. Gibbons, S. Lockley, R. Stevens, and M. Motta. 2012. 'Light Pollution: Adverse Health Effects of Nighttime Lighting', *Report 4 of the Council on Science and Public Health* (Chicago: American Medical Association).

Bogard, P. 2013. *The End of Night* (New York: Little, Brown & Co.).

Bortle, J.E. 2001. 'Introducing the Bortle Dark-Sky Scale', *Sky and Telescope* 101.2: 126-29.

Bunge, R. 1990. 'Construction Halted on Mount Graham Observatory', *Astronomy Magazine* 18.7: 22.

California Energy Commission. 2005. 'Nonresidential Compliance Manual' (Sacramento: State of California Printing Office).

Churchwell, E., B.L. Babler, M.R. Meade, B.A. Whitney, R. Benjamin, R. Indebetouw, C. Cyganowski, T.P. Robitaille, M. Povich, C. Watson, and S. Bracker. 2009. 'The Spitzer/GLIMPSE Surveys: A New View of the Milky Way', *Publications of the Astronomical Society of the Pacific* 121: 213.

Cinzano, P., F. Falchi, and C.D. Elvidge. 2001. 'The First World Atlas of the Artificial Night Sky Brightness', *Monthly Notices of the Royal Astronomical Society* 328: 689-707.

Dacke, M., E. Baird, M. Byrne, C.H. Scholtz, and E. Warrant. 2013. 'Dung Beetles Use the Milky Way for Orientation', *Current Biology* 23.4: 298-300.

Davis S., D.K. Mirick, and R.G. Stevens. 2001. 'Night-shift Work, Light at Night, and Risk of Breast Cancer', *Journal of the National Cancer Institute* 93: 1557-62.

Department of Energy, Energy Information Administration .2006. 'Electric Power Annual' (Washington, DC: U.S. Government Printing Office [GPO]).

Department of Transportation, Bureau of Transportation Statistics 2001, 'National Household Travel Survey' (Washington, DC: GPO).

Durda, D. 2013. 'The Chelyabinsk Super-Meteor', *Sky and Telescope* 125.6: 24.

Duriscoe, D.M. 2001. 'Preserving Pristine Night Skies in National Parks and the Wilderness Ethic', *The George Wright Forum* 18.4: 30.

Duriscoe, D.M., F. Falchi, P. Cinzano, and C.D. Elvidge. 2016. 'A Field-Verified Indicator of Sky Quality Based Upon the First World Atlas of Artificial Sky Brightness' (In preparation).

Duriscoe, D.M., C.B. Luginbuhl, and C.D. Elvidge. 2014, 'The Relation of Outdoor Lighting Characteristics to Sky Glow from Distant Cities', *Lighting Research and Technology* 46.1: 35

Duriscoe, D.M., C.B. Luginbuhl, and C.A. Moore. 2007. 'Measuring Night-Sky Brightness with a Wide-Field CCD Camera', *Publications of the Astronomical Society of the Pacific* 119: 192.

Environmental Protection Agency, Office of Transportation and Air Quality. 2006. 'Light-Duty Automotive Technology and Fuel Economy Trends: 1975 Through 2006' (Washington, DC: GPO).

Galilei, G. 1610, *Sidereus Nuncius*, trans. Albert van Helden (Chicago: University of Chicago Press, 1989).

Gallaway, T., R.N. Olsen and D.M. Mitchell. 2010. 'The Economics of Global Light Pollution', *Ecological Economics* 69.3: 658-65.

Gauthreaux, S.A., and C.G. Belser. 2006. 'Effects of Artificial Night Lighting on Migrating Birds', in *Ecological Consequences of Artificial Night Lighting*, ed. C. Rich and T. Longcore (Washington, DC: Island Press): 67-93.

Groenewegen, M.A.T., A. Udalski, and G. Bono. 2008. 'The Distance to the Galactic Centre Based on Population II Cepheids and RR Lyrae Stars', *Astronomy and Astrophysics* 481: 441.

Hahn, R.A. 1991. 'Profound Bilateral Blindness and the Incidence of Breast Cancer', *Epidemiology* 2: 208.

Hubble, E. 1929a. 'A Spiral Nebula as a Stellar System, Messier 31', *Astrophysical Journal* 69: 103.

———. 1929b. 'A Relation between Distance and Radial Velocity among Extra-Galactic Nebulae', *Proceedings of the National Academy of Sciences of the United States of America* 15.3: 168-73.

IARC. 2007. 'Painting, Firefighting, and Shiftwork: IARC Monographs on the Evaluation of Carcinogenic Risks to Humans', vol. 98 (Lyon: International Agency for Research on Cancer Working Group on the Evaluation of Carcinogenic Risks to Humans).

IDA. 2010. 'Visibility, Environmental, and Astronomical Issues Associated with Blue-Rich White Outdoor Lighting'. Online: http://www.darksky.org/resources (accessed December 2013).

Johnson, H.L., and M.W. Morgan. 1953. 'Fundamental Stellar Photometry for Standards of Spectral Type on the Revised System of the Yerkes Spectral Atlas', *The Astrophysical Journal* 117: 313-52.

Krupp, E.C. 1991. *Beyond the Blue Horizon: Myths and Legends of the Sun, Moon, Stars, and Planets* (New York: HarperCollins).

Levy, D.H., E.M. Shoemaker, and C.S. Shoemaker. 1995. 'Comet Shoemaker-Levy 9 Meets Jupiter', *Scientific American* 273: 68-75.

Luginbuhl, C.B., G.W. Lockwood, D.R. Davis, K. Pick, and J. Selders. 2009. 'From the Ground Up I: Light Pollution Sources in Flagstaff, Arizona', *Publications of the Astronomical Society of the Pacific* 121: 185-203.

Mace, B.L., and J. McDaniel. 2013. 'Visitor Evaluation of Night Sky Interpretation in Bryce Canyon National Park and Cedar Breaks National Monument', *Journal of Interpretation Research* 18.1: 39.

Malville, J.M. 1993. *A Guide to Prehistoric Astronomy in the Southwest* (Boulder: Johnson Printing Co.).

Moore, C.A. 2013. Personal communication.

Moore, C.A., A.M. Richman, and V.D. Chamberlain. 2011. 'Finding Inspiration in the Face of Endangered Starry Skies', *Astronomical Society of the Pacific Conference Series* 441: 5.

National Park Service Organic Act of 1916 (16 U.S.C. Sections 1, 2, 3 and 4).

Poot, H., B.J. Ens, H. de Vries, M.A.H. Donners, M.R. Wernand, and J.M. Marquenie. 2008. 'Green Light for Nocturnally Migrating Birds', *Ecology and Society* 13.2: 47.

Portree, D.S.F. 2002. 'Flagstaff's Battle for Dark Skies', *Griffith Observer* 66: 2.

Reiter, R.J., T. Dun-Xian, A. Korkmaz, T.C. Erren, C. Piekarski, H. Tamura, and L.C. Manchester. 2007. 'Light at Night, Chronodisruption, Melatonin Suppression, and Cancer Risk: A Review', *Critical Reviews in Oncogenesis* 13.4: 303-28.

Rich, C., and T. Longcore. 2006. *Ecological Consequences of Artificial Night Lighting* (Washington, DC: Island Press).

Ristinen, R., and J. Kraushaar. 2006. *Energy and the Environment*, 2nd ed. (New York: John Wiley).

Salmon, M., M.G. Tolbert, D.P. Painter, M. Goff, and R. Reiners. 1995. 'Behavior of Loggerhead Sea Turtles on an Urban Beach. II. Hatchling Orientation', *Journal of Herpetology* 29.4: 568-76.

Selingo, J. 2001. 'Astronomers, in Search of the Best Views, Confront History and Politics in Hawaii', *Chronicle of Higher Education* 47.38: 018-A19.

Shapley, H. 1918. 'Studies Based on the Colors and Magnitudes in Stellar Clusters', *The Astrophysical Journal* 48: 154.

Stark, H., S. Brown, K. Wong, J. Stutz, C.D. Elvidge, I. Pollack, T. Ryerson, W. Dube, N. Wagner, and D. Parrish. 2011. 'City Lights and Urban Air', *Nature Geoscience* 2: 730-31.

UN World Health Organization (WHO). 2010. 'Hidden Cities: Unmasking and Overcoming Health Inequities in Urban Settings', Geneva, World Health Organization. Online: http://www.who.int/kobe_centre/publications/hidden_cities2010/en/: *iv-ix*.

Williamson, R.A. 1984. *Living the Sky: The Cosmos of the American Indian* (Norman: University of Oklahoma Press).

REACH FOR THE STARS!
LIGHT, VISION AND THE ATMOSPHERE

Tim Ingold

Department of Anthropology, School of Social Science,
University of Aberdeen, Aberdeen AB24 3QY, Scotland, UK
tim.ingold@abdn.ac.uk

Abstract

What is the sky? I begin by comparing the answers that psychologist James Gibson and philosopher Maurice Merleau-Ponty give to this question. For Gibson, light delivers objects to our perception, but is not visible as such. Yet if there were no more to the sky than its luminosity, then the sky itself would be invisible, leaving no difference between day and night. Drawing on the example of van Gogh's painting, *Starry Night*, I show how light is understood by Merleau-Ponty not as radiant energy but as the experiential consequence of a fission/reaction that unites us with the cosmos even as it divides us from ourselves. Light, in other words, is a phenomenon of the *atmosphere*, brought about through the conflation of the cosmic with the affective. As a space of inhalation and exhalation, we alternately breathe in the atmosphere (fusion) and breathe it out (fission). I relate this alternation to one between line and colour, showing how colour lends atmosphere to the line, and how line gives colour to the atmosphere. I conclude that this alternation is fundamental to sentient life.

Keywords

Sky, weather, phenomenology, visual perception, starry night, colourful lines.

Introduction

I begin with the simplest of questions. What is the sky? What do we mean when we say we see the sky, rather than, say, the land, the ocean, trees, houses or people? Can you draw the sky? Can you paint it? Why do the stars seem so remote and so close at the same time? What is a sunbeam? Like all simple questions these, too, turn out to be devilishly hard to answer. In attempting this next-to-impossible feat, I shall set in play a cast of just two characters, both of whom have hugely influenced my thinking. One is the psychologist James Gibson; the other the philosopher Maurice Merleau-Ponty. On balance, I shall be rather critical of Gibson, and rather accepting of Merleau-Ponty. But this should not be taken as a measure of the worth of their respective contributions. The reason I have so much admiration for Gibson, despite my criticisms, is that he not only sought to answer but also dared to ask such simple questions as those posed above. He wanted to know how we perceive the world we naturally inhabit rather than the artificial world of the research laboratory: a world, as he put it, comprised of 'the earth and the sky with objects on the earth and in the sky, of mountains and clouds, fires and sunsets, pebbles and stars' (Gibson 1979: 66). Merleau-Ponty, by contrast, wondered how there could be a world with things to perceive in the first place. He wanted to know 'how the things become things, how the world becomes world' (Merleau-Ponty 1964: 181). In character and style, these two—the psychologist and the philosopher—could hardly have been more different: the one crisp, precise and to the point, the other airy and obscure. Indeed their respective characters bear an uncanny resemblance to that of which they speak: on the one hand, rays of light that go straight to a focus, on the other hand the diffuse and percolating atmosphere. Gibson's words pierce the void; with Merleau-Ponty you have to wait for them to sink in. The first strike, then, goes to Gibson.

Invisible Light

'Of all the possible things that can be seen, is light one of them?' So asks Gibson (1979: 54), in the course of setting out his ecological approach to visual perception. His answer is resoundingly in the negative. Light, he says, is the one thing we cannot possibly see. It is an answer that at first seems perverse, for surely we cannot see *without* light. In pitch darkness we see nothing. But nor do we see anything in a thick fog, even in broad daylight. This is because the radiant light coming from the sun is so scattered and diffused by vapour droplets in the air that any light reaching the eyes has already been effectively scrambled. It retains no structure, no pattern (Gibson 1979: 52). On a clear day, by contrast, we may suppose that light reflected from the surfaces of environmental objects and features reaches an eye so placed as to receive it without further distortion. To the forms and textures of these objects and features in the world there correspond a nested series of angles at the eye: thus the outline of a thing such as a tree subtends a larger angle, within which are nested the numerous and much smaller angles subtended by the occluding edges of leaves and branches, in so far as they can be made out. This set of solid angles comprises what Gibson calls the 'ambient optic array'. The structure of this array is, of course, particular to a certain point of observation. A single-point perspective alone will not suffice to inform the viewer of the shapes or forms of environmental features 'in the round'. We normally see things, however, not from fixed points but while moving among them, along a path of observation. As we move, the perspective structure undergoes continuous modulation. Underlying this modulation are certain invariants. It was Gibson's contention that these invariants—which emerge from the flow of ever-changing perspective structure along a path—fully specify the shapes, forms and textures of the things we see (Gibson 1979: 69-75).

The critical point here is that visual perception is about the extraction of information from the structure in the light and its modulations; it is not about the way light itself stimulates the eye, or triggers its photoreceptors. The alternative view, long ascendant in the psychology of perception, is that strictly speaking, light is *all* that we see. Nothing else enters the eye. It is thus left to the mind to conjure internal images of what might be 'out there', to contribute conceptual form to the raw material of sensory stimulation. We have, according to classical optics, no direct access to the world; all visual perception is necessarily indirect. If, in Gibson's ecological approach, you see the world but not light, in classical optics you see light but not the world. Now I have no wish to mount a defence of this latter position: it has, in my view, been amply discredited. My concern is rather to bring out a certain limitation, shared by both sides, in the understanding of light itself. On the one side, if to see means to register sensations triggered by the stimulation of retinal photoreceptors, then light is the energetic impulse that causes these receptors to 'fire'. On the other side, if to see means to extract invariant information from an ever-varying optic array, then, as Gibson puts it, 'all we ever see is the environment or facts about the environment, never *photons or waves or radiant energy*' (1979: 55, my emphasis). This statement gives the game away. For it reveals that Gibson is thinking of light in just the same sense as in classical optics: it is the physical cause, of which retinal stimulation is the effect. And although it is from the workings of the eye, in vision, that the science of optics takes its name, light in this sense has no need of eyes to exist. It needs eyes only to establish its relevance. The existence of light, for Gibson, is a physical datum, its relevance is an ecological one (Gibson 1966: 222).

Is there really no more to light than this? Nowhere are the limitations of a purely physicalist understanding more clearly revealed than in Gibson's attempts to demonstrate that light, far from being *only* what we see, is what we *never* see. Imagine yourself out on a dark night. Up above, stars twinkle in a cloudless sky, while at ground level electric lamps shine through the windows of nearby houses. You see starlight and lamplight, or so you say. Gibson, however, insists that you do not: 'A single point of light in an otherwise dark field is not "light"; it specifies either a very distant source of light or a very small source, a luminous object' (Gibson 1979: 54). How can light not be 'light'? To be sure, the stars are very distant, and the lamps very small. We know that because of what astronomers have told us about stars, and because of what everyday life has taught us about lamps. We know, too, that stars do not land on the ground, and that houses do not take off into the sky. For all these reasons, we are unlikely to confuse lamps with stars. Nevertheless, we might be forgiven for confusing both lamps and stars with light. In the world according to Gibson, it transpires, the stars you witness in the heavens are but specks, 'specified' by the light you do not see. And the lamps you see in the houses are likewise mere bulbs which indicate—among other things—that people are at home to switch them on. In this world, stars hang in the sky but do not shine; lamps hang from ceilings but do not glow. The light is like a messenger that delivers stars and lamps to the doors of your perception, but magically vanishes at the moment you let them in.

Empty Sky

As you ponder these thoughts, the moon rises over the horizon. Its silvery light casts faint shadows, revealing the contours of a landscape. But if you think you see the moonlight, says Gibson, you would be mistaken. Along with the forms of the landscape, he claims, the moon is an object *specified* by the light, and not, in itself, a show of luminosity. Observed closely, or perhaps through a telescope, you observe that the moon's surface is puckered by craters and other features, whose forms are specified by angles in the optical array nested within the angle subtended by the outline of the moon itself. Now the astronomer will reassure us that, of course, the moon does not really emit light, and that what we call 'moonlight' is actually the light of the sun, reflected from its mottled surface. So perhaps Gibson is right after all: the moon is given to us by light, but *is not* light. But now the new day dawns, and the sun rises. As it does so, the stars vanish, the moon fades, the landscape that had once appeared as silvery shadows stands out as a polychrome manifold of surfaces, while up above is that great mystery we call the sky, appearing to us as a sea of translucent colour: shades of blue, more intense towards the zenith, flecked with patches of white and grey that we call 'clouds'. It seems that we are bathed in light, yet still Gibson holds out: he continues to insist, against the odds, that we see objects specified by the light, not light as such. What goes for the moon, he contends, goes for the sun as well: it is delivered to us—by its light—as a round object suspended in the sky. But it doesn't shine. How come, then, that if we attempt to look at it, or if we look at a glossy surface that reflects it, we are dazzled and even blinded by its brilliance? 'Are these not sensations of light as such?' Gibson asks, and then promptly answers his own question in the negative. What we perceive is a state akin to pain, he says, arising from excessive stimulation. This is a fact about the body, not about the world. We perceive the pain and not the light (Gibson 1979: 55).

Strangest of all is Gibson's conclusion with regard to the sky. Once again he poses his own question—'What about a luminous *field*, such as the sky?'—only to respond with this most enigmatic of answers, 'To me it seems that I see the sky, not the luminosity as such' (1979: 54). The sky is luminous, but to perceive the sky is not to perceive its luminosity! What, we might wonder, is left of the sky once its luminosity has been subtracted? If light delivers the sky to our perception, but then vanishes, does not the sky vanish with it? Are we not left, on a cloudless day, with precisely nothing: mere emptiness, save for the ghost of a sun that does not shine, turning shimmering day into starless night? It is worth tracing the steps that lead Gibson inexorably to this perplexing result. The first step is to distinguish, as Gibson does, between *radiation* and *illumination*. The one is emitted from a source; the other lights up the world. Radiation, principally from the sun, becomes illumination by being scattered in all directions, by refraction through particles in the atmosphere and reflection from the mottled and textured surfaces of the earth. Step two: since the scatter is omnidirectional, for any selected point in the medium (the air), the ambient light converging upon it would come from all quarters. Third, to the extent that this ambient light is structured and not scrambled, it contains information that specifies features of the environment. But by the same token, fourth, unstructured ambient light specifies nothing; what we perceive, then, is emptiness. On lifting one's gaze from the landscape, across the line of the horizon, to the clear blue of the sky, the structured ambient light that specifies the opaque surfaces and textures of the landscape from which it is reflected therefore gives way to the unstructured ambient light that permeates the sky, leading to the perception of a translucent void, interrupted only by more textured regions that indicate clouds. The ambient light of the sky, Gibson concludes, is no different from ambient darkness: since it specifies nothing, there is nothing to be perceived. The illuminated sky, like black night, is emptiness itself.

Starry Night

Picture yourself once more on a starry night: perhaps the one famously painted by Vincent van Gogh (Fig. 1). The painting appeals to us precisely because it both resonates with our experience of what it *feels like* to be under the stars and affords us the means to dwell upon it—perhaps to discover depths in this experience of which we would otherwise remain unaware. Two things are immediately apparent. First, the night sky is not homogeneous, nor is it empty save for stars. It swirls with currents that resonate to the contours of the landscape which we can dimly make out in the light of a crescent moon. And secondly, the stars themselves are not inert specks in the firmament. On the contrary, they *pulse*. That is to say, their light is experienced not merely as a messenger—a vector of projection—that yields them up as objects of our awareness. Rather, we feel it from within, as an affect. Immersed in the swirling expanse, it is as though our minds and bodies were swept up in the flow, even as we remain rooted to one spot. Van Gogh, then, is not just painting stars. He is a star-struck painter: he sees, and paints, *with* their light. This is why the stars can be at once infinitely distant and yet touch the soul. It is not that vision puts the stars within reach so that we might snatch them from the sky like apples from a tree. Nor do we throw out a line to rope them in. As Merleau-Ponty puts it, vision 'is the means given me for being absent from myself' (1964: 186). To stand in place and open one's eyes upon the night sky is not to extend one's being along a continuum, from near at hand to far away, but to find it split between two poles, one emplaced with the body, the other at large in the heavens, mingling with the stars and flitting like an agile spirit from one to another as the focus of attention shifts. And yet these two poles are really one, for at the termination of their fission, continues Merleau-Ponty, 'I come back to myself' (1964: 186). We discover, perhaps to our astonishment, that the twinkling stars are our own eyes: that we don't just see them but see with them.

Figure 1. Gogh, Vincent van (1853–1890): *The Starry Night* (*De sterrennacht*), June 1889. Oil on canvas, 29 × 36 ¼ in. (73.7 × 92.1 cm). New York, Museum of Modern Art (MoMA), acquired through the Lillie P. Bliss Bequest. Acc. n.: 472.1941 © 2014. Digital image, The Museum of Modern Art, New York/Scala, Florence.

For what van Gogh paints is not the panorama of the sky in its totality, as it might be exhibited in a planetarium. His painting makes no claim to *represent* what he sees. It rather enacts, in line and colour, the birth of his vision which, as it opens upon the cosmos, seems to explode like a shower of fireworks. Wherever sensing meets the sensible, as Merleau-Ponty writes, or wherever our attention is let loose into the world, there is ignited a kind of spark (1964: 163-64). The night sky glitters with a thousand such sparks, which will burn for as long as they glow in our own eyes. Some burn bright, others fade, and in the painting you can follow the unfolding of the painter's attention as it wanders from star to star. A moment ago, it was with the stars near the top of the canvas, but now it has lowered to one nearer the horizon which, at this instant, appears incandescent. This light, glowing white in the picture, is not the radiant energy of the physical universe, whether conceived as waves or photons, nor is it some disturbance or agitation of a consciousness imprisoned in that cavernous endo-cranial space behind the eyeballs. It does not travel in straight lines that connect a point source with a receptor. It is no more emitted from a source than it enters the eye. Rather, like a spark, it bursts from the fusion of the two poles of vision, respectively corporeal and celestial, in directions orthogonal to the line of their connection. Every star, then, is not so much a hub from which shafts of light fan out in all directions, as a pivot *around and between* which (and other stars) the light seems to swirl, in concert with the swivelling eyes. This swirling corresponds with the temporal movement of our attentiveness. So long as attention is focused on a particular star, the light revolves tightly around it, but as attention wanders so does the light. Here and there, the star-sparks have already faded, leaving only flaccid and decaying swirls. And that is exactly how van Gogh has painted them![1]

As an affectation of being, then, light is the outcome of a fission/ fusion reaction that unites us with the cosmos in the very moment that it divides us from ourselves. Of course, there could be no experience of light without the incidence of radiant energy, or without the excitation of photoreceptors in the retina, but as a quality of *affect*—of what it feels like to inhabit an illuminated world—light is reducible to neither. Nevertheless, this experience is entirely real. We cannot afford to dismiss it as an illusion any more than we can write off the history of painting as an aberration caused by the overstimulation of excessively susceptible minds (Ingold 2000: 265). Nor, on the other hand, can we deny the reality of blindness for the visually impaired. Light is real for the sighted, precisely because it is none other than the spark of vision itself—the birth of visual awareness as it opens up to the cosmos. Thus the painter stands forever at that sliding moment—rather like riding the crest of a wave—at which the world is on the point of revealing itself, such that the perpetual birth of their awareness is, concurrently, the perpetual birth of the world. It is as though, at every moment, they were opening their eyes upon the world for the first time. And in this opening, the visual field— that is, the night sky in its entirety—is merged with the field of their attention. That is why the star, in our perception, sheds its light at once from the core of our being and from the furthest reaches of the cosmos.

---

1. This was not his first attempt, however. Nine months previously, in September 1888, van Gogh had painted *Starry Night Over the Rhone*. Bowing to convention, he had depicted each star as a dot from which short yellow streaks radiated out into a deep blue sky.

It simultaneously beams and beckons. I shall henceforth refer to this conflation of beaming and beckoning, or of the affective with the cosmic, by means of the term *atmosphere*.[2] Light, then, is neither physical nor psychic. It is atmospheric. And in his painting, van Gogh has given us the atmosphere of the night sky. I know no better rendering of it.

Sun-like Eyes

Following our painterly contemplation of the night, and a well-earned rest, we rise to discover that the sun is already up, and is shining brightly in an azure sky. We dare not look at it directly; we know its form, however, to be that of a disk of brilliant yellow. For Gibson, as we have already noted, this form is delivered up to us by the sun's light: we see the form and not the light as such, registering the strain on our eyes as a kind of pain. Yet the sun doesn't just hang in the sky. It, too, both beams and beckons. To witness the sun is to see by its own light, or in the poetic language of Johann Wolfgang von Goethe, 'if the eye were not sun-like, it could not see the sun' (Goethe and Luke 1964: 282). By 'sun-like', Goethe did not mean to imply a relation of formal resemblance, as if to highlight the spherical form common to both suns and eyeballs. His point was rather that the same sun that shines in the sky (the beacon) also shines from our eyes (the beam). It is what we see *with*. Seeing with sunbeams is like feeling the wind: it is an affective mingling of our own awareness with the turbulence and pulsations of the medium in which we are immersed. No more than the wind is the sun given to us as an *object* of perception. It rather gets inside and saturates our consciousness to the extent that it is constitutive of our own capacity to see or feel. In this vein, Merleau-Ponty described the relation of sunlight to vision as a kind of symbiosis—a way 'the outside has of invading us', and our way 'of meeting this invasion' (1962: 317). Where Merleau-Ponty wrote of symbiosis, however, I prefer the term *correspondence* (Ingold 2010: 243-44).

To see the sun, as Goethe had insisted, the eyes must already respond to its light. But conversely, the sun can only shine in a world with eyes capable of so responding. Eyes and sun thus co-respond. In his *Bedeutungslehre* or 'Theory of Meaning' of 1940, the Estonian-born biologist

---

2. The concept of atmosphere has recently become the subject of intense discussion, in fields ranging from meteorology to cultural geography, architecture and the philosophy of aesthetics. It is beyond the scope of this chapter to review the literature that has grown up around it, though I have made a start elsewhere (see Ingold 2012).

and founder of biosemiotics, Jakob von Uexküll, argued on these grounds that Goethe's insight was but half-formed. To complete it one should add the corollary: 'If the sun were not eye-like, it could not shine in any sky' (Uexküll 1982: 65). Von Uexküll's contention was that the sky, and the sun as a celestial light that illuminates the sky, can only exist in the phenomenal world of creatures with eyes. To be sure, were the sun to be conceived in a strictly physical sense, as an astronomical body rent by nuclear reactions, then it could perhaps be said to exist even if there were no creatures to see it, or in its light. This, to recapitulate, was Gibson's argument: namely, that light needs no eyes to exist; it only needs eyes to establish its relevance. For von Uexküll, however, the sun in its shining was to be understood not as a physical entity but as a manifest presence in the world of phenomena. And in this sense, just as the eye, as Goethe had observed, can see only by virtue of its correspondence with the sun, so the sun we perceive in the sky, and that lights the world of our experience, can exist only through its essential correspondence with the eye.

What then of the sky itself? Recall Gibson's observation, that what he sees is the sky and not its luminosity, yet that this sky, barring objects such as clouds that float in it or birds that fly in it, is pure emptiness. The sky presents a paradox for Gibson precisely because he cannot countenance the environment in any other way than as a world of objects set over against the perceiver and revealed through the patterns of ambient light reflected from their opaque, outer surfaces. The sky, however, has no surface. It is not a magically blue-painted dome that encompasses our lives within some giant bubble. To the contrary, it is openness or transparency itself. Nothing is there. How can we see the sky when there is nothing to see? For Merleau-Ponty, by contrast, to see the sky—just as to see the sun—is precisely to experience its luminosity from within. To contemplate the blue of the sky, he writes, is not to be set over against it as a cosmic subject to cosmic object, nor is it to grasp it cognitively by assimilating the raw material of sensory experience to some abstract idea of blueness. It is rather to fuse the cosmic with the affective. 'I am the sky itself as it is drawn together and unified', writes Merleau-Ponty; 'my consciousness is saturated with this limitless blue' (1962: 214). Or in a word, the blue sky is an *atmosphere.* I mentioned earlier how seeing with sunbeams is like feeling the wind. In a certain sense, then, one breathes the light of the sky as one breathes the air. For when we breathe, it is not just the body that takes air in, and lets it out, as though the mind could be left to float in the ether of the imagination. It is with our entire being— indissolubly body and soul—that we breathe. As Merleau-Ponty put it, 'there really is inspiration and expiration of Being'. This is not to speak metaphorically. The words 'inspiration' and 'expiration', Merleau-Ponty insisted, have to be taken quite literally (1964: 167). And in this double movement lies the essence of perception.

Sentient Being

For in truth, the sky is not empty save for birds and clouds, and celestial bodies such as the sun, moon and stars. It is full of the material stuff of air. Long forgotten by thinkers whose overwhelming focus has been on the earthly grounding of dwelling, who speak of landscape in ways that exclude the atmosphere, and for whom the very idea of materiality conjures up images of the solidity and durability of forms, the air is the very medium that makes perception possible. 'Can man live elsewhere than in air?' asks philosopher Luce Irigaray (1999: 8). The question is of course a rhetorical one to which the answer, as soon as it is posed, is obvious. Breathing the air, we also perceive *in* the air; it is not just that we would suffocate without it, we would also be struck senseless. Normally, we cannot see the air, though sometimes we can—as in the mist, or in the rising smoke from fires and chimneys, or in light snow when flakes, in their feathery descent, pick out the delicate tracery of aerial currents. Yet it is precisely because of the transparency of this life-sustaining medium that *we can see*. Moreover, in its vibrations, air transmits sound waves, so that we can hear, and in the freedom of movement it affords, it allows us to touch. All perception, as Gibson realised, depends upon it (Gibson 1979: 16). In an airless, solidified world, perception would be impossible. Thus our very existence as sentient beings is predicated on our immersion in the atmosphere.

In the phenomenology of Merleau-Ponty, to be sentient is to open up to a world, to yield to its embrace, and to resonate in one's inner being to its illuminations and reverberations. To be able to see is to open to the experience of light; to be able to hear is to open to the experience of sound; to be able to touch is to open to the experience of feeling. Bathed in light, submerged in sound and rapt in feeling, the sentient being rides the crest of the world's becoming, ever-present and witness to that moment when the world is about to disclose itself for what it is (Ingold 2011: 69). Thus in a sentient world there are no objects and subjects of perception; rather perception inheres in the creative movement of emergence, where 'things become things', to recall Merleau-Ponty's credo, and 'the world becomes world' (Merleau-Ponty 1964: 181). To perceive things, then, is simultaneously to be perceived *by* them: to see is to be seen, to hear is to be heard, and so on. This reversibility, most obvious in the exemplary instance of two hands touching, was for Merleau-Ponty fundamental to all perception, even to the perception of things we would normally consider inanimate. Thus in his work on landscape phenomenology, archaeologist Christopher Tilley reports that when he touches the stone of an ancient monument, he feels its touch on his hands: 'I touch the stone and the stone touches me' (Tilley 2004: 17). Admittedly, the reversibility entailed here is not quite of the same order as of a handshake. For the stone, in itself, is not sentient. But this does not, in Tilley's view, invalidate his claim that he is indeed touched *by* the stone. Precisely because it affects him bodily and structures his awareness, the stone, he thinks, may be said to possess an agency of its own.

Such things as stones, Tilley argues, 'are sensible without being sentient' (Tilley 2004: 19). By this he means that they are as much a part of the phenomenal world as are human bodies and, as such, are already *with* perceivers, just as bodies are, in the very process of perception. They are, as Merleau-Ponty put it in posthumously published notes, of the same *flesh* (Merleau-Ponty 1968: 248-51). Thus the archaeologist does not just touch the stone but touches *with* it. In the idiom of Goethe and von Uexküll, the hand that touches the stone is already stone-like. Otherwise put: stone is at once on both the hither and the far side of touch. And so it is too, says Merleau-Ponty, with the sun, the moon and the stars. Eyes that know sunlight, moonlight and starlight, like hands that know hardness and softness, roughness and smoothness, bring these qualities of light, as of feeling, into their own ways of perceiving (Merleau-Ponty 1962: 217). When I touch, stone touches, because the texture of stone has already invaded my tactile awareness. When I look, the sun, moon and stars look, since these celestial bodies, in their luminosity, have already invaded my visual awareness. And were I to listen, say, to a rumble of thunder that announces an impending storm, so the thunder listens because, in its sonority, it would have already invaded my auditory awareness. Neither stone, nor sun, moon and stars, nor thunder, are in themselves sentient. But *immersed in sentience*, they can, as it were, double back so as to touch, see and hear themselves. The stone touches through hands that have become stone-like; the sun and moon look through eyes that have become sun-like and moon-like, and the stars through eyes that are starstruck; likewise, the thunder listens through thunderstruck ears. Every perception of the world, in short, is part and parcel of the world's perceiving itself. In this 'coiling over', as Merleau-Ponty calls it, perceivers become one with what they perceive (Merleau-Ponty 1968: 140).

In Merleau-Ponty's key concept of the flesh, however, there remains a fundamental ambiguity. It clearly troubled him that the way in which the world penetrates the awareness of perceivers is *not*, in reality, the exact reverse of the way the latter perceive the world. For a self-sensing being, like a human, for one hand to touch another is precisely for the latter to touch the former. But the flesh of the world, Merleau-Ponty admitted, is not self-sensing. 'It is sensible and not sentient—I call it flesh nonetheless' (Merleau-Ponty 1968: 250). Under this one concept are subsumed, on the one hand, my being *with* stone, star or thunder, and the stone's, the star's or the thunder's being *with* me. The second kind of 'being with', we could say, is passionate. It is an inhalation of being, an invasion of consciousness. But the first is expressed in activity, in a movement of perception, launched on the current of exhalation. The one gathers and draws in the medium in which I am immersed, holding it in tension. The other releases the tension in bursting forth like a spark along a line of flight. The rhythmic alternation entailed here is comparable to that of the breast stroke in swimming, where the backward sweep of the arms and in-folding of the legs is followed by a forward thrust: the first is a movement of gathering or recollection, the second a movement of propulsion. And with this, we can return to what I have called the *fission/ fusion reaction* that drives all perception. In fusion, the stone, the star or the thunder is *with* me: it is in my hands, eyes and ears. But in fission, I have escaped from myself and am abroad in the cosmos, in among the elements. I am *with* them. The next step in my argument is to assimilate this alternation between fusion and fission, or breathing in and out, to one between colour and line.

Colourful Lines

You cannot draw the sky, but you can paint it. That, at least, was Gibson's opinion. Drawings are comprised of lines, and these lines, according to Gibson, delineate features of the environment that have come to the notice of the draughtsman and that he wishes to commit to a surface. These features are registered at the eye as the nested series of solid angles which Gibson calls the 'optic array'. What is not specified in the array cannot be drawn. Thus a line drawing can specify corners, edges, occluding edges (such as of an upright cylindrical object like a tree trunk or pylon), wires, cracks or fissures, and the horizon that marks the division between earth and sky. But the drawing *cannot* specify the shading, texture or crucially, the colour of a surface: only an 'abrupt discontinuity' in any of these qualities can be drawn (Gibson 1979: 287).

Moreover, in the absence of surface, you cannot draw translucence. Thus, while one might draw objects *in* the sky, such as clouds or the moon, whose outlines are specified by the angles they subtend at the eye, one cannot draw the sky itself, whether by day or by night. Now although Gibson (1979: 278) is adamant in his rejection of the more traditional view of drawing, tied to classical optics, according to which the draughtsman mentally projects, onto the page, an image that has first been formed in his mind, and then physically traces the outlines, the pencil-point of lead on the page still serves for him as an inverse of the pencil-point of light-rays at the eye. Thus the line traced by the moving hand emerges as a record of the invariants extracted from the optical array by the moving eye. To that extent, Gibson remains very much a Cartesian. Indeed Descartes himself preferred copper engravings to paintings, a preference that Merleau-Ponty traces to the premise that in presenting things by their outsides—their envelopes—engravings 'preserve the forms of objects' (1964: 172). That is, they record invariants in just the way that Gibson says drawings ought to do.

Seeing and drawing, thus understood, both participate in what Gilles Deleuze and Félix Guattari (2004: 186) call the 'white wall / black hole system'. Here, the black hole marks the site of subjectivity, and the white wall the plane of significance. Concealed behind or within the black hole lurks the Cartesian intellect, isolated and self-contained, on the white wall are projected its constructions, whether rendered in writing or as drawn designs. In seeing, white light reflected from the surfaces of objects in the world converges at the black pupil of the eye; in drawing, the typically black line, issuing from the mind of the hidden subject, by way of the hand, is inscribed upon the white surface of paper. Colour, in this system, is superficial, even deceptive. In contrast with the power of the line—engraved or drawn—to specify invariant form, colour figures as mere ornament, embellishment or 'make-up' with the power to seduce or charm but not, as in writing or drawing, to convey the processes of thought (Roque 1994). 'Truth', writes the anthropologist Michael Taussig, 'comes in black and white for our philosophers... Shapes and forms, outlines and marks, that is truth. Colour is another world...a luxury, an excess, a filler, a decoration' (Taussig 2009: 17-18). We have to fence it in with lines and marks—what Taussig here calls the 'boundary riders' of thought. If however we return to van Gogh's 'starry night', then this division between line and colour seems confounded. For while it is a painting comprised entirely of lines, every line is coloured. Here, as Merleau-Ponty remarks, 'depth, colour, form, line, movement, contour, physiognomy are all branches of Being, and...each one can sway all the rest' (1964: 188). They do not present themselves as answering to distinct problems or objectives, as between recording information and conveying mood, nor do they stand on opposite sides of a division between a rational mind and an inchoate world, or between thought and feeling.

Ever since Newton, we have been accustomed to the idea that as radiant energy, light comes in a range of wavelengths which, if differentially refracted by means of a prism, yield up all the colours of the spectrum. Recombined, they merge into 'colourless' white. Thus colour is equivalent to spectral differentiation. But if, as I have argued here, waves of radiant energy on the one hand, and on the other the capacity of photoreceptors in the eye to react to them, are conditions for the experience of light but do not amount to light as such, then we have to ask again: what *is* colour? Can we describe colours as differentiations not of wavelength but of affect? This, of course, is an old problem. It lay at the root of Goethe's celebrated spat with Newton, in his *Theory of Colours* of 1810. Colour, for Goethe, is not a physical datum but a phenomenon of correspondence, and every colour is a particular blend of the affective and the cosmic. At its most concentrated, it is black. Light, at its most intense, is white. Thus light dilutes colour, and colour dims light. 'White that becomes darkened or dimmed', Goethe observed, 'inclines to yellow; black, as it becomes lighter, inclines to blue' (Goethe 1840: 206, §502). We can see this in van Gogh's painting, where the brightest star, nearest the horizon, glows white, while those towards the zenith, as well as the moon, are fading to yellow. At the same time, the glimmerings of light in the night sky take it from black to shades of blue. In this scheme, colours are not variations of radiant light, spectrally arrayed on the white wall of projection as viewed through the black pinhole of the eye's pupil. For van Gogh as for Goethe, the black hole is a place not of emptiness but of infinite density, from which colours explode in the ignition of our visual awareness.

It follows that all colour, including that of the sky and the celestial bodies, is the product of a fission/fusion reaction. As against the Cartesian position—according to which the interior subject, at one with itself but divided from the cosmos, projects its meanings upon the white wall of the exterior—the seer, as in Merleau-Ponty's characterisation, is inwardly at one with the cosmos but divided from himself. There is no black-and-white opposition, then, between line and colour, as though the pupillary movement of a black point, issuing from within, were traced upon an external surface already saturated with the constituent hues of white light. Rather, every line has, or better *is*, colour, and every colour goes out along a line. Whether painted, drawn or written, lines pour from the fusion of the affective and the cosmic as colours pour from tar. 'Colour walks', writes Taussig. 'And as it walks, so it changes' (Taussig 2009: 36). It is not, therefore, a mere adornment, conferring an outer garb to thought or filling in its forms, but the very medium in which thought occurs. Like the atmosphere in the inclusive sense that I have delineated here, colour gets inside us and makes it so that whatever we do, say, draw or write is done with a certain affection or disposition. We inhale it as we breathe the air, and on the outward breath of exhalation we weave our lines of speech, song, story and handwriting into the fabric of the world. Thus colour lends atmosphere to the line; line gives colour to the atmosphere. Their relation is as intimate as in music, between harmony and melody. This was an analogy explicitly drawn by von Uexküll when he compared the life of every creature to a musical line, and correspondent lifelines to a polyphonic score (Uexküll 1982: 52-54). Colour and line, then, are as closely related as vertical and horizontal readings of the score.

Conclusion

As the atmospheric product of a fission/fusion reaction, light obeys very different rules from those to which we are accustomed from the science of optics. For one thing, as we have seen, it does not travel in straight lines, as rays, but curls like the sparks of a fire or its wreaths of smoke. For another, it is neither emitted from a celestial source nor registered by receptors in the eye, but follows the temporal correspondence of the seer's attention as it roams the heavens. It is, in these respects, comparable to sound, as it is to the wind. For is it not the *sound* of music that we hear when we listen to a melody? The acoustician, perversely, would insist that we do not. Sound, in his understanding, travels in a virtually straight line from source to recipient, by way of vibrations in the medium. To suppose that we hear sound on listening to music, he would say, is as illusory as supposing that we see light on watching the flickering of a candle flame or when gazing at the twinkling stars. As light delivers the star or the candle as an object of perception, so sound delivers music, understood—in the words of musicologist Eric Clarke—as 'a pattern of temporal proportions and pitch intervals' (Clarke 2005: 35). Thus the musical line goes one way and the line of sound goes another: the two lines exist in wholly different dimensions, as pattern differs from the vectors of projection by which it is rendered or discerned. It is as though music were drawn in black-and-white, which is of course exactly how it appears in standard musical notation, where black dots and lines are arranged in complicated patterns on white paper. Yet the musician will protest: for her, in performance, the melodic line she plays with her instrument *is* a line of sound, and moreover it is a line that is coloured with intensities along a range from the pitch black of silence to white noise.

Now this musical understanding of sound is precisely equivalent to the understanding of light that I have proposed here, and it suggests—as the musicologist Victor Zuckerkandl (1956: 344) once observed—that in opening our eyes and ears to the sky, vision and hearing effectively become one. And they merge with feeling, too, as we bare ourselves to the wind. For the wind, too, twists and turns, forming swirls and eddies. It may come from this or that direction, but the direction is not a point of origin, nor do I receive it like a tap on my cheek. Rather, the wind brushes by me on its journey to nowhere, and I feel it as I do my own body in its posture and movement. So to return to the questions with which I began. What is a sunbeam? It is the visual equivalent of a peal of sound, as when we hear the toll of a bell ringing in our ears, or of a gust of wind, as we feel it wrapping around our bodies. Why do stars seem at once so remote and so close? Because their light is generated in a reaction of fission and fusion. Can you paint the sky, or draw it? These are not alternatives, as the example of van Gogh's painting shows. For he paints with line, and the line is coloured. What do we mean when we say we see the sky? That we are present in the moment-by-moment birth of the atmosphere. And finally, what *is* the sky? I hesitate to give a final answer, since that would be to bring a kind of closure to what, more than anything, reveals the fundamental openness of the world in which we live. The sky is the kingdom of light, sound and air. It may perhaps be defined by a simple experiment. Place one finger between your eyes and touch the hard surface of your forehead. Reassure yourself that you are still there. Yet in the visual field, this tapping finger strikes no surface but rather looms as a ghostly presence that casts its shadow in the void. We are at once at home in our bodies and inhabitants of a world in which the body returns to us as a spectre. That world is the sky.

To conclude, let me return to Merleau-Ponty's notion of the flesh. Recall that even in his last writings, Merleau-Ponty remained confused about whether we are of the flesh of the world because of the way it is *with* us, or because of the way we are *with* it. Does he mean the fusion of affect with the cosmos to which I have applied the term 'atmosphere'? Or is he rather referring to the interlacing lines of flight or fission along which our own and others' lives are stretched? Elsewhere, I have called this interlacing the 'meshwork' (Ingold 2007: 80-82). Thus we can rephrase our question as follows: Is the flesh meshwork or atmosphere? My answer is that it is not one or the other but alternately both: atmosphere on the inhalation, meshwork on the exhalation. Meshwork and atmosphere are, if you will, two sides of the flesh, corresponding to the two senses of 'being with' that I have just distinguished. And the living, respiring being is the site where atmospheric immersion is transformed into the growth of the meshwork along its proliferating lines. In flight, the bird draws the sky, but gathers the atmosphere into its wings. When van Gogh paints, he gathers the colours of the night into his brush and goes on to weave his way around and between the stars. The magic of flight, and of painting, is epitomised in the famous story of Aladdin and the lamp. With a gentle stroke of wing or brush, as Aladdin stroked the lamp, whole worlds are unloosed, of vast horizons and empty skies, of immense possibility. All it takes is a soft touch—a little gesture, manual or visual—to rekindle the genie and release an atmosphere.

References

Clarke, E. 2005. *Ways of Listening: An Ecological Approach to the Perception of Musical Meaning*. Oxford: Oxford University Press.

Deleuze, G., and F. Guattari. 2004. *A Thousand Plateaus: Capitalism and Schizophrenia*, trans. B. Massumi (London: Continuum). Originally published as *Mille Plateaux*, vol. 2 of *Capitalisme et Schizophrénie* (Paris: Minuit, 1980).

Gibson, J.J. 1966. *The Senses Considered as Perceptual Systems* (Boston, MA: Houghton Mifflin).

———. 1979. *The Ecological Approach to Visual Perception* (Boston, MA: Houghton Mifflin).

Goethe, J.W. von 1840. *Theory of Colours*, trans. C.L. Eastlake (London: John Murray).

Goethe, J.W. von, and D. Luke 1964. *Goethe [Poems]: Introduced and Edited by David Luke, with Plain Prose Translations of Each Poem* (Harmondsworth: Penguin).

Ingold, T. 2000. *The Perception of the Environment: Essays on Livelihood, Dwelling and Skill* (London: Routledge).

———. 2007. *Lines: A Brief History* (Abingdon: Routledge).

———. 2010. 'Epilogue', in *Conversations with Landscape*, ed. K. Benediktsson and K.A. Lund (Farnham: Ashgate): 241-51.

———. 2011. *Being Alive: Essays on Movement, Knowledge and Description* (Abingdon: Routledge).

———. 2012. 'The Atmosphere', *Chiasmi International* 14: 75-87.

Irigaray, L. 1999. *The Forgetting of Air in Martin Heidegger*, trans. M.B. Mader (London: Athlone).

Merleau-Ponty, M. 1962. *Phenomenology of Perception*, trans. C. Smith (London: Routledge & Kegan Paul).

———. 1964. 'Eye and Mind', trans. C. Dallery, in *The Primacy of Perception, and Other Essays on Phenomenological Psychology, the Philosophy of Art, History and Politics*, ed. J.M. Edie (Evanston, IL: Northwestern University Press): 159-90.

———. 1968. *The Visible and the Invisible*, ed. C. Lefort, trans. A. Lingis (Evanston, IL: Northwestern University Press).

Roque, G. 1994. 'Writing/Drawing/Color', trans. C. Weber, *Yale French Studies* 84: 43-62.

Taussig, M. 2009. *What Colour Is the Sacred?* (Chicago, IL: University of Chicago Press).

Tilley, C. 2004. *The Materiality of Stone: Explorations in Landscape Phenomenology* (Oxford: Berg).

Uexküll, J. von 1982. 'The Theory of Meaning', trans. B. Stone and H. Weiner from *Bedeutungslehre* (ed. T. von Uexküll), *Semiotica* 42.1: 25-82 (originally published 1940).

Zuckerkandl, V. 1956. *Sound and Symbol: Music and the External World*, trans. W.R. Trask, Bollingen Series, 44 (Princeton, NJ: Princeton University Press).

Images in the Heavens: A Cultural Landscape

Bernadette Brady

University of Wales Trinity Saint David
Sophia Centre for the Study of Cosmology in Culture
School of Archaeology, History and Anthropology
Lampeter, Ceredigion SA48 7ED, Wales, UK
b.brady@uwtsd.ac.uk

Abstract

The constellation images with their historically persistent nature and adaptability fulfil many contemporary definitions of culture. From the earliest Elamite seals of the fourth millennium to the list-maps in the first century CE through Ptolemy's *Almagest*, the constellation images became established in Western cultures. With the invention of printing and the age of the great star atlases from the sixteenth to the nineteenth centuries, the constellation images continued to display cultural resistance by cartographers to Gothicise, Christianise, politicise, or simply remove them. This resilience has shown that the constellation images are in fact a living gallery of human history with images ranging from the Palaeolithic to the modern world. Furthermore, with their acceptance across a diversity of people and nations, the constellation images today have come to represent a form of world culture, in that they constitute a culture of humanity that is not linked by tribes, clans, nations, religions, or languages.

Keywords

Cosmology, culture, constellational imagery, sky, history of astronomy, cultural astronomy, celestial cartography.

Introduction

This paper investigates a story. It is a story that is remarkable in its resistance to change, yet at the same time receptive to the creative desires of humanity. Its roots lie potentially in the Palaeolithic period, yet it has carried its themes in an unbroken line from the Bronze Age to the twenty-first century. It is the story of the images humanity has placed in the sky, images embedded with human lifestyle, society, and even the gods. The history of this story shows that these sky images display a persistence through time, as well as evoke an almost universality of acceptance. Such a wide acceptance challenges the unspoken but assumed argument that the constellation images are an irrelevant historical relic. I contend instead that these images represent a cultural phenomenon that has transcended national and religious identities, at least within the West.

The notion of culture has diverse definitions. Raymond Williams (1958: 82) in the 1950s suggested that culture is both ordinary—how an individual is taught to act, behave, and respond—as well as creative. His premise was that culture is at once traditional, in the handing down of customs from one generation to the next, yet at the same time flexible and open to change, allowing for human creativity. A more contemporary approach to the question of culture is that of John Bodley (1999), who argued that culture is a shared social phenomenon that is learned, passes from one generation to the next, and involves the assignment of arbitrary symbolic meanings. For Bodley, culture is an observable phenomenon, and hence he recognised the importance of images and icons as carriers of a people's cultural information.

In contrast to Williams and Bodley, Terry Eagleton focused on how culture is created rather than how it is carried. He suggests that culture is the outcome of the human will encountering the determinism of nature. He sees the word 'agriculture' as an example of such a merging and points out how customs, ritual, and family knowledge emerge out of the human will pitted against or in union with the landscape (Eagleton 2000: 2). In his view of culture, he keeps his eyes firmly on the ground. Nevertheless, within Eagleton's earth-based definition, it is possible to consider the sky. For the sky is also part of nature; it also exhibits a persistent and unrelenting fixedness, and the human will has always engaged and negotiated with the 'heavenly gods'. Eagleton also argues that culture borrows from the determinism of nature, and through its traditions and history it imposes pressure on its human carriers for its continual existence: 'Culture is what we can change, but the stuff to

be altered has its own autonomous existence, which then lends it something of the recalcitrance of nature' (2000: 4). For Eagleton, a culture,
once established by the blending of humanity with nature, is hard to
remove.

Within Eagleton's definition, therefore, the determinism of nature,
earth, and sky is a vital ingredient for the formation of culture. He sees it
like the 'other parent' in union with the 'parent' of human imagination.
Within Bodley's definition, cultures, once formed, produce images and
symbols that, Williams would suggest, exist in a diversity of expressions
from the revered to the mundane. My aim is to show how the sky and its
images exhibit the features of Williams's, Bodley's, and Eagleton's
definitions of culture—a culture that has emerged from the blend of
humanity with the fixedness of the sky and one which displays an
autonomous existence stubbornly resisting change. At the same time, it is
a culture that through human creativity has scattered its images across
time into diverse objects, ranging from precious manuscripts and
ceilings, to mouse mats and coffee cups.

Images in the Sky

This journey in exploring sky images as a unique culture begins with
some of humanity's earliest art. The bull leaps out at the viewer from the
walls of the Lascaux cave (Fig. 1), dated from 17,000 BCE. With its
long horns and seven dots it appears to be the sky bull of Taurus marked
with the seven stars of the Pleiades. This image may, however, simply
be the statement, 'We saw seven bulls'. Of greater interest is that
scholars like Michael Rappenglueck (Whitehead 2000) suggest that it is
Taurus. The desire for it to be Taurus is a desire to pull those forgotten
artists and forgotten people with their forgotten culture closer to us, to be
united across time by a common sky, all belonging to a common culture.
Another piece of evidence for this desire comes from a much later
period.

This is the discovery of what may be a celestial bear within the
traditions of the native people of North America. A Pawnee sky map
dated earlier than the arrival of the white settlers in the sixteenth century
apparently shows a constellation of a bear using the same stars as Ursa
Major (Hagar 1900: 92; Buckstaff 1927: 282; also see Frazier 1979).
This has been explained either as a coincidence that the Pawnees inde-
pendently saw the stars of Ursa Major as a bear or that this constellation was a part of the oral tradition carried across the late Pleistocene

period by the first humans into the northern parts of the Americas conservatively established around 15,000 BCE (Goebel, Waters, and O'Rourke 2008: 1497).

Figure 1. The bull, Lascaux Cave, France, c. 17,000 BCE. Photo: Prof. Saxx, Wikimedia Commons.

Although not as speculative as the motivation of our Palaeolithic ancestors or the star maps of the Pawnee people, the debates on the origins of the constellation images are still diverse. Archaeoastronomers A. Crommellin in 1923 and later John Rogers (1998), S. Zhitomirsky (1999: 495), and Bradley Schaefer (2002: 316) argued that the Southern Greek constellations were established in a series of groups, ranging from the third millennium to the first millennium BCE. These constellations are the four giants of the heavens, Ophiuchus, Boötes, Auriga, and Hercules, as well as the southern vessel of the Argo and the constellation Centaurus. There was also a Mesopotamian contribution. Nick Kanas (2007: 28) argued that by the third millennium BCE the names of the constellations of the Bull, the Lion, and the Scorpion were recorded in Sumerian text. Jeffery Cooley (2013: 58-64), in his summary of Babylonian and Assyrian celestial text, noted that by the Middle Assyrian period (sixteenth to tenth century BCE), thirty-six bright stars were listed within constellations. B.L. Van der Waerden (1949: 13-14) contended that most of these Middle Assyrian constellations appear to correspond with our current view of the sky. These include eighteen constellations that describe the path of the moon. These were listed by Francesca Rochberg (2004: 127) as the Hired One (Aries), Great Bull of Heaven, the Twins, the Crab, the Lion, the Farrow (Virgo), the Scales (Libra), the Scorpion, Pabilsag (Sagittarius), the Goat Fish, the Great One (Aquarius), the Tails (Pisces), the Swallows (another part of Pisces), the Stars (the Pleiades), the True Shepherd of Anu (Orion), the Old Man

(Perseus), and the Crook (Auriga), although she also commented that the drawn images may not have been used until the middle of the first millennium BCE. However, the images were well established as descriptive text in the *Enuma Anu Enlil*, a text which originated in the last third of the third millennium BCE and expanded in the second millennium BCE (Hunger and Pingree 1999: 6-7). The text of the *Enuma Anu Enlil* is a collection of celestial omens, and it used the sky images as a way of locating a planet in the heavens. As Reiner put it, for example: 'If Jupiter reaches the navel of the Scorpion, in the land of Elam the market [price] of one kor of barley will be reduced to one bushel', that is, by four-fifths (Reiner 1999: 27).

Separate from these arguments regarding the history of the constellation images, the image of the bull and the lion is an ancient motif, and it makes up what Willy Hartner (1965: 1) has labelled a symplegma: an intertwining of two different objects which make up a symbol. He suggested that an Elamite seal from the fourth millennium BCE is that of a symplegma of the constellations of the Lion and the Bull. Despite other seals of other combative animals appearing within the corpus of Elamite seals, he further concluded that this particular symplegma represented a calendar event, as it described the naked eye astronomy of the spring night skies for that period (Hartner 1965: 15). At those latitudes for the fourth millennium BCE, the February sunsets would reveal the constellation of the Lion culminating as the Bull set in the west. Thus the setting of the Bull in the evening marked its death, with the new incoming season having as its icon the culminating Lion. Regardless of whether Hartner's assessment of the seal is correct, this symplegma of possible sky/animal blended imagery is also reflected in later Mesopotamian art, as shown in a relief from Persepolis dated c. 550 BCE (Fig. 2).

Figure 2. A later depiction of the Lion/Bull symplegma, Persepolis c. 550 BCE. Photo: Anatoly Terentiev, Wikimedia Commons.

Clearer examples of descriptive sky images appear later in Homer's *Odyssey* and *Iliad* and Hesiod's *Shield of Heracles*, works placed into text around the eighth century BCE (Lorimer 1951: 86-87). In these texts the constellations appear to be well established with personalised names. In *The Odyssey* Book V, Homer describes Odysseus's method of navigating his vessel across the ocean for eighteen days, a possible reference to the eighteen constellations of the moon:

> here he sat and never closed his eyes in sleep, but kept them on the Pleiades or watched Bootes slowly set, or the Great Bear, nicknamed the Wain, which always wheels round in the same place and looks across at Orion the Hunter with a wary eye (Homer 1986: 95).

In Hesiod's *Shield of Heracles*, which is more cosmological than astronomical, there is, however, a description of the constellation Perseus:

> There, too, was the son of rich-haired Danae, the horseman Perseus: his feet did not touch the shield and yet were not far from it... On his feet he had winged sandals, and his black-sheathed sword was slung across his shoulders by a cross-belt of bronze. He was flying swift as thought. The head of a dreadful monster, the Gorgon, covered the broad of his back, and a bag of silver—a marvel to see (Hesiod 1914: II, 216-25).

Coming after Homer and Hesiod was the work of Eudoxus of Cnidus (406–355 BCE), who wrote a 'handbook' for the globe—a work now lost but considered to be part of the source material for the *Farnese Globe*, a second-century Roman copy of a Hellenistic globe which displayed most of the now-considered classical constellations (Estey 1943: 114). This notion of the sky images carrying the knowledge of the celestial sphere or globe was also evident in the third-century BCE sky poem, *The Phaenomena*, by Aratus (315–240 BCE). Aratus was a student of Zeno, the founder of the Stoic school of philosophy. Aratus placed into text a description of the sky images and their relationship to each other, and he used these images to define the great circles of the celestial sphere:

> Between the Tropics a Belt, peers of the grey Milky Way, undergirds the earth and with imaginary line bisects the sphere. In it the days are equal to the nights both at the waning of the summer and the waxing of the spring. The sign appointed for it is the Ram and the knees of the Bull—the Ram being borne lengthwise through it, but of the Bull just the visible bend of the knees (Aratus 1989: L.511-15).

Due to the effects of precession, the great circles of the celestial sphere gradually move against the backdrop of the stars. Therefore, a description of how any circle passed through a particular celestial image is valid only for a certain period of some hundred or so years. In this way Aratus's poetic descriptions of the constellation imagery woven into celestial geometry allows the different parts of his poem to be dated.

Aratus wrote his poem in the third century BCE, but he did not use direct observation. Instead he used a collection of visual astronomy data, some of which can be dated by the use of precession to 2000 BCE +/– 300 years (Zhitomirsky 1999: 498; Roy 1984; Crommellin 1923). The implications of Aratus's poem are twofold: first, it indicates that some images of the Greek constellations were in use from the second millennium BCE, and second, in this early period these images were already used to carry knowledge of the celestial sphere (Brady 2013). Today the celestial coordinates of right ascension and declination define the equator, tropics, or the location of a star. In the first millennium BCE, however, it was the actual constellation images that defined the sky geometry. A star like Antares, for example, was located by looking for the red star in the heart or middle of the Scorpion (Ptolemy 1915: 39). The Tropic of Capricorn was defined by a line which ran through the 'Water-Bearer's feet and the Monster's tail' (Aratus 2010: 525-26). Thus, by this period, the constellations' images had moved from mythic/ divine creatures to carriers of astronomical data and were displaying what Eagleton (2000: 4) would suggest was their 'own autonomous existence'.

Consequently, in 323 BCE when Alexander the Great's half-brother, Philip III Arrhidaeus, became Pharaoh of Egypt, the Greek culture resisted the adoption of the rich sky imagery of the Egyptians. The Dendera Zodiac (Fig. 3) displays this phenomenon. Located in the temple of Hathor at Dendera and, according to R.A. Parker, dated within the Hellenistic period of around 50 BCE, it shows evidence of how the Greek constellation images colonised the Egyptian sky (Parker 1974: 63). The Dendera Zodiac is a stone star map that has twelve zodiac signs, as well as other mythological or divine figures representing constel- lations. There is much we can recognise in this sky map from 2000 years ago—the zodiac, for example. As Parker has argued, however, there is much here that is alien from our vantage point because the Egyptian sky components failed to be adopted into the Greek constellations that were already, by this time, saturated with useful navigational and celestial sphere information.

Figure 3. Photograph of the Dendera Zodiac, originally part of the ceiling in the temple of Hathor at Dendera about 50 BCE. This image is a true sky map showing a mixture of Greek/Mesopotamian images as well as Egyptian. Musée du Louvre. Image: Sebi, Wikimedia Commons.

Indeed, there is more that is familiar for the twenty-first-century viewer on a Babylonian border stone from 1500 BCE than on the great astronomical ceiling of Senmut, created in the same period by an Egyptian architect (Figs. 4, 5). While Senmut's ceiling is considered to be the oldest known astronomical display in the world, as Donald Etz (1997: 143) has pointed out, it raises little interest amongst historians of astronomy. This lack of Egyptian sky components in our contemporary images suggests that the blended Mesopotamian and early Southern Greek imagery had, before they encountered the Egyptian constellations, become culturally robust by being embedded with astronomical knowledge.

Figure 4. Section of a boundary stone showing the Hydra, Leo, and the Scorpion. Image: Trustees of the British Museum.

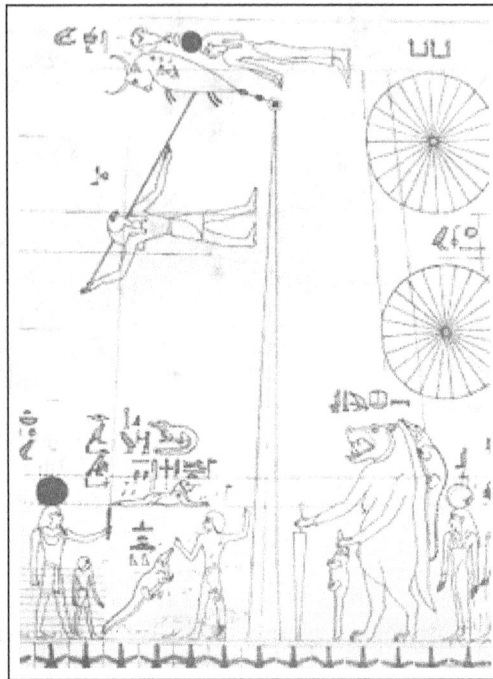

Figure 5. Section of the ceiling from the tomb of Senmut, 2nd millennium BCE. Image: Wikimedia Commons.

By the second century BCE, the astronomer Hipparchus (190–120 BCE) had compiled the first known star catalogue, which is believed to be one of Claudius Ptolemy's (90–c. 168) prime sources (North 2008: 98-99). Ptolemy was concerned with the positions of stars and noted, borrowed, and re-observed 1026 stars in order to help find the rate of precession.[1] Ptolemy used the tradition of the day and described each star in relation to its position within the now Hellenised images of the constellations. In doing so, far more than Aratus some 400 years earlier, he embedded fine image detail into his text. Each star was located and defined as part of, for example, a girdle, a buckle of a belt, the gem in a tiara, and so forth (Ptolemy 1998: 341-400). Figure 6 is an image of the stick figure of Boötes showing a few of Ptolemy's named stars via their position in that image. These finely detailed star-image locations are now known as the Ptolemaic positions. As Ptolemy's *Almagest* became a revered work from the classical period right through to the seventeenth century, the images themselves were protected by their astronomical usefulness and

1. Ptolemy actually listed 1028 stars but two of these were duplicates.

their association with his name. Indeed, as I shall discuss presently, only once in the last 2000 years were Ptolemy's star positions challenged, and that was in 1603 by Johann Bayer. Bayer's mirror-imaging of Ptolemy's positions, however, in which the right hand became the left, were dismissed and overthrown by his contemporary, Johannes Kepler, and again later in the eighteenth century by John Flamsteed.

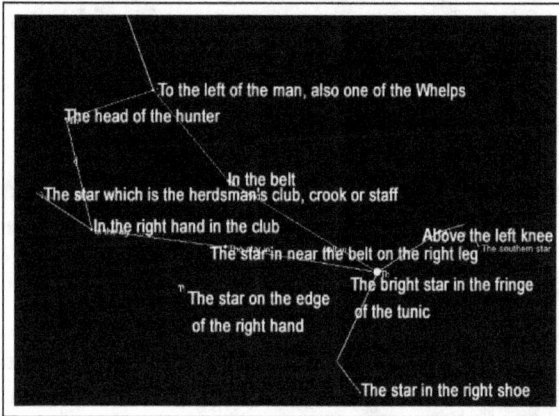

Figure 6. Boötes with some of Ptolemy's star's positions, named within the image so as to locate each star in its unique position in the sky. Image: Bernadette Brady.

Meanwhile, the sky images, from possibly as early as the fourth millennium BCE or, more conservatively, as late as the first millennium BCE, maintained their form and visual astronomy data until the end of the classical era. From this post-Ptolemaic period until the invention of the printing press, the images moved into medieval manuscript, frescos, and Islamic globes (Rogers 1998: 82). This was principally through illustrations based on Aratus's *Phaenomena*, in the case of Islamic works, or Cicero's Latin version of Aratus in the West (Beer 1967: 183). Often linked with Aratus's work was the *Poetica Astronomica* of Gaius Julius Hyginus (64 BCE–17 CE), a work that focused on the ethno-astronomical data of the mythology of the constellations as described by Ptolemy rather than naked eye astronomy (Whitleld 1995: 33; Condos 1997). Throughout the medieval era the constellation images fuelled by the work of Aratus and Hyginus underwent stylistic changes, yet they still maintained their association with Ptolemy's star/image descriptions.

Printed Maps

It was not until the invention of the printing press that the constellation images were seriously challenged. The first known printed sky maps were produced in 1482 by Erhard Ratdolt from Augsburg, Germany. Ratdolt was considered to be one of the masters of early printing, and he developed the techniques that gave the world the first book faceplate (Redgrave 1894: 6-7). As he developed printing skills far superior to others of his profession, he sought publications worthy of his talent. He produced two books that were both Latin versions of classical works. These books were the first printed edition of Euclid's geometry that, to the amazement of other printers, included the diagrams as part of the printed text, and the *Poeticon Astronomicon* by Hyginus (Ratdolt 1482), complete with images. With both these works Ratdolt was more concerned with the images and the typeface than with the accuracy of the printed constellations (Heath 1920). In his printing of the *Poeticon Astronomicon*, each constellation was a separate image and the stars were not precisely located.[2] He printed his constellations using a geocentric orientation, the view of the stars as seen from the earth, with the exception of the constellation Aquarius. His publications went through many editions and reached a large readership. From Ratdolt's and his readers' point of view, the important information was the image's link with the mythology, rather than their accuracy as star locators.

Ratdolt took his sky images from different, now unknown medieval manuscripts. In his selection he drew on the style of images used by Michael Scotus (1175–1232) who, in his *Liber de signis*, had moved away from the classical or Aratean style and produced Gothic and Romanesque images (Ackermann 2001). Ratdolt's Water Carrier (Fig. 7) is thus dressed in medieval clothing and pours his water into a dish, whereas Ptolemy describes him pouring water into the mouth of a great fish. The noble warrior king Orion (Fig. 8) is shown as a medieval nobleman in full battle armour, and the skin of a lion, which Ptolemy hangs from Orion's left arm, has been turned into a shield. Ratdolt may have tampered with Ptolemy's images to follow the medieval tendency for Gothic images. For a widely based readership, however, he removed the stars from their list maps and provided them as images on the printed page, freeing these sky images from the confines of frescos and rare manuscripts.

2.   Ptolemy's list-map places every star in a specific location *within* every image, using the image itself as the reference point. Ratdolt's stars were, however, randomly placed in the images, ignoring Ptolemy's descriptions.

Astronomers tended to consider Ratdolt's contribution to the world of celestial cartography as minor. Nevertheless, his mass production of sky images had an impact on cartography, because list-maps of the sky, such as had been produced by Ptolemy, were no longer thought to be adequate. If cartographers wanted their work to be widely accepted, they were now dependent on both the continual improvement of stellar plotting as well as on their ability to depict the imagery of the sky. Indeed, for over 300 years after Ratdolt, up to and including the *Uranographia* of Johann Bode (1747–1826), the role of the artist within celestial cartography was valued. If the images of the constellations are a culture in their own right, then by being instrumental in their mass production, Ratdolt is one of its significant contributors.

Figure 7. Erhard Ratdolt's Aquarius, in Hyginus, *Poeticon Astronomicon*, published by Erhard Ratdolt, 1482. Digitised book in public domain.

Figure 8. Erhard Ratdolt's Orion, in Hyginus, *Poeticon Astronomicon*, published by Erhard Ratdolt, 1482. Digitised book in public domain.

Some thirty-three years later, in 1515, the German artist, engraver, and mathematician, Albrecht Dürer (1471–1528), produced the first real astronomical star maps containing both images and accurate star positions. Rather than a globe, he produced mat maps showing a large portion of the sky in two polar projections: one containing eighteen northern constellations (Fig. 9) and the twelve zodiac constellations; and the other containing fifteen southern constellations. In producing the first recognised mat map of the heavens, Dürer also drew on the spirit of Ptolemy's list map by returning to the Aratean or classical images. However, he maintained the classical globe or external orientation to his maps, in which the images were oriented as if they were placed on a celestial globe such that one looked down onto the constellation from above, rather than the geocentric view of looking up to the constellations from the earth.

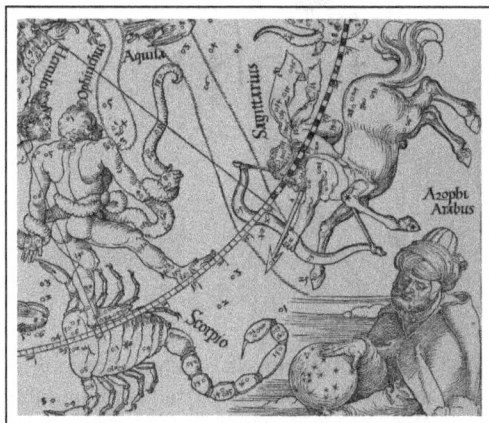

Figure 9. Section of the northern planisphere by Albrecht Dürer. Celestial Map of the Northern Sky, showing Scorpio, Ophiuchus and Sagittarius, 1515. Woodcut. Image: Trustees of the British Museum.

Dürer worked with Conradus Heinfagel (c. 1470–1530), a mathematician from Nuremberg, and so was able to include coordinates and scales with his celestial images. This meant that, for the first time, astronomers did not require the constellation image in order to locate a star. Antares was no longer found by looking to the heart of the Scorpion but could be located by Dürer's coordinate system. Up to the time of Dürer's work, cartographers were expected to be both mathematician and artist or mathematicians who worked with artists. Dürer, however, freed astronomy from the need for artistry; yet the cultural momentum of the constellation images was such that the link between art and mathematics was maintained for another 400 years. Although Dürer's maps had little impact at the time on the public, his development of a mat map laid the foundation for future cartographers, and he provided the now classical visual interpretation of Ptolemy's text-based images (Holden 1890: 20).

Dürer's or Heinfagel's choice of the globe-view for the orientations of the constellations did not, however, settle the question. If the bull of the Lascaux cave is a representation of a sky image, then it is drawn from the geocentric perspective, since drawing a sky image by looking up from earth is the natural view. In 1532 Johannes Honter (1498–1549), known as the Luther of Transylvania, produced *Imagines Constellationum Borealium* and *Imagines Constellationum Australium*. These two star maps were published as part of the collected works of Claudius Ptolemy (Ptolemy 1541). Honter was influenced by Dürer's and Heinfagel's mathematics, yet he returned to Ratdolt's geocentric perspective (Warner 1979: 123). In the early sixteenth century there had been a resurgence of the Ptolemaic and Aristotelian geocentric models of the solar system (Heninger 1977: 53). Honter's decision to create his celestial maps from the geocentric perspective, therefore, may have been a reflection of this new enthusiasm for Ptolemy, conveniently in rapport with the new Lutheran doctrine of simplicity and reality—to wit, the stars viewed as they appear to everyman and everywoman. Additionally, Honter rejected the classical images and changed some of the figures into northern Europeans dressed in heavy clothes and with thick beards. His work proved popular and went through many editions, making a lasting impact. Unlike Dürer and Heinfagel, whose mathematics and new idea of scale and coordinate system made their work useful for actually locating the stars in the sky, Honter's maps were mathematically flawed, the coordinate system being a full 30° out of alignment. Nevertheless, and perhaps surprisingly, this mathematical fault did not detract from the work's popularity. As Kanas has claimed, people wanted the maps for their constellation images (2007: 142).

It was some fifty years after Honter that the first accurate geocentric sky maps were produced. Giovanni Paolo Gallucci (1538–1621) was a mathematician and astrologer who lived in Venice in the mid-to-latter part of the sixteenth century. In 1588 he produced *Theatrum Mundi, et Temporis*, an astrological handbook that contained tables and diagrams for explaining celestial mechanics, as well as a set of star maps. In this work Gallucci presented all forty-eight of Ptolemy's constellations using the accuracy of Copernicus's new star catalogue. Gallucci (1614: 91) also used his knowledge of perspective and geometry and linked a trapezoidal projection to a stellar coordinate system so that the location of the stars could be read from the margins in both celestial latitude and longitude. It was Gallucci, therefore, who produced the first useful celestial atlas; it was geocentric in its orientation and accurate in its positioning of stars. In this seeming burst of freedom and creativity, Gallucci produced truly remarkable images for his atlas. He depicted the classical constellations in a style that appears modern. In this respect he was at the same time handing on the classical images to future genera-tions while also exhibiting his own creativity. His images depict Boötes the Hunter as an ancient hunter-gatherer, barefoot, and wearing only a loin cloth or short tunic, while his Cassiopeia foreshadows Picasso's pink period, showing an uninhibited and relaxed classical woman reclining on her throne (Fig. 10).

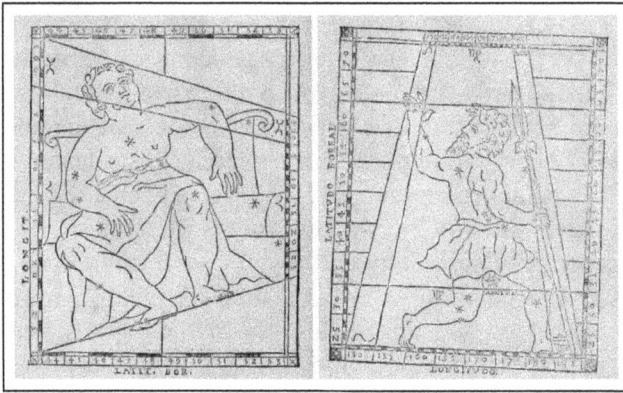

Figure 10. Gallucci 's *Theatrum Mundi, et Temporis*, 1614, Boötes (right) and Cassiopeia (left). Images: Gallucci, Giovanni Paolo, *Theatrum Mundi, et Temporis*, Granada: Sebastian Muñoz, 1614. Digitised book in public domain.

By this stage, the long history of the expression of star images had seen many style changes yet nevertheless had remained consistent with regard to their subject matter of hunters, warriors, mythical creatures, animals, scales, crowns, and insects. These images were also now represented in two ways: the globe-view and the earth-view. By the late sixteenth century, however, another factor came into play. In 1598 Tycho Brahe (1546–1601) completed the most comprehensive and extensive star catalogue since Ptolemy and thus laid the foundations for a new genera- tion of cartographers. The most influential of these was Johann Bayer (1572–1625). In 1603 he produced the *Uranometria*, which was regarded as the best scientific celestial cartography endeavour of its day. Bayer's work not only contained the forty-eight Ptolemaic constellations, it also included twelve new southern constellations and thus began the effort to name the southern sky (Bayer 1603). The *Uranometria* contained fifty-one star charts and was a true atlas, as each page had a grid coordinate system, enabling a star's position to be read in relationship to the sky as well as to other constellations. In addition, Bayer developed the system first used fifty-one years earlier by Alessandro Piccolomini (1508–1578), who labelled the stars in order of brightness within a constellation using alphabetical letters (Piccolomini 1552). Piccolomini chose Latin, but Bayer employed the less Catholic Greek letters. His maps were accurate and followed the geocentric orientation established and made acceptable by Ratdolt and Honter. These maps were popular with non-astronomers because of their beauty, but Bayer turned all of his figures outwards to face the outer solar system. Although Ptolemy had described the star Betelgeuse as 'the right shoulder of Orion', Bayer's warrior Orion now became left- handed (Fig. 11). Bayer's desire to allow his figures to look outward rather than down upon the human race outweighed the cultural pressure to maintain Ptolemy's traditional star positions. For reasons known only to himself, Bayer was willing to sacrifice one of the cartographer's ancient traditions in order to achieve this reversal.

Figure 11. Orion from Johann Bayer's *Uranometria* 1603. In this image Orion holds his club in his left hand. Image: Wikimedia Commons.

Johannes Kepler (1571–1630) disagreed with Bayer's reversal of Ptolemy's image-based star positions. In 1606 in Prague, Kepler published a single constellation figure, *De Stella Nova in Pede Serpentaria*, which showed a new star (Fig. 12). This star had appeared in Ophiuchus at the same time as a triple conjunction of the planets Mars, Jupiter, and Saturn. His figure is clearly Bayer's Ophiuchus from 1603, but it now turned around to restore Ptolemy's star positions. Bayer produced a beautiful and accurate celestial atlas, yet no other cartographer followed his example, even though his work was considered of great importance astronomically. His system for defining the order of magnitude of the stars within a constellation by the Greek alphabet is universally accepted and carries his name but not his reversed images.

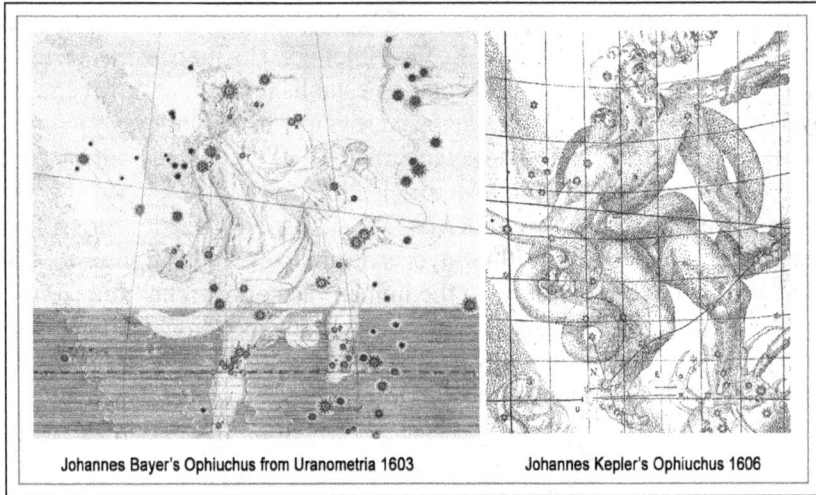

Johannes Bayer's Ophiuchus from Uranometria 1603   Johannes Kepler's Ophiuchus 1606

Figure 12. A comparison of Johann Bayer's Ophiuchus from *Urano-metria*. Image courtesy of Barry Lawrence (Ruderman Antique Maps—RareMaps.com) showing the reversal of stellar positions and Johannes Kepler's response in 1606. Kepler's image: Wikimedia Commons.

In this period Julius Schiller (1580–1627) produced a celestial atlas that attempted to replace all the classical constellations with Christian images. There had been a movement within monastic circles from the sixth century with Gregory of Tours's *De cursu stellarum*, which Christianised some of the constellations to allow the monks to tell the time by the stars without evoking any pagan imagery.[3] Schiller, however, after help from Bayer, in 1627 took this earlier Christian concept and expanded it and published the *Coelum Stellatum Christianum* (Schiller 1627) which represented the celestial hemispheres as the two parts of the Bible. The constellations of the northern hemisphere focused on the New Testament, while the Old Testament was embodied in the southern hemisphere images. Aquarius became Abraham and Isaac, Aries became Christ's Manger, Cancer turned into the Scourge of Christ, and Boötes became Saint Sylvester. In 1661, Andreas Cellarius (1596–1665)

3. McCluskey 1998: 106.

produced a new edition of Schiller's Christian constellations. Published in Amsterdam as *Harmonia Macrocosmica*, Cellarius improved the artistry of the original images and, indeed, made the concept of a Christian sky more popular by abolishing all the 'pagan' images (Cellarius 1661). This was to be the first serious attempt in the history of constellations from the Sumerian text of 3000 BCE to the then-present day to replace all the constellation images, and it was unsuccessful. Due to Cellarius's 'apostolic fever', other astronomers did not accept his images (Ashworth 1981: 60).

Politics brought another challenge to the expression of the sky's images. In 1690, Elizabeth, the wife of Johannes Hevelius (1611–1687) posthumously published his great *Prodromus Astronomiae*. In this work Hevelius introduced ten new constellations including a political one named *Scutum Sobiescianum* (Hevelius 1690), which was the coat-of-arms of his patron (Ashworth 1981: 60). When this coat-of-arms was later renamed *Scutum*, the Shield, it lost its political overtone. The starry sky was now, however, moving into the arena of political propaganda and this continued into the late seventeenth and early eighteenth centuries, during which a variety of celestial atlases and globes were produced. One notable example was by Erhard Weigel (1625–1699), a professor of astronomy at the University of Jena, Germany, who in 1699 produced a celestial globe that was an optical planetarium.[4] Weigel did not draw on the classical images of Ptolemy but rather the coats-of-arms of the royal families of Europe. In Weigel's sky the all-conquering and all-powerful warrior Orion, whom the Egyptians considered their pharaoh, became the double-headed Austrian Eagle (Franklin Institute). His imagery was designed either to flatter the European courts or to make a statement—perhaps true, perhaps propaganda—about the prevailing European balance of power. Like the Christian constellations of Schiller and Cellarius 150 years earlier, however, as Jürgen Hamel (2010: 34) concluded, Weigel's cartographic work was more agitprop than astronomy.

At this time the question of longitude was one that occupied the minds of British astronomers. To help this endeavour, John Flamsteed (1646–1719) slowly compiled a catalogue of stellar observations over a period

---

4. The globe was constructed in a manner that allowed a lamp to be placed in a hollow centre. The light from this lamp shone through an embossed copper sphere, which used holes to represent the stars. The observer looked into the globe through one of four large holes, and could see stars in their correct positions as points of light. Weigel also produced a globe large enough to enable a person to walk inside.

of forty-three years (Kanas 2007: 172). Flamsteed held the position of the first Astronomer Royal of England 1675–1719 and named this catalogue the British Catalogue of Stars (Flamsteed 1729). But it was not until 1725 that his star catalogue *Atlas Coelestis*, having been edited by his wife Margaret, was published posthumously. Flamsteed published *Atlas Coelestis* in part to correct the reversal of the figures of the constellations in Bayer's work of 1603. Bayer's work had become popular due to its accurate stellar positions, as well as the quality of its images. Flamsteed considered this work to represent a major flaw in celestial cartography. Thus he went to considerable trouble to find an artist capable of drawing the images to his satisfaction, eventually finding Sir James Thornhill, the man who had created murals in many of Christopher Wren's great buildings, including St Paul's Cathedral (Whitleld 1995: 100). Flamsteed wanted to restore Ptolemy's star positions and re-establish the classical geocentric imagery—with the figures looking down on humanity—and to ensure that all his measurements were perfect. His perfectionism delayed the publishing of his observations and star catalogue, which frustrated Isaac Newton (1642–1726) and Edmond Halley (1656–1742), who needed Flamsteed's star catalogue for their own work in trying to calculate longitude. They pressured Flamsteed to release his work; Flamsteed's response was recorded in a letter he wrote in 1705 quoted by Deborah Warner (1979: 82): 'Sir I. Newton would have the great catalog printed without the maps. I cannot consent to so sneaking a proposition.' Newton and Halley prevailed, however, as Flamsteed sent them a preliminary manuscript of his catalogue and some of his observations under the condition that only his observations were to be published. Despite this request, Newton and Halley printed 400 copies of Flamsteed's complete catalogue without crediting its author. Flamsteed tracked down and destroyed some 300 copies (Kanas 2007: 173). Apart from Flamsteed's desire to protect his work, his prolonged reluctance to release his catalogue was due in part to the huge effort that went into preparing the images; this suggested that he considered the role of the classical images of the constellations to be of equal value to the star locations themselves.

By the early nineteenth century, accurate and complete celestial maps were becoming very dense as new stars and nebulae were discovered through the use of the telescope. With all this new visual information competing for space on the cartographer's map, the question of the need for the constellation images was reconsidered. By the dawn of the nineteenth century, Johann Bode (1747–1826) in Berlin was completing what came to be known as the last great star atlas, the *Uranographia* of 1801. Bode was a self-taught astronomer and became the director of the Berlin Academy of Science, a position he held for over 40 years (Hockey

2007: 141). He produced the *Uranographia* by using Ptolemy's star-image positions and the classical geocentric orientation (Bode 1801). He used the work of Bayer, Hevelius, and Flamsteed for the new constellations and stars. His atlas contained ninety-nine constellations, with at least five asterisms or subgroups. Ptolemy's work had contained 1026 stars; Bode's masterpiece contained over 17,000 stars and 2500 nebulae. From this point forward, according to Kanas (2007: 183-84), professional star atlases for astronomers were stripped of images. Yet some of the images in Bode's *Uranographia*—images such as the Bull, the Lion, the Snake, as well as more complex images such as Pabilsag the fearful warrior of the Babylonian zodiac—had and continued to maintain a visual integrity for over 5500 years. Pabilsag, from an eighth-century neo-Babylonian boundary stone, for example, demonstrates the remarkable constancy in image with contemporary renditions of the constellation Sagittarius (Fig. 13).

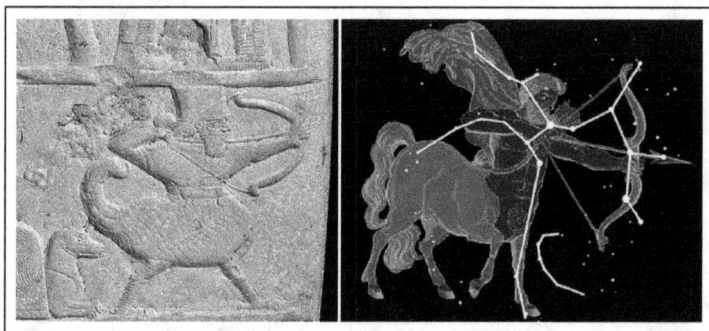

Figure 13. Pabilsag from eighth-century neo-Babylonian boundary stone (image courtesy of the British Museum) and a contemporary image of Sagittarius. Starlight celestial software (permission given).

By the early twentieth century, astronomers' maps, stripped of their artistry and mythology, were visually barren to the uninitiated or uneducated. In 1922 astronomers decided officially to organise the constellations of sky, and the International Astronomical Union divided the celestial sphere into eighty-eight constellations, which included all of the classical constellations along with forty-four new constellations. By 1930 the boundaries between the constellations were being defined in terms of right ascension and declination (Davenhall and Leggett 1997). Just as the Greeks had difficulty in standardising the location of the seasonal zodiac signs amongst the stars, however, such astronomical boundaries need to be altered periodically, as precession skews the constellation images against the mathematical grids.

With astronomy no longer perpetuating the images of the constellations in the artwork of the great celestial atlases, the images have moved
into popular culture. In the early twenty-first century there is a profusion
of zodiacal images, from jewellery to clothing to body tattoos. Heaven's
objects are used for the naming of confectionary, such as the Milky Way
chocolate bar, while constellation names are appropriated in an endless
list for casinos, cinemas, insurance companies, shipping lines, newspapers, navigational devices, and even 'Taurus' pistols. As Williams,
cited earlier, stated, culture is both ordinary and creative. The zodiac sign
coffee cup in the office is deeply ordinary and at the same time a creative
use of a largely universally recognised constellation image for the
identification of one's cup. Despite the starry images having lost their
utility in astronomy, their robustness in everyday life is widespread.

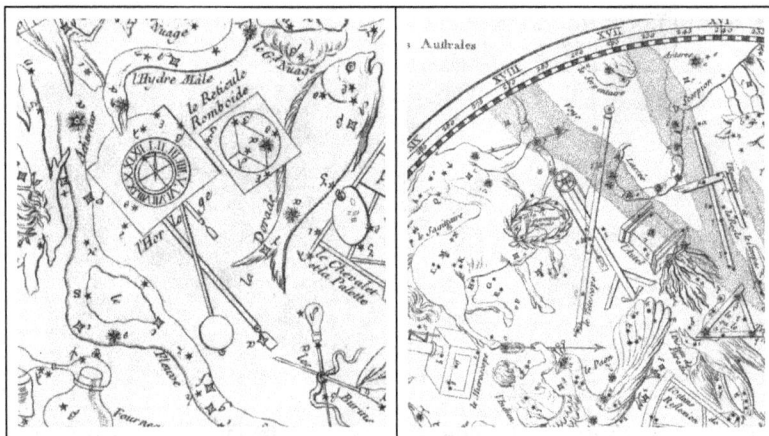

Figure 14. Nicolas Lacaille (1713–1762) images from *Atlas Celeste*,
Telescopium (right) and Horologium (left). Images: courtesy of Ian Ridpath.

By acknowledging the age of many of the stellar images, the sky can
be viewed as a cultural gallery. Our Palaeolithic ancestors potentially
placed some of the images we have today in the sky, such as perhaps the
bull in the Lascaux cave. As Richard Allen has shown, a constellation
like Boötes, seen as a herdsman and the hunter, was ancient by the time
of Homer, and may be an artefact from our Neolithic ancestors (1963:
93). The constellations of Orion, the Pharaoh of the Egyptians and the
ancient Greek warrior, and Auriga the Charioteer, thought to be a
shepherd and remodelled by the Greeks (Jobes and Jobes 1964: 126), are
also voices from the Bronze Age. Constellations such as Telescopium
and Horologium, for their parts, which were added to our sky in the

eighteenth century, are artefacts of early modernity (Fig. 14). In contemporary times there are the deep-space imagery, galaxies, and nebulae that humanity continues to name, such as the Horse Head nebula, the Sombrero, and the Eye of God.

Conclusion

The heavens have always been a palate for human imagination. It would seem that their story emerged when the images from Mesopotamia blended with the giants of the southern Greek constellations. These images then became linked with the scientific thinking of the Greeks who used them to carry information of star locations and the celestial sphere. Empowered and protected with this knowledge, they resisted merging with the Egyptian view of the heavens, and 2000 years later, having gained authority by virtue of their antiquity, they survived the efforts of Christianity to repaint the heavens and repelled the political propaganda of the eighteenth century. As they lost their usefulness in terms of astronomy, they nevertheless maintained a place within the world of amateur sky viewing, enhanced in the twenty-first century by applications on hand-held telephones and other devices. Their images and names have thus continued to gain vitality in popular culture. Instead of becoming a relic or being placed in a museum of disused scientific notions, these ancient images of the sky have grown in cultural importance yet further with the discovery and naming of the southern skies and the advent of deep-space photography.

This discussion of the perpetuation of images from antiquity to the present day may seem obvious, but the robustness of these images is suggestive of similarities between diverse cultures. In reconsidering the arguments of Bodley (humanity's tendency to generate symbols created culture), Williams (culture is diverse in its everyday representations), Eagleton (culture is created wherever humanity encounters the 'recalcitrance of nature'), and Hartner (the idea of a symplegma), I contend that a culture is formed by the symplegma of humanity with the sky.

When the 'nature' component of a culture-forming symplegma is a landscape, then the resulting culture is territorial, tribal, political, or nation building, and 'owned' by a particular human group. On the other hand, when the 'nature' component of the symplegma is a shared night sky that knows no national boundaries, then its human observers create a culture that transcends such borders. To reiterate, when viewed in this manner the constellation images emerge out of a symplegma of humanity and the sky. They gain their mythology and stories from the imagination of their human parent and their divine immortal nature from their sky parent. They constitute a culture of humanity that is not bound by tribe, clan, nation, religions, or language.

References

Ackermann, S. 2001. 'Bartholomew of Parma, Michael Scot and the Set of New Constellations in Bartholomew's Breviloquium de Fructu Tocius Astronomie', in *Seventh Centenary of the Teaching of Astronomy in Bologna, 1297–1997*, ed. F.B. Pierluigi Battistini, Alessandro Braccesi, and Dino Buzzetti (Bologna, Italy: Cooperative Libraria Universitaria Editrice): 77-98.
Allen, R.H. 1963. *Star Names: Their Lore and Meaning* (New York: Dover).
Aratus. 1989. 'Phaenomena', in *Callimachus, Hymns and Epigrams Lycohpron, Aratus* (Cambridge, MA: Harvard University Press): 206-303.
———. 2010. *Phaenomena* (Baltimore, MD: Johns Hopkins University Press).
Ashworth, W.B. Jr. 1981. 'John Bevis and his "Uranographia" (ca. 1750)', *Proceedings of the American Philosophical Society* 125: 52-73.
Bayer, J. 1603. *Uranometria: Omnium Asterismorum Continens Schemata, Nova Methodo Delineata, Aereis Laminis Expressa* (Augsburg, Germany: Christophorus Mangus).
Beer, A. 1967. 'Astronomical Dating of Works of Art', *Vistas in Astronomy* 9: 177-223.
Bode, J. 1801. *Uranographie* (Berlin: Frideric de Hahn).
Bodley, J.H. 1999. *Cultural Anthropology: Tribes, States, and the Global System* (Pullman: Washington State University Press).
Brady, B. 2016. 'Star-Paths, Stones and Horizon Astronomy', in *Seac 2011 Stars and Stones: Voyages in Archaeoastronomy and Cultural Astronomy*, ed. F. Pimenta et al., BAR International Series (Oxford: Archaeopress): 58-63.
Buckstaff, R.N. 1927. 'Stars and Constellations of a Pawnee Sky Map', *American Anthropologist* 29: 279-85.
Cellarius, A. 1661. *Harmonia Macrocosmica* (Amsterdam: Johannes Janssonius).
Condos, T. 1997. *Star Myths of the Greeks and Romans: A Sourcebook* (Grand Rapids, MI: Phanes Press).
Cooley, J.L. 2013. *Poetic Astronomy in the Ancient Near East: The Reflexes of Celestial Science in Ancient Mesopotamian, Ugaritic, and Israelite Narrative* (Winona Lake: Eisenbrauns).
Crommelin, A.C.D. 1923. 'The Ancient Constellations Figures', in *Splendor of the Heavens 2* (London: Hitchinson & Co.): 640-69.
Davenhall, A.C., and S.K. Leggett. 1997. *Constellation Boundary Data (Davenhall+ 1989),VI 49*. Online: http://vizier.cfa.harvard.edu/viz-bin/VizieR? source=VI/49.
Eagleton, T. 2000. *The Idea of Culture* (London: Blackwell).
Estey, F.N. 1943. 'Charlemagne's Silver Celestial Table', *Speculum*18: 112-17.
Etz, D.V. 1997. 'A New Look at the Constellation Figures in the Celestial Diagram', *Journal of the American Research Center in Egypt* 34: 143-61.
Flamsteed, J. 1729. *Atlas Coelestis* (London: n.p.).

Franklin Institute. 2013. Celestial Globe. Online: http://www.l.edu/learn/sci-tech/celestial-globe/celestial-globe.php?cts=space.

Frazier, K. 1979. 'Stars, Sky and Culture', *Science News* 116: 90-93.

Gallucci, G.P. 1614. *Theatrum Mundi, et temporis* (Granada: Por Sebastian Muñoz).

Goebel, T., M.R. Waters, and D.H. O'Rourke. 2008. 'The Late Pleistocene Dispersal of Modern Humans in the Americas', *Science* 319: 1497-502.

Hagar, S. 1900. 'The Celestial Bear', *Journal of American Folklore* 13: 92-103.

Hamel, J. 2010. 'The Heraldic Astronomical Silver Globe by Erhard Weigel in the Astronomical-Physical Cabinet in Kassel (German Title: Der heraldische Silber-globus von Erhard Weigel im Astronomisch-Physikalischen Kabinett Kassel)', *Acta Historica Astronomiae* 41: 34-64.

Hartner, W. 1965. 'The Earliest History of the Constellations in the Near East and the Motif of the Lion–Bull Combat', *Journal of Near Eastern Studies* 24: 1-16.

Heath, S.T.L. 1920. *Euclid in Greek* (Cambridge: Cambridge University Press).

Heninger, S.K.J. 1977. *The Cosmographical Glass, Renaissance Diagrams of the Universe* (San Marino, CA: The Huntington Library).

Hesiod. 1914. 'Shield of Heracles', in *The Homeric Hymns and Homerica*, ed. H.G. Evelyn-White (Cambridge, MA: Harvard University Press): n.p.

Hevelius, J. 1690. *Prodromus Astronomiae* (Danzig: n.p.).

Hockey, T., ed. 2007. *Biographical Encyclopedia of Astronomers* (New York: Springer).

Holden, E.S. 1890. 'Contributions of Raphael and of Albrecht Dürer to Astronomy', *Publications of the Astronomical Society of the Pacilc* 2: 19-21.

Homer. 1986. *The Odyssey* (New York: Penguin Books).

Hunger, H., and D.E. Pingree. 1999. *Astral sciences in Mesopotamia* (Leiden: Brill).

Jobes, G., and J. Jobes. 1964. *Outer Space: Myths, Name Meanings, Calendars* (New York: Scarecrow).

Kanas, N. 2007. *Star Maps, History, Artistry, and Cartography* (New York: Springer).

Lorimer, H.L. 1951. 'Stars and Constellations in Homer and Hesiod', *The Annual of the British School at Athens* 46: 86-101.

McCluskey, Stephen C. 1998. *Astronomies and Cultures in Early Medieval Europe* (Cambridge: Cambridge University Press).

North, J. 2008. *Cosmos: An Illustrated History of Astronomy and Cosmology* (Chicago: University of Chicago Press).

Parker, R.A. 1974. 'Ancient Egyptian Astronomy', *Philosophical Transactions of the Royal Society of London. Series A, Mathematical and Physical Sciences* 276: 51-65.

Piccolomini, A. 1552. *Della Sfera del Mondo e Delle Stelle Fisse* (Venice: Al Segno del Pozzo).

Ptolemy, C. 1541. *Ptolemy: Cl. Ptolemaeus, Omnia, quae extant opera, Geographia excepta* (Basel: Henri Petri).

———. 1915. *Ptolemy's Catalogue of Stars: A Revision of the Almagest*, ed. C.H.F. Peters and E.B. Knobel (Washington: Carnegie Institute).

———. 1998. *Ptolemy's Almagest* (Princeton: Princeton University Press).

Ratdolt, E. 1482. *Hyginus, Poeticon Astronomicon* (Venice: Erhard Ratdolt).

Redgrave, G.R. 1894. *Erhard Ratdolt and his Work at Venice* (London: Bibliographical Society).

Reiner, E. 1999. 'Babylonian Celestial Divination', in *Ancient Astronomy and Celestial Divination*, ed. N.M. Swerdlow (London: MIT Press): 21-37.

Rochberg, F. 2004. *The Heavenly Writing, Divination, Horoscopy, and Astronomy in Mesopotamian Culture* (Cambridge: Cambridge University Press).

Rogers, J.H. 1998. 'Origins of the Ancient Constellations II: The Mediterranean Traditions', *Journal of British Astronomical Association* 108: 79-89.

Roy, A. 1984. 'The Origins of the Constellations', *Vistas in Astronomy* 27: 176-85.

Schaefer, B. 2002. 'The Latitude and Epoch for the Formation of the Southern Greek Constellations', *Journal for the History of Astronomy* 23: 313-50.

Schiller, J. 1627. *Coelum Stellatum Christianum* (n.p.: Augusta).

Waerden, V.D.B.L. 1949. 'Babylonian Astronomy II: The Thirty-Six Stars', *Journal of Near Eastern Studies* 8: 6-26.

Warner, D.J. 1979. *The Sky Explored: Celestial Cartography, 1500–1800* (New York: A.R. Liss).

Whitehead, D. 2000. *Ice Age Star Map Discovered.* BBC News. Online: http://news.bbc.co.uk/1/hi/871930.stm.

Whitleld, P. 1995. *The Mapping of the Heavens* (San Francisco: Pomegranate).

Williams, R. 1958. 'Culture Is Ordinary'. Online: http://www.wsu.edu/gened/learn-modules/top_culture/culture-delnitions/ raymond-williams.html.

Zhitomirsky, S. 1999. 'Aratus' "Phaenomena": Dating and Analysing its Primary Source', *Astronomical & Astrophysical Transactions* 17: 483-500.

INDEX

A

AAAS. See American Association for the Advancement of Science

Abu Ma'shar, 114, 116

Acadia National Park in Maine, 210

accuracy of imagery, xiv, 142, 146, 152, 154, 155, 157, 244, 247

agency, 50, 53, 226

Albertus Magnus, 109

Almagest, 55, 102, 116, 146, 152, 154, 234, 242

ambient light, 220, 224

'ambient optic array', 217

American Association for the Advancement of Science (AAAS), 17

Amman, Jost, 134

Andromeda, 60, 62-64, 69, 70, 72, 103-105, 204

Antares, 240, 246

Antinous, 146

Antwerp, xiv, 114, 125-28, 132-39

Apollo, 117; as comet, 31

Aquarius, 48, 51, 82, 237, 244, 245, 250; Cloak of, 51

Arabic astrology, 120

Aratus, 64-66, 68, 69, 75, 102, 106, 108, 110, 145-47, 149, 239, 240, 242, 243

archaeoastronomy, x, xvii, 2, 5, 8, 9, 11-14, 17, 18
  brown archaeoastronomy, 18
  green archaeoastronomy, 18
  Mesoamerican, 17
  Pre-Columbian, 17

archaeology, x, 2, 3, 5, 6, 8, 9, 13, 15-17, 37, 38

Arcturus, 152

Argo, the, 58, 150, 237

Aries, 48, 50, 82, 102-105, 237, 250

Aristophanes, 60

arte, 94, 131

artificial lighting, 205

Ascendant, 44, 46-50, 97, 98; as 'the steersman', 49

asteroids, 36, 207

astrolabe, 97, 98, 101, 103, 105

Astrolabium Planum, 96-101, 111

astrological frescoes:
  encyclopaedic, 149
  horoscopic ceilings, 150
  that commemorate a specific event, 150

astrology, xiii, xiv, xvii, 2, 5, 44, 46, 48, 49, 52, 53, 54, 87, 90, 93, 94, 101, 109, 114-17, 120, 138, 151, 152

Astronomers without Borders, 187

astronomical timelapse photography, 172

Aten, as comet, 30

Atkinson, Richard, 6, 8

Atlas Coelestis, 252

atmosphere, xvi, 28, 151, 168, 192, 197, 198, 207, 208, 219, 223-25, 230-32; definition, 223

August Perseids, 31

Augustine, 157

Augustus, 25, 79, 80

Auriga, 237, 238, 254

Aveni, Anthony, 17, 18

www.ingramcontent.com/pod-product-compliance
Lightning Source LLC
Chambersburg PA
CBHW070240290326
41929CB00046B/2118